TAKING
South Park
SERIOUSLY

Edited by

Jeffrey
Andrew
Weinstock

STATE UNIVERSITY OF NEW YORK PRESS

Published by
STATE UNIVERSITY OF NEW YORK PRESS, ALBANY

© 2008 State University of New York

For information, contact State University of New York Press, Albany, NY
www.sunypress.edu

Production by Marilyn P. Semerad
Marketing by Susan M. Petrie

Library of Congress Cataloging-in-Publication Data

Taking South Park seriously / Jeffrey Andrew Weinstock.
    p. cm.
Includes bibliographical references and index.
ISBN 978-0-7914-7565-2 (hardcover : alk. paper)
ISBN 978-0-7914-7566-9 (pbk. : alk. paper)
1. South Park (Television program) I. Weinstock, Jeffrey Andrew.

PN1992.77.S665T35 2008
791.45'72—dc22

                                                                    2007042264

                    10   9   8   7   6   5   4   3   2

Contents

Part Two
Identity Politics

Part Three
South Park Conservatives?

Part Four
Specific Critiques

Illustrations

Acknowledgments

Edited collections are odd beasts—they are collaborative efforts that require substantially more cooperation than your usual monograph. With that in mind, I would first like to thank the contributors to the collection for making this process about as smooth as any editor could hope for. I've enjoyed working with all of you and appreciate not only your intellectual insights, but also your engagement throughout the process. My thanks to Larin McLaughlin, Andrew Kenyon, Marilyn Semerad, and the team at SUNY Press for their enthusiasm about the collection and guidance. The students in my pop culture classes at Central Michigan University served as willing and able guinea pigs in trying out some of these ideas and provided valuable feedback. (Note: no students were harmed in the making of this collection!) My colleagues at CMU have been a consistent source of encouragement whether they knew it or not, especially Ari Berk, Kris McDermott, Mark Freed, Brooke Harrison, Heidi Holder, and Stephenie Young. Lastly, my special thanks to Astrid, Sophie, and the feline army for watching with me and keeping me grounded.

Taking
South Park
Seriously

JEFFREY ANDREW WEINSTOCK

Taking *South Park* Seriously

When I first circulated a call for submissions for this collection, I was surprised to find that the solicitation was propagated online and provoked a certain amount of confused derision—not among academics, from whom one still might expect it, but among the general public. To both my amazement and amusement, while running an Internet search for articles on *South Park*, I discovered my brief call for essays included on a blog of sorts called "Spitting Image," along with the comment, "There's 'something appealing, something appalling' in this." This pronouncement was then followed by one of the strangest appraisals of contemporary academia that I have ever encountered: "this is how it is to be a university professor. you must be critical of any accepted narratives and generate a bigger better one all so that you can get more money, more students, more fame. its sort of boring." Not only is it unclear to me which "accepted narrative" the author presumed this collection would be critical of, but the author clearly has a distorted idea of professorial salaries, financial compensation for academic publishing, and class sizes at most universities! Then there was a posting of the call for papers on a site called "Digg.com," which prompted the response, "One more reason to laugh at professors of english." And the appearance of my call for papers on the *Free Republic* site prompted a long discussion thread that included memorable comments such as "This is what tax dollars SORRY ES I like South Park this is ridclous LOL!" "A class on South Park . . . My kids are majoring

1

in Engineering or they can forget about me paying for their college," and my absolute favorite, "Cartman would kick Professor Weinstock's butt."

Despite the intriguing imagining of academia offered on the "Spitting Image" site, derisive attitude toward "english" on digg.com, and the surreal image of a giant cartoon cutout kicking my butt, the most appealing and appalling discussion of my initial call for participation in the volume appeared, in all places, in a forum on the South Park Studies.com Web site. An initial posting noted my call for papers and a discussion thread ensued in which presumably *South Park* fans derided the idea of any serious consideration of the program. Although many participants in the conversation curiously mistook the initial posting to mean a class was being offered on the topic rather than a book being published (as did some participants on the *Free Republic* thread), the comments still have the same derisive resonance. One very bitter participant posted (in all caps), "REALLY PROVES WHAT A WASTE OF TIME AND MONEY COLLEGE IS. YOU LEARN VERY LITTLE OF VALUE AND ITS STILL NEXT TO IMPOSSIBLE TO GET A JOB WITH YOUR DEGREE. THIS JUST MAKES A MOCKERY OF OUR AMERICAN COLLEGE SYSTEM." Another less caustic posting echoed what appears to be a commonplace conceptualization of university salaries by noting, "Academics are quite happy to utilise any part of popular culture to draw attention and potential income," and pondered both who I thought the audience for this book would be (a fair question!) and whether permission had been obtained to quote or give examples from *South Park*.

What I find most fascinating about these dismissive comments in general and the ones on the South Park Studios.com site in particular is that the participants in the conversation in all likelihood are fans of the program or they would not be there in the first place—and many of them vigorously resist the idea that *South Park*, a program they enjoy, could have anything of interest to say about modern culture. Instead, all of the bemused or aghast comments noted previously that rebel at the idea of taking *South Park* seriously confirm that the perception of a deep divide between something called "high" or "elite" culture and something called "popular" or "mass" culture remains alive and well in American culture.

Senseless Vile Trash?

Part of what makes *South Park* so much fun to consider from an academic perspective is the fact that the program is hyperaware of itself as participating precisely in a debate about the value and influence of popular culture. Consider, for instance, the episode entitled "Death," aired during *South Park*'s very first season, in which South Park Elementary third grade teacher Mr. Garrison (who often incorporates references to television programs such as *The*

Love Boat and *Barnaby Jones* into his lessons), lectures his class on why they should not watch the animated program *Terrance and Phillip* (which, as all *South Park* aficionados know, is a program, much beloved by the children, that is built entirely around fart jokes): "Shows like *Terrance and Phillip*," explains Mr. Garrison, "are what we call 'toilet humor.' They don't expand your minds. These kinds of shows are senseless vile trash. You should be spending your time enlightening your mind with more intelligent entertainment." Mr. Garrison's comments come in the context of a parental movement, led by Kyle's mom, Sheila Broflovski, to get *Terrance and Phillip* pulled from the air because of her conviction that the minds of the town's children are being "tainted by the garbage on television that they see." Mrs. Broflovski here ironically ends up sounding quite a bit like the usual standard-bearers of high culture who are quick to defame pop culture for its lack of sophistication and presumed pernicious effects.

Clearly, this scenario in which concerned parents protest what they consider to be the degrading effects of a crass cartoon self-referentially foregrounds similar attacks on the program *South Park* itself, such as that by Action for Children's Television founder Peggy Charren, who rather inexplicably characterized the program in 1998 as "dangerous to democracy" (Marin 57), Focus on the Family's Bob Smithouser, who characterizes the program as "extremely mean-spirited" and "deplorable" (Fagin 38), petitions online to ban the program because of its presumed anti-Christian values (see "Ban *South Park*" and "Ban *South Park* it is anti-christ"), or various school districts that have at one time or another banned *South Park* clothing and paraphernalia.[1] Not surprisingly then, the episode paints the "concerned parents" as hysterical, hypocritical, and, most damning, insincere. Not only do the parents transform themselves into ridiculously ineffectual kamikazes who, to be "taken seriously" (and with rather eerie pre–9/11 resonances) use a giant slingshot to hurl themselves to their deaths against the Cartoon Central skyscraper, but also they themselves bandy about and enjoy the same kind of "toilet humor" that they find so disgraceful in *Terrance and Phillip*—part of the plot of the episode is that the adults have all contracted cases of "explosive diarrhea" that originated with Kenny, and they laugh at comments such as Mr. Garrison's colorful pronouncement, "I've got the green apple splatters."

Beyond this, however, the parents' self-righteous zeal is shown to have much more to do with self-aggrandizement than with sincere concern. As William J. Savage Jr. observes, the episode reveals the writers' awareness of "the unspoken subtexts in parental protests over television shows and the logic of censorship: this debate revolves around the power over who consumes what, who decides what sort of humor is acceptable for whom, and the desire for some parents to impose their own standards on everyone" (217). Ultimately, according to Savage, the episode presents the argument that "when parents put the onus for their children's behavior on the content of television, it is a dodge, a way of evading responsibility for problems which might very well have roots elsewhere" (218). The episode ends moralistically with Stan and Kyle directly addressing the viewer:

> STAN: You know, I think that if parents would spend less time worrying about what their kids watch on TV and more time worrying about what's going on in their kids' lives, this world would be a much better place.
>
> KYLE: Yeah. I think that parents only get so offended by television because they rely on it as a babysitter and the sole educator of their kids.

As Savage points out, this conclusion is itself a kind of dodge because the content of television programs *is* something going on in children's lives, but the larger point is that the episode demonstrates a conscious awareness of the debates revolving around both *South Park*'s crude humor and the logic of media censorship more generally. According to the episode, the parents' sanctimonious indignation is in reality nothing but a power grab, a way to exert their wills over others. Although the episode never defends the content of *Terrance and Phillip*, and, by extension, does not defend its own scatological or provocative content, it attacks those who would impinge on the free expression and enjoyment of others.

This position is in keeping with the series' general political philosophy in which the unpardonable sin is the attempt to control someone else's speech.[2] However, the conclusion to "Death" is a dodge in more ways than one. Not only is television something going on in the lives of children, but the episode sidesteps entirely the thorny issue of whether television programs such as *South Park* actually do have the potential to influence children (or adults) negatively. Other episodes in fact clearly depict the children (most frequently Cartman) as easily manipulated by television and cinema. For example, in "Weight Gain 4000," Cartman mistakes fat for muscle and increases his already substantial girth after viewing a commercial for a product called "Weight Gain 4000"; in "Chinpokomon," all the children fall under the influence of, first, commercials for, and then messages encoded in, the Japanese game, "Chinpokomon"; and in "The Passion of the Jew," Mel Gibson's movie, *The Passion of the Christ* (2004), leads Cartman to adopt a genocidal program against the Jews and Kyle to doubt his own faith.[3] In contrast to these episodes that unambiguously depict the influence of media messages on children, "Death" makes use of a sort of Freudian "kettle logic" by asserting simultaneously that watching television, if not harmless, is certainly better than other forms of mischief kids can get into (when *Terrance and Phillip* is taken off the air, the kids consider breathing gas fumes, smoking crack, and watching pornography); that limitations on free expression are more damaging than any ideas kids may get from watching television; and that television does not teach kids anything they do not already know or cannot pick up from other sources.⁴ *Terrance and Phillip* (and, by extension, *South Park* itself) may be "senseless vile trash," but, says "Death," its toilet humor is amusing and far less dangerous than the hypocrisy of those who conceal their intolerance and egoism behind a façade of compassionate concern.

Pop Cultural Capital

"Death" is a useful text to introduce this volume because it so clearly condenses numerous important issues concerning *South Park* the contributors will address. Among the questions the episode raises are the extent to which an animated program can engage in cogent social commentary and political critique (the episode also addresses euthanasia—Stan's grandfather, having celebrated his 102nd birthday, attempts to enlist Stan's aid in killing himself), the effects of television viewing on children, and the suspect motivations of those who seek to curtail or censor various forms of expression. More generally, the episode engages with cultural constructions of childhood and the appropriate roles for parents and educators in shaping child development. And, perhaps most notably, the episode self-reflexively interrogates its own status within American culture by raising (and ultimately not really answering) the question of whether it itself is "senseless vile trash"—and, if so, whether that is necessarily bad.

What consideration of "Death" and *South Park* more generally reveal is that the knee-jerk rejection of popular culture texts as lacking value and complexity is deeply problematic and tends to reveal more about prevailing ideologies and the critics' priorities than about the texts themselves. In particular, such dismissals arguably privilege certain class-inflected forms of knowledge and pleasure over others and manifest an almost willful refusal to look carefully at the content of popular culture texts. One learns how to watch *South Park* as surely as one learns how to take in Shakespeare (we learn for instance that Kyle is almost always right and Cartman is almost always wrong; that if Kenny dies, he most likely will be back again in the next episode; that Chef's advice invariably has more to do with libido than with the actual problem at hand, and so forth), and one is forced to dig as deeply into his or her database of pop culture references to make sense of the former as he or she is into Greek mythology for the latter. The big difference is not that texts by Shakespeare and James Joyce and T. S. Eliot and the other paragons of high culture require training to interpret and *South Park* does not, but rather that some types of knowledge are esteemed as more valuable within Western culture than others. Nowhere under the rubric of "culture" in the sense of "being cultured" is included conversance with what is generally referred to as pop culture—forms of entertainment open to the masses.

One could say a great deal on this topic of high culture versus pop culture—one could demonstrate, for instance, that elite culture touchstones such as Shakespeare and Chaucer have moments every bit as bawdy as anything in *South Park* (see Melissa Hart's "'South Park,' in the Tradition of Chaucer and Shakespeare")—and much work has been done to demonstrate the ways in which canonical authors' works are not at all "universal" or "timeless," but are instead very much products of their times that do not invariably or unproblematically cross great cultural divides. However, my point here is not to dismantle the high culture/pop culture divide entirely, but rather to question it at the onset in light of dismissive attitudes toward programs such as *South Park*—and similar volumes that take pop culture phenomena as their focus—on the part of both academics and the general public. Suffice to say that I and the contributors to this volume take *South Park* seriously—that is, we presume that it is meaning-bearing, complex, socially significant, and worthy of analysis.

South Park's Histories

All texts are invariably and inevitably products of their historical moments and *South Park* is no different: It has a history, it is a product of historical forces, and it quite consciously incorporates and contends with a variety of specific histories. The remainder of this introduction, prior to turning to the chapters themselves, provides background about the series and the social forces governing its emergence. Rather than being in any way complete or exhaustive, this background highlights the complexity of cultural analysis. As anthropologist Clifford Geertz has famously discussed in relation to something as simple as deciding between a wink and a blink, interpreting the cultural significance of an action or text requires a sort of "thick description" that attends to the place of a signifier within the broader field of signification.

In terms of the specific history of the program, that the "discovery" of the show seems to be a parody of the cherished American dream of accidental stardom is entirely fitting. As frequently recounted in the popular media, *South Park* creators Trey Parker and Matt Stone, both Colorado natives, met at the University of Colorado at Boulder where Stone majored in math and Parker, who never graduated, studied music theory and produced the film *Cannibal! The Musical* (1996). According to Parker, the two bonded in a film class because they "were the only ones who didn't want to make black-and-white films about lesbians" (Marin 59). (Parker's film, *Giant Beaver of Southern Sri Lanka* [1989], featured a little girl dressed as a beaver ravaging a town.) Stone's recollections are more surreal as, in an interview with *Rolling Stone's* David Wild, he remembers being impressed with the fact that while other college students subsisted on noodles or beans and rice, Parker had a big roast on his counter ("Evil Geniuses" 34). (Alas, none of the *South Park* commentators draw a connection between *Cannibal! The Musical* and the roast.)

Although the specific details at this point vary slightly depending on the source, the story of *South Park*'s origins seems to follow these lines: Parker and Stone relocated to Los Angeles where their *Cannibal! The Musical* impressed FOX executive Brian Graden enough to work with the network to try to develop a pilot. However, Graden could not interest anyone in *Cannibal*—or in other ideas he tried to develop with Parker and Stone, including a television series about "two apes who hang upside down and sing" (Collins 76)—so, to help them pay the rent and buy food (according to Stone, the two were down to one meal a day [Wild, "Evil Geniuses" 34]), he paid them $1,200 in 1995 to produce a holiday video for his industry contacts based on an animated short the boys had produced at the University of Colorado about four little boys, aided by a dashboard-size Jesus, who stop a killing spree by Frosty the Snowman. The result was the now legendary "The Spirit of Christmas," a five-minute refined version of the Frosty story in which Jesus and Santa Claus duke it out over who has the bigger claim on the holiday while the kids cheer them on.

Collins quotes Graden as saying that he had intended to send it to the "500 people on [his] executive kiss-a__ list," but, despite it being "the funniest thing [he'd] ever seen," he decided he could not send it to the studio heads, so it was instead distributed to forty of his friends, most of whom, according to Graden, were not even part of the entertainment industry (76). Nonetheless, the video became an "underground bootleg obsession" (Marin 59) that won them many high-profile fans (according to a 1997 *People Weekly* article, actor George Clooney dubbed 100 copies of the video for friends [Tomashoff 17]) and catapulted Parker and Stone to stardom. Marin notes that the boys received numerous offers, including one to direct *Barney's Great Adventure* (1998), but went with Comedy Central because when Parker asked, "How do you feel about talking poo?" they responded, "Love it!" (59). McDonald adds that the original idea for the program was to call it *The Mr. Hankey Show* and have it star what undeniably is television's most loveable piece of talking poo, but that Graden persuaded Parker and Stone to focus more on the four boys and their town (24). The pilot episode involved more than 5,000 actual construction-paper cutouts and each action was filmed individually (24).

South Park premiered in August 1997 and was touted as the first made-for-television cartoon to warrant a TV-MA rating that designated it for mature audiences only. Indeed, part of Comedy Central's marketing strategy has been to emphasize *South Park*'s potentially offensive humor with advertising taglines such as "Alien abductions, anal probes, & flaming farts: Why they invented the V–chip." The Christmas episode that ran on December 17, 1997, drew a 51% share among men age 18–24 in the 47 million homes receiving Comedy Central and a 5.4 rating—the biggest rating in Comedy Central's history at that point and the second highest rating on cable for that week (Ross). By early 1998, advertising rates during *South Park* were selling for more than ten times the network's standard prime time rate; the program's list of advertisers included AOL, Calvin Klein, CBS, The Gap, RadioShack, Snapple, Sony, and Volkswagen; and sales of *South Park* merchandise had already topped $30 million (Ross).

The program also predictably roused the ire of individuals and organizations concerned about its crude humor and irreverence toward all forms of authority. As noted, religious organizations assailed the program, concerned about its crude humor and language, and *South Park* merchandise was banned from a handful of elementary school grounds. Despite these attacks, *South Park*—in sharp contrast to another "edgy" program called *Nothing Sacred* about a Catholic priest that appeared on ABC in 1997 and was quickly cancelled after offended Christian viewers protested—has had no trouble retaining advertisers.

The success of *South Park* freed Parker and Stone to develop other projects. In 1997 they released *Orgazmo*, a feature film written, directed, and starred in by Parker and produced and acted in by Stone; 1998 saw the release of the critically disparaged *BASEketball*, a David Zucker sports parody starring Parker and Stone. In 1999 the duo brought *South Park—Bigger Longer & Uncut* to the big screen, where it was nominated for an Academy Award for best original song ("Blame Canada"), which Richard Corliss lauded in *Time* as "ruthlessly funny," but which was reviled by many defenders of "traditional morals," such as the Christian ChildCare Action Project Ministry, describing the film as an "extraordinarily vulgar, vile, and repugnant movie" and as "INCREDIBLY dangerous" (qtd. in Gardiner 51). In 2004 the pair released *Team America: World Police*, a feature film that uses marionettes to satirize the American War on Terror and celebrities turned activists, and included a scene of puppet sex so racy that it had to be edited for the film to receive an R rating. As of this writing, the program has now surpassed 100 episodes and is in its eleventh season.

South Park is of course most immediately the product of its creators' experience, talents, and imagination—all combined with an element of chance. In various interviews, Parker (who is the voice of Stan, Cartman, Mr. Garrison, Officer Barbrady, Mr. Mackey, Phillip, and Mr. Hankey) and Stone (who is the voice of Kyle, Kenny, Jesus, Jimbo, Terrance, Pip, and Big Gay Al) suggest historical origins for various characters and plot conventions. Parker generally identifies with Stan, and Stone generally identifies with Kyle (McDonald 23). More specifically, Mr. Garrison allegedly is based on Parker's British literature professor and Parker has an older sister, Shelly, who wore orthodontics headgear and bullied him. Stan's love interest, Wendy Testaburger, purportedly is based on Parker's former fiancé who walked out on him (McDonald 23–24). Parker's father is a geologist, as is Stan Marsh's father on the program. Bizarrely—and perhaps apocryphally—Parker revealed at the U.S. Comedy Arts Festival in Aspen, Colorado in 1998 that Mr. Hankey was a product of his own childhood trauma. According to Parker, as a young child of three or four, he had difficulty remembering to flush the toilet and his father, in an effort to provide the necessary motivation for his recalcitrant child, informed him that failure to flush causes Mr. Hankey to emerge, sing a little song, and then *kill you* (Collins 75). (This comment leads Collins to conclude that *South Park* "explore[s] the surreal terrors of childhood" [75]. In the program, Mr. Hankey is a kindly figure who brings toys on Christmas to all the good boys and girls with enough fiber in their diets.) Not quite as absurd, but still rather odd, in an interview with *Newsweek*, Isaac Hayes (who voiced Chef) mentions that as a child, he had a friend in Memphis who owned a gay dog. While Hayes does not identify this as the origin for the gay dog Sparky (George Clooney is the "voice") in the episode "Big Gay Al's Big Gay Boat Ride," this would be a surprising coincidence if it were not (Marin 60–61).

In contrast to these autobiographical incorporations, what many have noted as the program's most notable repetition compulsion—the recurring death and resurrection of Kenny—seems to have originated mainly as a result of historical contingency combined with Parker and Stone's willful antiauthoritarianism. As Parker and Stone tell it, Kenny died in their original five-minute short, "Frosty vs. Jesus." However, when Graden commissioned them in 1995 to produce his Christmas video, *The Spirit of Christmas*, the two brought Kenny back because few people had seen the original short. Then, when they signed on with Comedy Central to develop the series, they felt they should start with the four boys again—and that's when they realized "how much we liked the fact that Kenny dies, so we kept killing him" (Parker qtd. in Wallace 15). Stone then adds that Comedy Central network executives opposed the recurrent death and resurrection of Kenny because it "destroyed the logic of the show." With characteristic maturity, this only fueled their desire to incorporate this aspect—which they did until they felt it was expected of them: "So as soon as we set the role [sic] that Kenny must die in every episode, we immediately broke it. In one episode, Kenny didn't die, and everyone got very upset with us because we f***ed with their rules. As soon as there's one there, that's when we break it" (Stone qtd. in Wallace 15).

In these respects, *South Park*—as is the case with any cultural text in any medium—clearly is the product of the experiences, desires, and vision of its creators, combined with an element of chance. However, in a more global sense, the program is what one might refer to as "congealed history"—the materialization of converging lines of historical forces that shaped the possibility of the program, structure its form, and explain its spectacular success.

Among these historical forces are the new political economy of cable television, the history of prime time animation and evolving animation technologies, and the broad and contentious spectrum of American ideology, including, importantly, attitudes toward racial difference and "political correctness." Although I cannot do justice to the complexity of these three topics within the restricted space of this introduction, I would be remiss not to at least gesture toward the importance they have had on the emergence of *South Park* as a contemporary cultural phenomenon.

Niche TV

To begin, *South Park* clearly owes the fact of its existence—at least in its current form—to the existence of Comedy Central and, more generally, to what Paul Wells has referred to as the development of "niche channels" and "dedicated broadcaster outlets" including the Cartoon Network, the SciFi Channel, ESPN, the Food Network, and others (4). Although little so far has been written about it, the development of cable and satellite television has had a profound impact on the lives of millions of people in the United States and around the world and has fundamentally altered program development and, arguably, viewership practices. Many television viewers today take for granted the fact that one can turn on the television and select from literally hundreds of programs. However, those old enough to remember "antiques" such as manual typewriters and Betamax video recorders can also remember a time when television viewer choices in the United States were restricted to a handful of stations—typically, the trio of ABC, NBC, and CBS, along with Public Broadcasting. The development of first cable television and then satellite television greatly expanded viewer choice and, concomitantly, competition for the major networks. The networks have responded to the diversification of the television marketplace by developing their own cable offerings (NBC, for example, is connected to the SciFi Channel, the USA Network, and Bravo; CBS is related to Showtime; ABC is connected to the Disney Channel and ESPN), and through an increased homogenization of network television whereby each major network offers variations on the same popular themes and formats (if one network launches a medical drama or dance contest, the others counter with something similar) and reserves more experimental or adventurous programming for cable—keeping open the possibility that if a program does especially well on cable, it can be transferred to network television in syndication (which has happened with *South Park*).

Cable television thus provides a fertile breeding ground for unorthodox programming and the risks that cable programs can take are heightened by the fact that censorship standards are far more lax on cable. The Federal Communications Commission's (FCC) regulatory domain with respect to indecency remains restricted to the public airwaves, notably VHF and UHF television and AM/FM radio. Cable and satellite television, in contrast, is largely free of regulatory oversight and instead is governed by internally developed network regulations, ever mindful of the need to attract and retain advertisers.

South Park clearly takes full advantage of the opportunity that cable programming affords for off-color (to put it mildly) humor and representations—Parker notes in an interview with Jeff Otto that Comedy Central gives them the freedom to do "any topic [they] want," including topics that network television would not touch. While a list of "daring" representations would be extensive, a few of the more outrageous ones would have to include Martha Stewart inserting a whole Thanksgiving turkey into her ass, Mr. Slave inserting Paris Hilton into his, Christopher Reeve sucking on fetuses as a way to rehabilitate himself, and the animation of Oprah Winfrey's vagina and anus. Also notable is an entire episode, "It Hits the Fan," built around "curse words" in which the word "shit" is repeated uncensored 162 times. (This episode includes Mr. Garrison's unforgettable rendition of "Hey, there, shitty shitty fag fag, shitty shitty fag fag, how do you do?" sung to the tune of the title song from Chitty Chitty Bang Bang [1968].)

South Park is occasionally censored—a scene in which Shelly throws lit matches at Stan, for example, was cut at the request of Comedy Central out of fear that children might imitate the act (McDonald 24) and, notably, an image of the prophet Mohammed was censored without Parker and Stone's approval during part two of the episode, "Cartoon Wars." (Mohammed had previously been shown without network concern in the pre–9/11 episode, "The Super Best Friends.") Nonetheless, South Park is clearly a phenomenon related to the rise of cable television with its more lenient censorship standards and immense range of programming. Its outrageousness is one important means through which it distinguishes itself within this broad field.

Animation History

Although South Park's indebtedness to the specific history of television animation is the topic of chapter 4 (see Weinstock's "Simpsons Did It"), it is worth mentioning briefly here because discussing South Park's emergence as a cultural phenomenon without having the history of television animation and South Park's differential relationship to contemporary animated programs as points of reference is impossible. In various interviews, Parker and Stone acknowledge that they are fans of the 1980s Saturday morning cartoon Space Ghost (both Parker and Stone note that they love Space Ghost because "it's barely animated" [Wallace 14]), that they are "huge fans of Beavis and Butt-head, and huge fans of Mike Judge [the creator of both Beavis and Butt-head and King of the Hill]" (Wild, "Under Attack" 86), and that they found much to enjoy in *Ren & Stimpy* (Wild, "Evil Geniuses" 36). *South Park* explicitly references *The Simpsons* on at least two occasions ("*Simpsons* Already Did It," in which Butters, as his evil alter ego Professor Chaos, attempts to come up with an original plan to cause mischief, but finds that all his ideas have been used on *The Simpsons*, and "Cartoon Wars," in which Bart Simpson himself makes a cameo appearance in part 2) and *South Park* launches an assault on the FOX program *Family Guy* in "Cartoon Wars" for its frequent reliance upon non sequiturs. In various other episodes, *South Park* implicitly references other animated programs by adopting particular animation styles for part or all of an episode. For example, "Korn's Groovy Pirate Ghost Mystery" is both plotted and animated like *Scooby-Doo*; "Osama Bin Laden Has Farty Pants," in which Cartman antagonizes Osama Bin Laden is clearly styled after an episode of *Loony Toons*, with Cartman playing the role of Bugs Bunny; and "Good Times with Weapons" switches back and forth between *South Park's* trademark low-tech style and the general stylistic features of "Japanimation." In all these instances, *South Park* reveals the extent to which it is a part of a specific history of television animation as it both pays homage to and attempts to distinguish itself from particular programs.

All or Nothing

Finally, *South Park's* success cannot be considered without situating the program against the broad backdrop of American ideologies and identity politics. Here we need to acknowledge that the program's political orientation has in fact been the subject of much discussion and debate. Brian C. Anderson's

FIGURE 1
South Park in manga vision.

book, *South Park Conservatives: The Revolt against the Liberal Media Bias*, paints the program broadly as an antiliberal satire and Parker and Stone themselves are fond of foregrounding the apparent irony that they provoke the most controversy by advancing conservative viewpoints. However, as inclusions in this volume by Becker and Fallows (chapters 8 and 9, respectively) observe and as Parker and Stone themselves are aware, demarcating the program as ideologically conservative does not tell the whole story. Stone notes in an interview with *Time* magazine's James Poniewozik, "you could also easily write a book called *South Park Liberals*, because we've attacked a lot of funny stuff that conservative people and institutions do in America. But we're the only show that rips on Rob Reiner and antismoking laws and hippies, so we get that label [conservative]." And, indeed, various episodes of the program adopted socially progressive positions vis-à-vis such issues as homosexuality, euthanasia, and religious zealotism in general.

Although "libertarian" is the political rubric that seems best to fit the show, Judith Kegan Gardiner offers a fuller description of the program's politics in her analysis of the *South Park* movie. She writes that the film's "ethics" are "unempathically tolerant, polymorphously perverse, ambiguously gay affirmative, and disruptive of heteronormativity but also misogynistic, classist, and ethnocentric" (51). What Gardiner is getting at here is the film's—and the series'—overarching ethic of what may be referred to as inclusivity via mockery—an ethic articulated clearly in the "Cartoon Wars" episodes as either everything is available for mockery or nothing is. This "all or nothing" approach to satirizing identity politics is the cagey stratagem that the program deploys to defuse criticism of its potentially offensive representations of historically disenfranchised populations, and it provides the necessary alibi for socially sensitive viewers to laugh at "politically incorrect" humor—the idea being that if everyone is offended equally, no one is singled out, and therefore anyone who takes offense is being overly sensitive and "can't take a joke." *South Park* thus gives the viewer license to trespass on taboo ground and laugh at its parodies of ethnic and social minorities—and this arguably constitutes a great deal of its appeal at the start of the twenty-first century.[5] But this fact raises a series of important questions—ones Samuels and Groening (chapters 5 and 6, respectively) pursue—including why does this sort of humor appeal to viewers and is it really the case that to offend everyone is to offend no one? Do self-aware viewers tune in simply to see what outrageous thing *South Park* will show today and laugh good-naturedly as we recognize "that *South Park* is really making fun of us—both the people who recognize the ignorance-based stereotypes that humanity has cultivated, and the people who buy into those stereotypes" (Hart)? Or does *South Park*'s democratic approach to offensiveness obscure real histories of inequity and provocatively liberate a fundamental but generally repressed aggressiveness on the part of the viewer toward exoticized others? Succinctly stated: Is poking fun at a middle-class white man really the same thing as poking fun at an African American (or a Native American or an Asian American or a Hispanic American or the physically challenged, and so on), and does a member of a social or ethnic minority have any "right" to be indignant at the redeployment of derogatory stereotypes?

South Park's "anti–PC" ethic is not the only provocative component of the program of course, nor is it the only—or even the most obvious—means through which the program participates in the contemporary U.S. political arena. The program's accelerated production schedule, that is, episodes can be put together in a week's time, allows it to achieve a level of currency generally only reserved for news programs. For example, the program aired an episode built around the right to die ("Best Friends Forever") the same week that Terri Schiavo died after having had her feeding tube removed. In this episode, Kenny is killed because Heaven needs him to assist in an apocalyptic battle against Satan. However, the future looks dark when Kenny is revived and kept alive artificially. Heaven emerges victorious only when Kenny is allowed to die. Similarly, the two "Cartoon Wars" episodes that aired in April 2006 engaged with censorship of the image of the Muslim prophet Mohammed after riots in Denmark and elsewhere following the publication of political cartoons that many Muslims found offensive. Comedy Central actually censored this episode, and blacked out the image of Mohammed.

Again and again, *South Park* intrepidly wades into the American ideological fray and no American sacred cow is spared its satiric attack. Among the topics the program addressed at one time or another are environmental issues such as global warming, hybrid cars, and the depletion of the rain forest; religious issues surrounding Mormonism, Scientology, Judaism, Christianity, and Islam; and social issues such as gay marriage, stem cell research, animal rights, celebrity worship, and the sexualization of children. Again and again, *South Park* demonstrates the extent to which it is invested in its particular historical moment and analysis of the program must therefore bear this in mind.

The Book

Turning now to the chapters in this volume, they have been grouped into four parts, each of which is focused on a particular feature or aspect of *South Park*. Part 1, Pleasures of *South Park*, deals with a topic all too often omitted from academic textual analyses: pleasure. The chapters in Part 1 attend to the ways in which the program seduces the viewer and provides for a pleasurable viewing experience. Chapter 1, "'Bigger, Longer, & Uncut': *South Park* and the Carnivalesque," by Alison Halsall, examines the program in light of Russian literary critic M. M. Bakhtin's writings on Rabelaisian carnival. Halsall explores the ways in which *South Park* interweaves levels of parody and satire to ridicule many of the figures and symbols that are iconic of American culture and asserts that *South Park*'s carnival humor, the pride that creators Parker and Stone take in rejecting official dogma and in mocking "high" cultural references, makes it so deliciously addictive.

Halsall's chapter serves as an appropriate lead-in to Brian L. Ott's chapter, "The Pleasures of *South Park* (An Experiment in Media Erotics)," in which Ott explores the ways in which the program "speaks directly to the body." The central question organizing this contribution is not *what* does *South Park* say to viewers, but *how* does it arouse viewers? To answer this question, Ott probes six scenes from the show, each of which illustrates a specific type of transgressive pleasure: the abject, the carnivalesque, the intertextual, the ironic, the liminal, and the depthless. Ultimately, according to Ott, thinking carefully about the ways in which *South Park* produces pleasure helps to explain why people are drawn to particular programs.

Part of the pleasure of watching *South Park*, according to Jason Boyd and Marc R. Plamondon, is precisely the enjoyment viewers derive from the occasional musical numbers. In their "Orphic Persuasions and Siren Seductions: Vocal Music in *South Park*," the authors analyze the role of two types of song in both the *South Park* movie and the series—what the authors refer to as Orphic songs and Siren songs. Boyd and Plamondon argue that these songs function as powerful satiric tools that "normalize" outrageous plot conventions and seduce viewers into morally ambiguous positions that "complicate the complacency many viewers have about the certainty of their convictions and about where their sympathies lie."

Rounding out Part 1 is my own contribution, "'Simpsons Did It!' *South Park* as Differential Signifier," which explores *South Park*'s persistent intertextuality. This chapter asserts (as I've done throughout this introduction) that the cultural significance of *South Park* cannot be assessed properly without taking into consideration the ways in which the program appropriates from and militates against the history of television cartoons and the ways in which it attempts to distinguish itself from other competing shows including *The Simpsons* and *Family Guy*. Part of the fun of *South Park* is precisely the way in which it self-referentially foregrounds its own status as animated program within the broader context of cartoon history.

The chapters in Part 2, Identity Politics, examine the program's representations of and general attitude toward ethnic and social minorities. The section begins with Robert Samuels's psychoanalytic approach to the *South Park* movie, "Freud Goes to South Park: Teaching against Postmodern Prejudices and Equal Opportunity Hatred." *South Park*, according to Samuels, enacts what he refers to as a "rhetorical reversal" whereby one is taught to be intolerant of tolerance and tolerant of intolerance. Samuels views this reversal as part of a larger social effort to challenge and reverse progressive efforts to fight stereotypes and prejudices in American culture and emphasizes the ways in which pop culture representations have the power to provide the rhetorical foundation for a political reversal of victims and victimizers. Implicit in his chapter is a powerful justification for incorporating pop culture texts into the classroom and his chapter concludes by calling on responsible pedagogues to teach against "equal opportunity hatred."

Stephen Groening's contribution, "Cynicism and Other Postideological Half Measures in *South Park*," shares Samuels's cynical approach to *South Park*. According to Groening, *South Park* appeals to an audience consisting of media-savvy individuals who acknowledge the distortions and misrepresentations inherent in television and other forms of mass culture and yet act as if these representations have no consequences. Focusing as does Samuels on the program's egalitarian offensiveness that obscures real historical inequities, Groening asserts that *South Park* fosters a form of "postideological" cynicism that runs wholly counter to the commitment necessary for political engagement.

The last chapter in Part 2, Lindsay Coleman's "Shopping at J-Mart with the Williams: Race, Ethnicity, and Belonging in *South Park*," is more sanguine about *South Park's* representations of racial stereotypes than Samuels and Groening. Coleman begins by noting that ethnic and personal slurs are the stuff of even the most mundane conversations in the program and through such intemperate rhetoric *South Park* joins a long tradition of decidedly impolite, racially charged comedy. However, Coleman contends that in creating an atmosphere of pervasive social derision, Parker and Stone accomplish a dual objective: They first illustrate the deeply ingrained prejudice underlying all aspects of American social life and then, having done this, they ironically establish a "counterhegemony" that privileges racial minorities. Thus, Coleman also views the program as enacting a rhetorical reversal, but one that ultimately undermines rather than reinforces bigoted thinking.

Part 3, South Park Conservatives?, consists of analyses of *South Park's* "worldview." Each of the three chapters included in this cluster attempts to weigh into the debate over how to characterize the program's political stripes. With interesting connections to Groening's chapter, Matt Becker in his chapter, "'I Hate Hippies': *South Park* and the Politics of Generation X," contends that the political sensibilities of both *South Park* and its creators align most clearly with a Generation X world view—one characterized by political cynicism, apathy, and disengagement. Becker's chapter asserts that *South Park* is politically inconsistent and includes simultaneously radical, reactionary, and non- or apolitical leanings that relate intimately to the political worldview of Generation X.

For Randall Fallows, *South Park's* reluctance to embrace any political viewpoint fully is part of its general critique of rigid dichotomized thinking. Fallows maintains in chapter 9, "*South Park* Heretics: Confronting Political Orthodoxies through Theater of the Absurd," that one thing that nearly all the episodes have in common is the notion that the United States has become a country that goes to absurd extremes. Although according to Fallows the show rarely offers realistic solutions to contemporary problems, it frequently reveals the ridiculous quality of all-or-nothing thinking that has become increasingly common in American culture and politics. By parodying the extreme views to which both liberals and conservatives often adhere, *South Park* encourages the viewer to think beyond a mere repetition of ideological clichés and explore more creative ways of dealing with old problems. Fallows links the program's satiric approach to political orthodoxy to the tradition of Theater of the Absurd, which reached its apex during the early part of the Cold War and which dramatized and ridiculed similarly extremist thinking.

Adopting a very original approach to *South Park* and its politics, Michael W. DeLashmutt and Brannon Hancock link the program not with the Theater of the Absurd but with biblical prophecy. In "Prophetic Profanity: *South Park* on Religion or Thinking Theologically with Eric Cartman," the authors argue that its satirical nature places *South Park* in a long line of subversive and corrective pronouncements central to the prophetic within the Christian tradition and conclude that in keeping with the prophetic tradition, the program "spew[s] its centrist truth at a complacent American populace." The authors see *South Park* as performing an important social function with biblical precedent.

Part 4, Specific Critiques, moves the reader from general characterizations of the program's politics to focused readings of the program's treatments of particular topics and each of the two chapters included in this section demonstrates the ways in which *South Park* targets particular aspects of modern life for satiric critique. In "'You Know, I Learned Something Today . . .': Cultural Pedagogy and the Limits of Formal Education in *South Park*," James Rennie makes the case that with its narrative reliance on the schoolhouse, *South Park* routinely undermines the pedagogical influence and function of formal education and shows that the most important lessons come from the least likely of sources. Consequently, Rennie sees *South Park* as mounting an important critique of contemporary public education and its role in youth culture and development.

Damion Sturm's contribution focuses in on another central target of *South Park*'s irreverence: contemporary celebrities. In "'Omigod, It's Russell Crowe!': *South Park*'s Assault on Celebrity," Sturm maintains that *South Park* offers a challenge to the cult of celebrity in the United States—and Western culture more generally—by repeatedly undermining the value of contemporary celebrity. Sturm shows, through parody, how *South Park* provides both a comical and insightful critique of celebrity, exposing and mocking the processes of "celebrification" and questioning the authenticity, value, and place of celebrities in American culture.

All the chapters herein take *South Park* seriously and assume that any program attracting millions of viewers week after week constitutes a cultural phenomenon worth scrutinizing carefully. Together, these chapters cover a lot of ground. Not surprisingly, however, given the increasing attention to *South Park* as presenting cogent political satire, the volume as a whole emphasizes the program's politics and their implications for understanding American culture.[6] Clearly, only so many approaches can be incorporated into a single volume. Therefore, rather than being definitive, I hope that this volume instead will serve as a fruitful starting point for future considerations of the importance of *South Park* and other popular culture phenomena that follow in its wake.

Notes

1. Although many accept as common knowledge online that many schools have enacted bans, I have only been able to find specific references to two cases: Thomas Elementary School in Plano, Texas (Scoville), and Hickory Flat Elementary School in Canton, Georgia (Marin 60).

2. Consider for instance the satiric approach to "political correctness"—perceived by the series' creators to be a form of censorship—as depicted in the "The Death Camp of Tolerance" during season six. In this episode, Cartman, Kyle, Stan, and Kenny, after protesting Mr. Garrison's outrageous gay-themed antics (which include inserting a gerbil into the rectum of his new, bondage-clad teaching assistant, Mr. Slave, so that he can get fired and sue the school system for discrimination against homosexuals), are sent to a gulag-style "tolerance" camp at which, under the supervision of German-accented monitors, they are forced to color pictures including persons of varying races for hours on end.

3. Beyond these episodes, television and other forms of popular media play an enormous role in the series in general.

4. Freud develops the idea of "kettle logic" in *The Interpretation of Dreams* in relation to the contradictory logic of dreams. He illustrates the notion through a funny anecdote: "[A man was] charged by one of his neighbours with having given him back a borrowed kettle in a damaged condition. The defendant asserted, first, that he had given it back undamaged; secondly, that the kettle had a hole in it when he borrowed it; and thirdly, that he had never borrowed the kettle from his neighbor at all" (153).

5. Notably, *South Park*'s approach to identity politics has been appropriated by Comedy Central's satiric *Mind of Mencia* and short-lived *Chappelle's Show*, both of which present themselves as "equal-opportunity offenders" and further defuse potential criticism of potentially offensive stereotyped representations by having the representations originate with members of ethnic minority groups themselves.

6. Poniewozik observes in his 2006 interview with Parker and Stone that "[. . .] in '97 all people talked about was the vulgarity. Now all they talk about is the social commentary."

Works Cited

Anderson, Brian C. *South Park Conservatives: The Revolt Against the Liberal Media Bias.* Washington, DC: Regnery, 2005.

"Ban *South Park.*" 10 Aug. 2006. <http://www.petitiononline.com/bspsc0/petition.html>.

"Ban *South Park* it is anti-Christ." 10 Aug. 2006. <http://www.petitionspot.com/petitions/southparkisagainstjesusandchristianity>.

Collins, James. "Gross and Grosser." *Time* 23 Mar. 1998: 74–76.

Corliss, Richard. "*South Park: Bigger Longer & Uncut.*" *Time* 5 July 1999: 75.

Fagin, Barry S. "Goin' Down to South Park." *Reason* 32.1 (2000): 38–41.

Freud, Sigmund. *The Interpretation of Dreams.* New York: Modern Library, 1950.

Gardiner, Judith Kegan. "Why Saddam Is Gay: Masculinity Politics in *South Park: Bigger Longer & Uncut.*" *Quarterly Review of Film and Video* 22 (2005): 51–62.

Geertz, Clifford. *The Interpretation of Cultures: Selected Essays.* New York: Basic Books, 1973.

Hart, Melissa. "'South Park,' in the Tradition of Chaucer and Shakespeare." *Chronicle of Higher Education* 25 Oct. 2002: B5.

Marin, Rick. "South Park: The Rude Tube." *Newsweek* 23 Mar. 1998: 56–62.

McDonald, Stef. "25 Shocking Secrets You Need to Know about *South Park.*" *TV Guide* 28 March 1998: 22–25.

Otto, Jeff. "Interview: Trey Parker and Matt Stone." 31 July 2006. <http://filmforce.ign.com/articles/612/612094/1.html>.

Poniewozik, James. "10 Questions for Matt Stone and Trey Parker." *Time* 13 Mar. 2006: 8.

"Professor Takes on 'South Park' in Forthcoming Essay Collection." 7 Aug. 2006. <http://dig.com/tech_news/Professor_Takes_on_South_Park_in_Forthcoming_Essay_Collection>.

"Professor Takes on 'South Park' in Forthcoming Essay Collection." 7 Aug. 2006. <http://www.freerepublic.com/focus/f-news/1532069/posts>.

Ross, Chuck. "Advertisers Flock to Comedy Central's Racy 'South Park.'" *Advertising Age* 12 Jan. 1998: 3.

Savage, William J., Jr. "'So Television's Responsible!': Oppositionality and the Interpretive Logic of Satire and Censorship in *The Simpsons* and *South Park.*" *Leaving Springfield: The Simpsons and the Possibility of Oppositional Culture.* Ed. John Alberti. Detroit: Wayne State University Press, 2004. 197–224.

Scoville, Jen. "Too Crass for Class." *Texas Monthly: The Big Beat.* 10 Aug. 2006. <http://www.texasmonthly.com/ranch/bigbeat/beat.emay.98.php>.

"South Park Studios: BBS: Stan, Kyle, Kenny and Cartman Moving into Academic." 7 Aug. 2006. <http://www.southparkstudios.com/fans/bbs/viewtopic.php?t=15665>.

"Spitting Image: May 2005 Archives." 8 Aug. 2006. <http://www.spitting-image.net/archives/2005_05.html>.

Tomashoff, Craig. "Kids Behaving Badly." *People Weekly* 11 Aug. 1997: 17.

Wallace, Danny. "Kick Xmas, Dude!" *Melody Maker* 75.51 (Dec. 1998): 14–15

Wells, Paul. *Animation and America.* New Brunswick, NJ: Rutgers University Press, 2002

Wild, David. "South Park under Attack." *Rolling Stone* 8 July 1999: 85–86.

———. "South Park's Evil Geniuses and the Triumph of No-Brow Culture." *Rolling Stone* 19 Feb. 1998: 32–37.

PART ONE

The Pleasures of *South Park*

CHAPTER 1

"*Bigger Longer & Uncut*"

South Park and the Carnivalesque

ALISON HALSALL

The humor in *South Park* relies heavily on spectacle. It derives many of its laughs from fart jokes, racial slurs, talking turds, a kid in a Hitler costume at Halloween, and a child who shows his love for his girlfriend by vomiting. Its humor is not easily summarized in terms of its ideological agenda, and it is this very resistance to summary that makes *South Park* so open-ended, so polysemic, and therefore so productive as a vehicle for popular resistance. In August 1997, *Time* magazine lamented *South Park*'s inferiority in comparison to *The Simpsons* and *Beavis and Butt-head* because of its lack of engagement with "the emptiness of suburban life or the ugliness of youthful nihilism or the perniciousness of pop culture" (Nixon 15). Along with demonstrating that Trey Parker and Matt Stone's show does indeed grapple with these three issues, I will contend that much of *South Park*'s humor originates from what Russian literary critic Mikhail Bakhtin has discussed in terms of "Rabelaisian carnival" because the program interweaves levels of parody and satire to mock many of the figures and symbols that are iconic of American culture. The liberating comic energy of carnival provides what many have found to be a welcome antidote to staid and conservative American social values. *South Park*'s carnivalesque humor and the pride that creators Parker and Stone take in rejecting official dogma and in mocking "high" culture make *South Park* so deliciously liberating and important as a popular text.

South Park presents a microcosm of the United States. Unlike the suburban utopia of the *Archie* comics, which is characterized by its homogenous population and its principles of conformity and rule following, *South Park* portrays suburbia as a site of hypocrisy, rampant ignorance, supercilious sanctimony, and spectacular irreverence. Carnival laughter is a method by which popular culture in general, and *South Park* in particular, provides liberation from constraint. This laughter breeds irreverence, which in turn encourages freedom from rituals and rules, social expectations, hierarchical divisions, and official dogma. In an age of "political correctness," *South Park* eschews the correct; indeed, it revels in the socially inappropriate as it pushes, oversteps, and ultimately decimates boundaries of social decorum. The subversive power of laughter derives from its involuntary quality, from its ability to get in under our defenses and our personal ideologies. What is so useful about laughter and vulgarity—and particularly the profanities in *South Park*—is that they scuttle the norms of official speech. The laughter that this show encourages comes from the release from "proper" linguistic discipline. Carnival laughter is also linked to the "low" bodily principle—to the body and to the earth. Popular culture, and the scatology of *South Park*, reminds us that the body is inherently dirty and this dirtiness, this impurity, this untidiness is resistant to the metaphorical cleanliness of the American social order. Through the carnivalesque principles of *South Park*, its interrogation of language, and its use of grotesque realism, Parker and Stone construct a transformative vision of the world that "excrementalizes" the U.S. sociopolitical landscape.

South Park as American Carnival

In *Rabelais and His World*, Mikhail Bakhtin explores the tradition of the carnival, a tradition that abolishes the boundaries separating the public and private spheres and establishes an inverted order in which the lower orders become kings for a day. Folk carnival humor mocks all dogma and authoritarianism, and takes three forms, according to Bakhtin. These particular forms are completely distinct from the official, ecclesiastical, feudal, and political discourses of medieval times—and, by extension, contemporary life as well. These forms include: ritual spectacles (usually comic shows and pageants from the marketplace), comic verbal compositions (parodies that allow laughter to penetrate the highest religious cults and thoughts), and various genres of billingsgate (curses and oaths, familiar speech, often with an emphasis on the bodily and the erotic). In his study of French author Rabelais, Bakhtin explains the principle of grotesque realism, a reliance on appetite and excretion, as reflecting the spirit of carnival. This chapter demonstrates that Parker and Stone's clever animated episodes and feature-length films make use of these elements in their characterization of South Park as American carnival. To downplay the carnivalesque qualities of *South Park* is to ignore the cathartic release that Parker and Stone's satirical potty humor generates.

As Weinstock summarizes in the introduction to this volume, the four boys of *South Park*—Stan, Kyle, Eric, and Kenny—debuted in 1995 in a 5-

minute animated short by Parker and Stone called *The Spirit of Christmas*. The episode depicted an evil snowman terrorizing a town and concluded with Jesus and Santa Claus throwing punches over the true meaning of Christmas. The spectacular irreverence, "political incorrectness," and the combination of incongruous and bizarre situations and themes that characterize *South Park*'s aesthetic thus have been self-consciously present since the program's very beginning. Nine 30-minute *South Park* episodes first aired on cable television's Comedy Central in a late-night television slot from August to December 1997 and the program was astonishingly successful even before the end of the first season. By mid-1998 in Australia, for example, on the Special Broadcasting Service Channel *South Park* was the second most watched program after the World Cup soccer finals (Nixon 13). Parker and Stone deliberately turned down development deals with New Line, Warner Brothers, and Dreamworks before signing with Comedy Central, which guaranteed them full creative control over the series. The late-night time slot also allowed them to retain the vulgarity and bawdy humor that *South Park* used to signal America's preoccupations of the moment. Not long after its premiere, Comedy Central launched an advertising campaign effectively summarizing the program's interests (as well as offering a pithy summation of Bakhtin's notion of the carnivalesque): "Alien Abductions, Anal Probes & Flaming Farts. *South Park*. Why They Created the V–Chip."

Turning to the program itself, even before we enter Parker and Stone's suburban world of lowbrow humor and political incorrectness, *South Park*'s theme song alludes to the show's many levels of satire and parody, mocking as it does the "wholesome" introductory songs for children's animated programs. The "quiet mountain town" of South Park is supposedly located in Colorado. As is the case with Springfield in *The Simpsons*, South Park is both every place and no place. It is a small, suburban town known as much for its "humble folks with friendly faces" as for its "rednecks," a town that Parker and Stone use to project and exaggerate many of the qualities—and particularly the flaws—that they see typifying U.S. society. Gone are the sentimentality and gentleness of Disney's *Snow White and the Seven Dwarfs* (1937); gone are the wholesome domestic values of *Supergirl* from the 1950s; gone is the exaggeration of the American conception of masculinity in *Superman*; gone is the emphasis on the family as the domestic unit. Kenny's lyrics, whose muffled words we cannot understand, encapsulate the parodic impact of *South Park*. Kenny's indistinguishable words function as metaphors for *South Park*'s repeated attempts to frustrate the clear and straightforward conveyance of meaning.

Welcome to South Park: home of dysfunction, delinquency, and degradation. Corruption and American individualism rule. South Park functions as a miniature representation of all of the United States and, as such, is rife with social, political, and racial tension. For all intents and purposes, it appears to be a typical small, U.S. town. Any parallel with the innocuous Riverdale in the *Archie* comics, however, is destroyed by the presence of unlikely places such as Dr. Mephisto's lab and a secret government base, locations that demonstrate Parker and Stone's use of absurd, bizarre, and incongruous combinations to parody the foibles of the American national consciousness. Similarly, South Park's "all-American" façade of "humble folks with friendly faces" is unsettled by characters such as Big Gay Al, Mr. Garrison with his alter ego hand puppet Mr. Hand, and a series of visiting celebrities ranging from George Clooney, the Baldwin brothers, and Barbra Streisand, to Jesus and Satan. This combination of the absurd and the ludicrous allows Parker and Stone to revel in the delightfully productive contradictions typical of American culture.

In Charles Schulz's *Peanuts* and Bill Watterson's *Calvin and Hobbes*, children and even animals are used to voice social critique. Ironically, the children in *South Park* are criticized for having social voices. Each character is constructed and deployed as a particular type: Stan Marsh is the average kid, Kyle Broflovski is the Jewish kid, Eric Cartman is the fat kid, and Kenny McCormick is the poor kid. Parker and Stone actively discourage the perception of their figures as anything but generic types because, through them, they satirize the arbitrary generalizations that stereotypes permit. Token is the African-American kid on *South Park* whose very name points to the creators' fascination with character types. Cartman embodies the ugly American; he is the personification of greed and conspicuous consumption. His spectacularly classist, racist, and sexist statements stand in striking contrast to the professed American ideals of goodness, equality, and justice for all. Cartman's appearances on the program provide moments of carnival pleasure: While watching, the viewer delights in the oaths and politically incorrect expressions that this character so freely utters.

Kenny, too, is a stereotype. When asked why Kenny has to die in each episode, Parker and Stone answer in unison during an interview on the *South Park Volume 1* DVD: "Because he's poor." Not only does this answer point to the specific outcomes that characters from certain cinematic, televisual, and literary genres are guaranteed because of their class, gender, and ethnic status (think, for example, of the promiscuous girl who typically dies in a slasher film), but Parker and Stone's reply also foregrounds their use of stereotypes. Kenny's role on the show and in the film is to *be* poor, to enact poverty, to "perform" the poverty that was widespread in the 1990s during the era of the Bush Sr. and Clinton administrations. In effect, the rats that attack Kenny's body after each of his gruesome deaths draw attention through hyperbolic, gross exaggeration to the fundamental degradation that the poor body is destined to experience in a society that appears less interested in social reform than in military interventions. The rats ravaging Kenny's abused corpse point to the carnival's degradation of the body and provoke liberating and ambivalent laughter from the viewer.

Just a few minutes of watching the average *South Park* episode confirms that the program actually thrives on character stereotypes that enact one-dimensional thinking. The primary colors used on the show and the more than 5,000 two-dimensional cardboard cutouts that they first used in their animation style depict this unsophisticated thinking visually. Parker and Stone originally attempted to make their show look as primitive as possible, thereby enhancing the possibility for satirical manipulation. These two-dimensional figures discourage any visual complexity and function as shallow cutouts highlighting the woodenness of the characters.[1] Consequently, within only a few moments of one episode, viewers can identify the characters as specific types. In this way, *South Park* clearly rejects Disney's attempt to capture realism, depth of field, and three-dimensionality: Instead, Parker and Stone savor the "redneck" ideology that dominates this suburban town by these flat, poorly drawn characters that emphasize first the primitiveness of the animation itself, and second the witless thinking that distinguishes many of the characters. As Scott McCloud argues in *Understanding Comics*, cartooning, in its tendency to render in the abstract, simplifies the image, which in turn amplifies meaning in a way realistic art cannot (30). Parker and Stone's two-dimensional cutouts thus are poised to be effective at tackling difficult sociopolitical issues facing the United States.[2]

In the movie *South Park: Bigger Longer & Uncut* (1999) satirized celebrities appear with photographs of their faces superimposed on their cartoon bodies, as is the case with Hitler, Saddam Hussein, and Gandhi—three of the unfortunates who inhabit hell. This superimposition of a photographed head on a crudely rendered cartoon body points to the two-dimensional character as a screen onto which Parker and Stone project their specific satirical object. Humor arises from the contrast between the "realistic" face and the absurd and incongruous activities that the creators have them perform. Because all of the characters are recognized by their enlarged heads rather than by their bodies (except for Eric Cartman!), the characters become important not for how they look, but rather for what they say and how they act. And it quickly becomes clear that almost all of the characters are exaggerated, talking heads that spout anti-Establishment views, vulgarity, and, at times, homophobic, racist, and classist messages. Most importantly, and in keeping with the liberation provided by carnival laughter, Parker and Stone's characters consistently utter the unutterable; no one is safe from the creators' mockery, including the creators themselves.

Parker and Stone employ self-reflexive irony that is typical of postmodernist thought to poke fun at the creative process and the connection between product and artist. In their American carnival, the creators themselves are as much a focus of their humor as their subjects. In one of the scenes in the *South Park* movie, the four boys discuss movies as vehicles for education, specifically the education that they receive from their cartoon heroes Terrance and Phillip's recent film *Asses of Fire*. They justify their attendance at the movie by claiming that it teaches them what their own parents will not say, namely vulgarity and an appreciation for bawdy body humor. When Cartman dismisses the animation in *Asses of Fire* as "all crappy," and the talk-show host Conan O'Brien asks Terrance and Phillip about how they would respond to the accusation that their "show is nothing but immature fart jokes," the self-reflexive irony depends on the association the viewer is supposed to make between the "crappiness" of the animation of the Terrance and Phillip cartoon and the inherent "crappiness" of the animation of *South Park* itself. In the *Terrance and Phillip Show*, Parker and Stone deliberately produce a show that depends on bathroom humor—the same charge critics level at *South Park* itself. In this way, the Terrance and Phillip cartoon gives the audience and scholars a hint about how the show's writers and producers want the audience to think about the cultural status of the medium as well as its ideological content (Savage 198).

Laughter and *La Resistance*: Laughter as Resistance

Texts that become tools of popular culture critique generally are characterized by a certain measure of interpretive ambiguity and by a resistance to providing any heavy-handed, didactic narration of intention or meaning. *South Park* is full of contradictions, and these contradictions make this popular cultural text "polysemic," possessed of many, often conflicting, meanings. In its polysemy *South Park* embodies the spirit of the American Revolution, liberty, and passion for resistance. What makes *South Park* so potentially ambivalent, however, is that while some might view the film or the individual episodes as criticisms of prejudicial, conservative, self-serving Americanism, others may clearly align themselves with the ignorant, sexist, or racist values that individual characters express. This problematic position taking is evident in some of R. Crumb's underground comics that are certainly subversive in terms of their open and explicit engagement with sexuality and drug culture, but also could be interpreted as reinforcing stereotypes, both racial and sexist. It is this polysemy, this invitation to have contradictory interpretations of the materials, which makes *South Park* such a productive popular culture text. In its carnivalesque irreverence, *South Park* is similar to *MAD Magazine*, which (especially in the 1950s) rebelled against culture-mongers and the Comics Code's seal of approval. *South Park* is entirely post-Code in its determination to be vulgar and inappropriate and to engage explicitly with "touchy" sociopolitical issues.

One particular concept that routinely comes under attack in individual *South Park* episodes and in *South Park: Bigger Longer & Uncut* that demonstrates Parker and Stone's determination to poke fun at all iconic elements of

American culture is the idea of the American hero. David Hasselhoff, for example, iconic ubermensch of *Baywatch* and *Knight Rider*, appears in an episode (or at least his head does) in which he and his nose feature as the objects of the Mr. Garrison's gay wish-fulfillment fantasy. This is representative of the way Parker and Stone consistently "queer" heroes or icons in an effort to make the sacred profane and to disturb conventional parameters of heroism. Satan in the *South Park* movie is another example of this "queering" tendency. Parker and Stone transform Milton's antihero into an effeminate "queen," whose passive sexual presence stands in contrast to Saddam Hussein's hypersexual appetite. In queering Satan, Parker and Stone situate Satan's homosexuality as liberating from conventional conceptions of heroism, and the carnival laughter they provoke emerges through the homosexual subtext they locate in a Christian figure.

However, this process of queering (not surprisingly) goes both ways. Another sequence in the film redeploys a U.S. athlete as an unlikely superman. The qualities that conventionally are associated with superheroes such as Batman, Supergirl, and Spider-Man (rationality, moral steadiness, superhuman strength, keen vision, and understanding) for example, are superimposed on the figure of Brian Boitano, the U.S. figure skater known in part for his effeminacy and for his "unmanly" sport. The sequence's humor stems from the juxtaposition of Boitano's frilly pink shirt and his delicacy and grace as a figure skater with the superheroic qualities that the children project onto him. The kids describe his hyperbolical resourcefulness in fighting grizzly bears in the Alps, overthrowing evil robot kings in the future, and beating up Kubla Khan in the past. In effect, the children recast this effeminate sports figure as a masculine superhero who will "save the maidens fair," and insist that he would not "take shit from anybody." In this way, Parker and Stone resituate the effeminate Boitano as the archetypal hero, and in the process pinpoint the absurdities that fuel the very concept of American heroism.

South Park characteristically "busts up," satirizes, or parodies accepted texts in its carnivalesque undermining of commonly held truths and generic conventions. The *South Park* movie, for example, parodies the musical genre—taken, popularized, and eventually commodified by the Walt Disney Company—to address sensitive issues such as sexuality and race that Disney's more conservative films address only superficially (and often regressively). Like Buster Brown who "busted up" bourgeois ideals of class, race, and gender in the comics at the beginning of the twentieth century, *South Park* "busts up" notions of suburbia, authority, the body, sexuality, war, and even Christmas through its pervasive intertextuality and its vulgarity. *South Park: Bigger Longer & Uncut* parodies throughout the musical numbers that typify Disney fairy tales, including songs the protagonists croon as they dream about a different future. Satan, for example (a variation on the hypermasculine Beast figure), sings about his aspirations for a better life. Unlike the Disney song in which the Beast longs for Belle to accept him in spite of his hairy face and beastly body, Satan questions the arbitrariness of the concept of "evil." Satan, the movie suggests, is imprisoned in hell not because of his "evil" heretical beliefs, but because of his alternative sexuality. The rainbow icon (typically used in children's animated cartoons as an icon for idyllic happiness) is reassigned in this scene as a code for viewers that Satan's dilemma is not about his ethics but rather about his sexual preferences. Parker and Stone have no sacred cows. Every concept, theme, and identity category is fair game in their suburban carnival.

Fart Jokes and the V-Chip

The subversive power of laughter stems from its involuntary quality and its ability to get past our defenses and our personal ideologies. What is so productive about vulgarity—and particularly the profanities in South Park—is that it violates the norms of official speech. As Bakhtin argues, the language of the carnival is both abusive and regenerative; words both humiliate and revive. Carnival language provides liberation and renewal

> The familiar language of the marketplace became a reservoir in which various speech patterns excluded from official intercourse could freely accumulate. In spite of their genetic differences, all these genres [abusive expressions, profanities, and oaths] were filled with the carnival spirit, transformed their primitive verbal functions, acquired a general tone of laughter, and became, as it were, so many sparks of the carnival bonfire which renews the world. (Bakhtin 17)

The South Park movie clearly stages the conflict between official and unofficial language. Mrs. Broflovski wages a holy war on "dirty language," and the children form "La Resistance" to protest the policing of speech. Significantly, Cartman's rampant use of curses eventually defeats the archenemy Saddam Hussein. The carnival laughter that Parker and Stone encourage comes through the release from "proper" linguistic discipline. In the "Uncle Fucka" sequence in South Park: Bigger Longer & Uncut that features a clip from Asses of Fire, the Terrance and Phillip movie that provokes such an uproar in the small town because of its alleged vulgarity, the creators of South Park again parody a Disney musical. Instead of providing the bland, saccharine-sweet messages typical of such Disney films as Snow White or Cinderella (1950), this song is a parody of the creative possibilities the liberal and unrestrained use of profanity allows. "Fuck off, you donkey-raping shiteater" is only one of the delicate phrases that the four boys glean from this sequence in the Terrance and Phillip movie, which they in turn direct at any authority figure who has the misfortune of coming their way. The language in *Asses of Fire* relies principally on bawdy humor, referring liberally as it does to bestiality, homosexuality, and incest. In fact, one of the worst abuses—"you don't eat or sleep or mow the lawn, you just fuck your uncle all day long!"—is one that suggests that the behavior of Terrance, Phillip, or both is inappropriate simply because they abandon their everyday routine in favor of sexual activity, or worse, sexual activity with a relative. Evident here is the manner in which the oaths that *Asses of Fire* and *South Park: Bigger Longer & Uncut* feature focus compulsively on bodily functions and the possibilities they offer for creative liberation from socially appropriate behavior. Further, the gut-wrenching, cathartic response these curses provoke relies on the gross-out factor.

This profanity is then addressed in Mr. Mackie's sequence on euphemisms. Mr. Mackie, the school guidance counselor, has been charged with rehabilitating the children from their addiction to swear words. Mackie encourages them to substitute inane euphemisms for vulgar words, phrases that replace an offensive word with an expression that is milder, less precise, and fundamentally less accurate. Instead of saying "ass, say buns," he advises. Moreover, Mackie encourages the children to substitute his own strange verbal tic, "M'kay," if they cannot dream up a euphemism for one of their own swear words. In effect, this sequence satirizes the North American tendency toward political correctness in which less precise words are substituted for specific expressions. It also satirizes the simple-mindedness of the adult population obsessed with the corruption of innocence. Most important, it signals a kind of linguistic hypocrisy. His song teaches the children that they can denigrate homeless prostitutes but they had better not say "shit." In sum, Mackie's lesson is that language is the gateway to a bourgeois lifestyle and to social conformity. After this session, Mr. Mackie declares the children magically "cured," and they promptly run off to the cinema for another viewing of *Asses of Fire*, further demonstrating the draw that unofficial language and bawdy subject matter can have on popular audiences.

This engagement with the question about the effectiveness of language to reveal or conceal meaning is centered most specifically on the adults in *South Park*. In this respect, Parker and Stone employ the children as voices of social critique: Stan, Kyle, Eric, and Kenny stand in contrast to the adult world, which provides no authority worthy of their respect. Their teacher, Mr. Garrison, is especially ineffective as an educator, chastising a student for being a "complete retard" for offering the wrong answer to a question. Furthermore, the parental figures demonstrate their virulent intolerance when they prepare to wage war on Terrance and Phillip for teaching their sons dangerous toilet humor. Clearly, Parker and Stone condemn the self-censorship that the Mothers Against Canada endorse through the latter's decision to implant the V–chip, a little microchip that sends a small jolt of electricity through a child each time he or she swears, in their children. In effect, the V–chip represents the policing of language. In this instance, "V" stands for vulgarity and violence, two of the elements that the Comics Code and the Mothers Against Canada condemn. However, "V" also stands for vacant, vague, and vapid. The sanitized language that the Mothers Against Canada encourage is abstracted of all vitality. The parents' prejudice is made hyperbolic when they identify Terrance and Phillip's foul language and lowbrow humor as "crimes against humanity," and encourage the escalation of full-scale warfare between the United States and Canada to eradicate the supposed threat that these two cartoon figures represent to proper language. Not only do Parker and Stone ridicule the intolerance, which fuels the mothers' activism when Kyle's mom generalizes about Canadians as being "all the same with beady little eyes and square heads," but they also satirize scapegoating in general through the ease with which the mothers latch arbitrarily onto an enemy (in this instance, an entire country) on which to focus their hate. Undoubtedly, the compulsive focus that the *South Park* film gives to oaths helps the viewer delight in this unofficial and offensive language, and ironically generates an important critique of linguistic sanitation. Through the vigorous use of profanity, Parker and Stone rob contemporary political-speak of its abstract wordiness by bringing everything down to the level of the body.

Language can also impose a false sense of closure on a particular subject, as can be seen most obviously in the moralistic messages that conclude many children's animated programs. *South Park* arguably resists all forms of didacticism and dogmatism. If it does use moralistic statements, it is to highlight the inanity of the candy-coated endings of family-oriented sitcoms on American television. Usually a 30–minute episode of *South Park* ends with Stan or Kyle turning abruptly to the camera to say, "You guys, I've learned something today," and then delivering a trite statement about the importance of acceptance or having confidence in oneself. In such scenes, the robotic unnaturalness of the character's movements mimics the corny moral that is devoid of any true meaning. The black-and-white introductions Parker and Stone make at the beginning of individual *South Park* episodes on the DVD versions also satirize the false sentiment of such statements and the supercilious moralistic messages in children's programs. In the introduction to the "Mr. Hankey, the Christmas Poo" episode, for example, Parker and Stone clarify the "moral": Everyone should celebrate Christmas, they claim, not because of its endorsement of family values, but because of its commercialism. Again, Parker and Stone blur the sacred and the profane, in this instance, to gut holidays of their traditional meanings.

Fundamentally, what *South Park* trains its audience to do through this satire of corny morals is to rebuff sentiment and empathy. Emotional

FIGURE 2
Mr. Hankey waves hello.

involvement is not encouraged on *South Park*: Not a single character in *South Park* elicits a complicated emotional reaction from the viewer. Indeed, through the portrayal of repeated violent acts, the viewer becomes immune to the "reality" of this violence and is discouraged from registering any emotional reaction. What is produced instead is a sort of free-floating, intense enjoyment of socially unacceptable behavior. For example, Kyle and his little brother, Ike, enjoy playing a game called "kick the baby" in which Ike is kicked through a window or off the screen. As we watch, we never feel sorry for Ike; instead, the way he sails through the air is what is most funny about the scene. Moreover, one of the conventions of the episodes and the film is to kill Kenny in spectacularly bloody ways. His death is always followed by the cheerful refrain, "Oh my God, they've killed Kenny. You bastards!" The repeated murder of Kenny and the response expected and elicited from the kids on the show (and the audience watching) desensitize the viewer to the murder. In effect, the phrase, "Oh my God, they've killed Kenny," becomes a cliché, a hackneyed, empty phrase, and discourages any emotional reaction from the viewer. The humor lies, of course, in the children's refusal to act in a socially appropriate fashion.

Talking Turds: Scatology in *South Park*

One principal method through which carnivalesque popular culture manages to evade the constraints of social discipline is by focusing on bodily pleasures, by lowering pleasure to the level of the body. In his work on Rabelais, Bakhtin outlines the "concept of grotesque realism" (18) typical of folk humor, a concept that relies primarily on this bodily principle. An emphasis on the body, Bakhtin maintains, accentuates degradation and locates the popular pleasure in the body instead of raising expectation to a "higher," more refined pleasure that fewer can enjoy (21). In this way, carnival laughter is linked to the "low" bodily principle that, according to Bakhtin, both degrades and rejuvenates. For Bakhtin words of abuse, oaths, and expletives reflect a "grotesque concept of the body [. . .]. Oaths or other unprintable expressions degrade the object according to the grotesque method; they send it down to the absolute bodily lower stratum, to the zone of the genital organs, the bodily grave, in order to be destroyed" (28). *South Park*'s reliance on body humor is clearly indicated by the subtitle of their feature-length film, which reads like a title for gay porn or (as contributor to this volume, Robert Samuels, argues) an allusion to a Jewish stereotype. Moreover, the "Uncle Fucka" sequence pinpoints the links between expletives and the grotesque bodily principle of the Rabelaisian carnival. This sequence takes bodily humor and vulgarity to such an extent that, when Terrance and Phillip stage a fart-off in front of a Canadian Mounted Police officer, characters get out of their cars in a traffic jam to join them in this celebration of gas!

Carnival reminds us that the body is inherently dirty, and this impurity is resistant to the metaphorical cleanliness of the social order. *South Park* is famous for its scatology, its study of excrement.[3] *South Park* resists cleanliness and purity. No better example demonstrates Parker and Stone's concern with the scatological than Mr. Hankey, the Christmas Poo, the talking piece of shit who "comes out of the toilet once a year to give presents to all the little boys and girls who have fiber in their diets." Mr. Hankey is excrement incarnate: He jumps out of the toilet and leaves a brown mark, a smear, a stain, on every surface he touches as a reminder to the viewer of the inherent dirtiness of the human body no matter how much we try to aestheticize it.[4] Mr. Hankey's stains systematically mess up the cleanliness of the social order. This confrontation of the viewer with the undesirable, the vulgar, and the grotesque elicits the visceral reaction that Parker and Stone long for. In bringing humor down to the level of the body, *South Park* refuses cultural sanitization (and sanitation at all, for that matter!) through the gross-out factor.[5]

What makes Mr. Hankey such a complicated piece of shit, however, is the fact that he is also a parody of one of the most widely recognized icons of

American popular culture, Mickey Mouse, complete with plump brown body, gloved hands and large, happy eyes. Both are lovable, kind, and spout inanities. Consider Mr. Hankey's nonsensical expression to Kyle: "Gosh, Kyle, you smell like flowers." Parker and Stone pervert this world-renowned cultural icon by suggesting that he is nothing more than a piece of shit; further, their codification of Mr. Hankey as a "Christmas Poo" characterizes Christmas, "that charged consumerist node at the center of the world's largest consumer culture" (Hurley 204), as shit. This talking turd, used to remind characters that "everyone, regardless of [his or her] religion, should celebrate Christmas," smears the importance of the Christian holiday and mocks the consumerist tendencies that this holiday is known to evoke. As a brown smear, Mr. Hankey operates repeatedly as a force of disruption. Significantly, in the "Mr. Hankey, the Christmas Poo" episode, Hankey helps to thwart the sanitization of the Christian holiday that the mayor and inhabitants of South Park are promoting, especially in their nondenominational and therefore inoffensive holiday pageant designed by Philip Glass. In the episode "A Very Crappy Christmas," Mr. Hankey's noted absence from the town leaves the inhabitants with no Christmas spirit; again, then, the absence of this piece of holiday shit disrupts the "regular" commercialism that Parker and Stone use to characterize the Christmas season.[6]

Scatology and satirical irreverence operate side-by-side in Parker and Stone's suburban carnival, *South Park*. As a vehicle for resisting official U.S. dogma, Parker and Stone's individual *South Park* episodes and their feature-length animated film, as well as their marionette extravaganza *Team America: World Police*, demonstrate their strategy of using lowbrow humor to undercut and deflate established American cultural icons and ideologies. What is clear about *South Park* is that, despite its two-dimensional style of animation, the form and structure of the film and individual episodes are intensely sophisticated because of their polysemic pliancy, postmodern intertextuality, and self-reflexive irony. Through the comic energy of the carnival, Parker and Stone provide a cathartic (and irreverent) alternative to established American social values.

Notes

1. A significant economic pay-off is found in the aesthetics of *South Park*. The characters have been easily converted into an army of plush toys, and the quirky commodities on the show have been reproduced in real life: Any child can buy a box of Cartman's favorite snack, Cheesy Poofs, for example. In the 6 months after the cartoon premiered, 1 million T-shirts and $30 million in merchandise were sold. This popularity has not diminished. In fact, generally speaking, *South Park* merchandise outsells all comparable products (including *Simpsons* products) by a ratio of 10:1 (Nixon 13).

2. In *Team America: World Police* (2004), their marionette extravaganza, the *South Park* creators up the ante in terms of aesthetic and ideological speculation. Employing discomfortingly human-looking puppets, Parker and Stone continue to parody noted celebrities in their carnivalesque critique of U.S. foreign policy and America's War on Terror.

3. *Team America: World Police* takes a no-holds-barred approach to excrement. The sex scene involving Gary and Lisa, two members of Team America, features on the unrated DVD version not only intercourse in a wide array of positions, but Gary urinating in Lisa's mouth and Lisa defecating in his. Not surprisingly, this scene was edited for the theatrical release.

4. Parker and Stone even include a mock advertisement in the middle of one of the "Mr. Hankey" episodes that parodies ads for children's play sets. The children in the mock commercial fish in the toilet bowl for a turd, then create their own Mr. Hankey with the tools that come with the play set. Somehow the baby in the ad manages to get hold of her own Mr. Hankey and ingests it, leaving a brown stain on her cheek.

5. James S. Hurley notes the ironic financial result that Mr. Hankey as paradoxically cuddly and disgusting figure has for consumer culture. During the 1998 U.S. Christmas season, the Mr. Hankey "stuffed turd" was one of the hottest commodities of all the *South Park* tie-in products (Hurley 204).

6. The difficulty that this character offers also lies in the fact that, like Mickey Mouse, Mr. Hankey is a minstrel figure, a figure who is conventionally a member of a band of entertainers with blackened faces, performing songs and music ostensibly of African-American origin. Mickey epitomizes the conservative ideology and the morally simplistic themes Disney films endorse, as first seen in *Steamboat Willie* (1928). Influenced by Al Jolson in *The Jazz Singer* (1927), Mickey as a simple and naïve mouse functions as an enduring symbol of racial intolerance (Warren). The implicit racism of Disney's signature cartoon figure becomes evident once we draw the link between Mr. Hankey and Mickey Mouse, two lovable minstrels, and realize that Parker and Stone have redeployed Disney's Mickey as a piece of shit, a talking turd who is used to satirize the commercial and capitalistic tendencies of American—and, indeed, global—culture.

Works Cited

Bakhtin, Mikhail M. *Rabelais and His World*. Bloomington: Indiana University Press, 1984.

Hurley, James S. "Marketing Transgression, or Capital Talks Shit." *The Minnesota Review* 50–51 (October 1999): 197–207.

McCloud, Scott. *Understanding Comics: The Invisible Art*. New York: Kitchen Sink Press, 1993.

Nixon, Helen. "Adults Watching Children Watch *South Park*." *Journal of Adolescent and Adult Literacy* 43.1 (Sept. 1999): 12–16.

Savage, William J. "'So Television's Responsible!': Oppositionality and the Interpretive Logic of Satire and Censorship in *The Simpsons* and *South Park*." *Leaving Springfield: The Simpsons and the Possibility of Oppositional Culture*. Ed. John Alberti. Detroit: Wayne State University Press, 2004. 197–224.

Warren, Jonathan. "The Country Mouse and City Rabbit: Annie as Conservative Poster Girl." Lecture for Comics and Cartoons. York University, Toronto. 7 Nov. 2002.

CHAPTER 2

The Pleasures of *South Park*

(An Experiment in Media Erotics)

BRIAN L. OTT

One of my favorite scenes from *South Park* depicts 8-year-old and recently deputized local police officer Eric Cartman patrolling the streets of South Park on his Big Wheel. During a routine traffic stop, Cartman confronts Stan's father, Randy Marsh. The subsequent exchange, which is "shot" *Cops*-style, ends with Cartman whacking him on the knee with his nightstick and yelling, "Respect my authoritah!" I refer to this as one of my favorite "scenes" because I do not have favorite "episodes" of *South Park*. It just is not that kind of show. *South Park* is driven by, or more appropriately "animated" by, memorable moments, images, and catchphrases (most of which expeditiously find their way onto the Internet and/or T–shirts), rather than by sustained narrative complexity. I say that not by way of disparaging the series, but of drawing attention to its rhetorical mode. Formally and aesthetically, *South Park* is, in a word, "postmodern," which literary critic Terry Eagleton defines as "a depthless, decentered, ungrounded, self-reflexive, playful, derivative, eclectic, pluralistic art" (vii). Add to that the fact that *South Park* appears on television, which is widely regarded as "the postmodern medium par excellence" (O'Day 112), and it raises an important question: What is the role and function of the critic when confronted with postmodern textuality?

Historically, critics—be they art, literary, or media centered—have sought to "unlock" the mysteries of a text, to "uncover" its deep meaning or hidden ideology. But postmodern textuality confounds this task and perhaps even renders it impossible. Unlike the modernist text, which has discrete boundaries and celebrates a final signified, postmodern textuality is diffuse and privileges the boundless signifier. No singular, static, unified message then exists to recover or exhume in postmodern textuality.[1] Rather than being organized to say "something," postmodern textuality recombines the countless somethings that have already been said. It makes no claim to innocence, originality, or authenticity. As such, the critical "methods" of modernism—Marxism, structuralism, semiotics, feminism, and psychoanalysis—are poorly suited to address postmodern textuality. That, of course, has not stopped critics from trying, from naïvely arguing that "texts" such as *South Park*, which use ethnic, racial, gender, and sexual stereotypes self-consciously and ironically, are racist, sexist, and homophobic. Not all critics have fallen into this trap, however. Those who recognize that we live in a culture of excess, of intertextual webs, and an endless play of signifiers, have turned to deconstruction to show the instability of texts.[2]

Instead of working to uncover a text's hidden meaning, deconstructionists seek to show how meaning is always deferred.[3] Their central concern, therefore, like that of modernist critics, continues to be with meaning, although admittedly its dispersal, rather than its coherence. I find this approach to postmodern textuality equally unsatisfying because it tends toward a philosophy of nihilism.[4] As a poststructuralist, I concur that texts do not "speak" with a single, unified, or stable voice. But as a pragmatist, I am specifically interested in the use-value of media texts in our everyday lives. Thus, this chapter searches for an alternative critical practice, one that is neither hermeneutical nor deconstructionist. Instead of pursuing textual meanings, be they discrete or diffuse, I follow the lead of critics such as Susan Sontag and Roland Barthes and go in search of textual pleasures. My aim is to map the contours of a theory of media erotics by examining postmodern textuality in terms of *significance* rather than signification.[5]

Toward that end, I reverse the typical critical formula. Rather than "employing" (some might say "imposing") theory to judge a text, I seek to spin theory from a text. I turn to *South Park* not simply to illuminate *this* text, but also to illuminate the character of postmodern textuality and to proffer a theory of media erotics because, as Barthes explains in *S/Z*, "each (single) text is the very theory (and not the mere example)" (12). Because pursuing the meaning or ideology of *South Park* is fruitless, I will instead explore its *meaningfulness*—the way it speaks directly to the body. My central question is not *what* does *South Park* say to viewers, but *how* does *South Park* arouse viewers? To answer this question, I probe six scenes from the show, each of which functions as a transgressive pleasure: the abject, the carnivalesque, the intertextual, the ironic, the liminal, and the depthless. Although I examine these erotic modes independently, they are often deeply interconnected. Indeed, their affectivity lies largely in the ways they cross-pollinate one another.

Before turning to these erotic modes, however, I wish to comment briefly on the content and form of this chapter. With regard to pleasure, I address only those pleasures that I regard as principally, or at least potentially, counterhegemonic. Thus, the chapter scrupulously avoids regimes of pleasure rooted in identification, narrative form, and voyeuristic practices of looking. As I have demonstrated elsewhere, such pleasures reproduce dominant ideologies and subjectivities (Ott, "(Re)Locating"). With regard to the chapter's form, I have consciously attempted to speak in the "language" of television whenever possible. Because an image-based work was impractical, I adopted a more fragmentary and reflexive style than is typical of most academic writing. Like television, this chapter offers several "channels" of content, each of which is relatively self-contained and can be read or surfed by the reader in any order. In the spirit of television, which unceasingly quotes from the past, this chapter too frequently engages with the work of other scholars as a way of acknowledging how scholarship itself is recombinant.

The Abject

South Park is notoriously sexual, scatological, and sexually scatological. If something can come out of or go into someone's anus, it probably has on *South Park*. From flaming farts and alien anal probes to lost gerbils and Mr. Hankey, the Christmas Poo, this series is obsessed with asses and especially their holes. Selecting my favorite "anal scene" from *South Park* is, therefore, no simple task. That said, with regard to pleasure, the "whore off" between Mr. Slave and Paris Hilton in the episode, "Stupid Spoiled Whore Video Playset," stands alone. After the young girls in South Park begin dressing and behaving like Paris Hilton, Mr. Slave challenges Paris Hilton to a whore off in the hopes of teaching the girls that being a "whore" is nothing to be proud of. On a stage in front of the whole town, Paris and Mr. Slave compete to determine who the bigger whore is. Following sex with a group of men, Paris successfully inserts a whole pineapple into her vagina. Calmly standing up to take his turn, Mr. Slave leaps into the air and lands on Paris's head, where he squirms until she is completely engulfed in his anus. The scene ends with an intra-anal shot of Paris Hilton crawling through Mr. Slave's bowels looking for an exit (which visually repeats the same scenario previously played out with a gerbil in "The Death Camp of Tolerance" episode).

The whore off scene from *South Park* is a particularly clear example of what critical theorists today refer to as the abject. As Julia Kristeva explains in *Powers of Horror*, the abject is related to perversion, pollution, corruption, and defilement (15–17). As each of the concepts suggests, abjection arises from the transgression of social taboos or the crossing of culturally constructed boundaries. Because the "body is a model which can stand for any bounded system" (Douglas 142), its boundaries—the distinction between internal and external marked by bodily orifices—are common sites for staging the abject. Thus, anything discharged from the body, such as excrement, spittle, blood, tears, or mucus, can give rise to abjection.[6] Indeed, the most dangerous pollution of the body, the greatest social taboo, is the readmittance of anything that has previously been issued from the body (Douglas 151–52). For this reason even the mere mention of eating shit evokes intense disgust and revulsion. In light of *South Park*'s utter disregard for boundaries and its celebration of the abject, we should not be surprised that the show has repeatedly featured characters tasting or eating shit. But it is the rear entry, which is also a reentry, of Paris Hilton's body into Mr. Slave's body that best illustrates the show's abject pleasure.

To understand the complex relationship between the abject and pleasure in *South Park*, we must make two key distinctions. First, *South Park* does not simply depict the violation of social taboos; it enlists viewers' participation in them. By "watching" the show repeatedly transgress the boundaries of social acceptability, viewers complete the communication circuit vital to the show's violations. Indeed, if there were no viewers—no witnesses to the violations—then the transgressions would cease to signify transgressiveness. Transgression has "symbolic" significance only to the extent that an audience exists who recognizes it as such. Second, the abject operates on a "material" as well as a symbolic level. In other words, it acts directly on the body in somatic ways. Just as the thought of eating shit can evoke a bodily shudder, abject depictions on *South Park* can trigger bodily pleasures. As noted, abjection is above all about transgression, and according to Susan Rubin Suleiman, "The characteristic feeling accompanying transgression is one of intense pleasure" (75). In describing the state brought about by transgression as "one of intense pleasure," Suleiman is differentiating abject pleasure from everyday pleasure. Abjection is an "intense" pleasure precisely because it is registered by the body; it is felt in addition to being seen. "When *South Park* is at its best," Alyssa Katz notes, "it triggers the laugh reflex through an unstoppable will to transgress" (35).

The Carnivalesque

A central aspect of *South Park* and one that distinguishes it from much of the other programming on prime-time television is its focus on children. *South Park* revolves around the lives and exploits of four 8-year-old boys, Stan Marsh, Eric Cartman, Kenny McCormick, and Kyle Broslowski. Because the boys spend much of their time playing—whether it be Cartman playing "Lambs" or the gang playing "junior detectives"—play is a central element of the show. The episode, "The Return of the Fellowship of the Ring to the Two

Towers," for instance, begins with Kyle, Stan, and Cartman playing *Lord of the Rings*. Clad in full Middle Earth regalia, the three are in search of a quest worthy of their skills when Stan's father asks the boys to deliver a rented copy of *Lord of the Rings* to Butters's house. The boys are happy to oblige and deliver the tape, which unbeknownst to them is a pornographic movie titled, *Back Door Sluts 9* (accidentally put in the wrong video case by Stan's father). On learning of his mistake, Mr. Marsh assigns the boys a new task—to recover the "evil" tape. The boys retrieve the tape, but observing the strange hold it has over Butters (who, after having seen it, attempts to hump Stan), decide that they must consult the high elf. Once at the elf's home, Token (South Park's sole black child) is assigned the task of privately viewing the video to discover its power. After only a few minutes of viewing, Token returns and announces, "I don't want to play anymore."

This scene is a staging of Token's loss of innocence and his premature induction into adulthood. Having seen the "adult" video, Token has lost his desire to "play" with the other children. To appreciate the cultural significance of this scene, distinguishing between child and adult forms of play is helpful. Adult forms of play, such as golf, poker, and even pornography, are highly structured activities that follow preestablished rules. Moreover, adult play typically *progresses* toward a particular aim or outcome, such as winning. Children's play, by contrast, is more improvisational and open-ended. According to Brian Sutton-Smith, it "center[s] on having fun, [. . .] choosing freely, [. . .] pretending, enacting, fantasy and drama" (49). Because children's play is typically not directed toward a particular outcome, it fosters experimentation and "values immediate gratification and personal inventiveness over inherited tradition and predetermined cultural meanings" (Ott, "(Re)Locating" 204). For Kyle, Stan, and Cartman, the pornographic video is not a video at all; it is a magical object with strange powers. As children grow up, they are steadily drained of their creative impulses, and (re)trained to play in highly structured ways. When Token watches the video, he is no longer able to see it as something other than what it is. Unable to transform the pornographic video into something other than a pornographic video, as a child might imaginatively transform a box into a house, he ceases playing. By creating a world that is seen through the eyes of children, *South Park* challenges normative rituals and encourages a textual pleasure that is homologous with children's play.

The pleasure derived from children's play is quite different than the pleasure derived from adult play. Because children's play is not so tightly bound by social codes, it is analogous with Freud's notion of the *pleasure principle*—the pure, uninhibited gratification of desire. At birth, all humans are governed, according to Freud, by the pleasure principle. As they move into adulthood, the pleasure principle is tamed by the reality principle and desires are repressed in the name of social convention (Freud 595–97). Although pleasure does not disappear as we age, it is transformed from a momentary, uncertain, and destructive pleasure into a restrained, structured, and assured pleasure (Marcuse 13). While adult play is specifically constructed in opposition to work, it is no less structured than work and is thus a hegemonic pleasure. Because children's play is more open and unstructured, the pleasure associated with it is more resistive.

To put it another way, children's play is carnivalesque because carnival not only celebrates laughter and excess, but also challenges, typically through symbolic inversion or world-upside-down depictions, the very rules that replicate the social order (Bakhtin 197).[7] And, as cultural critic John Fiske observes, elements of the carnivalesque style are common to some televisual genres. According to Fiske, for instance, "Cartoons and comedies frequently invert 'normal' relationships and show the adults as incompetent, unable to understand, and the children as superior in insight and ability. [. . .] The pleasure involved is carnivalesque, for it is the pleasure of the subordinate escaping from the rules and conventions that are the agents of social control" (*Television Culture* 242–43). What *South Park* affords viewers is a temporary psychic escape from the burden of structure.[8] In seeing the world through the eyes of children, which is itself a resistive category (Hartley 36), viewers are momentarily liberated from the constraints of the prevailing social order. They are invited to engage the show and the world not as responsible individual adults, but as children at play.[9] Such liberation is an intense but fleeting pleasure because when one turns off *South Park*, he or she must reenter the world of social rules and conventions.

The Intertextual

In another of my favorite scenes from *South Park*, two handicapped fourth graders, Timmy and Jimmy, square off in a particularly brutal fisticuffs ("Cripple Fight"). As science-fiction aficionados are sure to recognize, the scene is a shot-for-shot recreation of the fight between "Rowdy" Roddy Piper and Keith David in John Carpenter's 1988 film *They Live*. It even features little Jimmy yelling, "You dirty mother-(bleep)!" This sort of gesture or nod to previous pop cultural texts is a regular feature of *South Park*, which has—since its inception—been filled with direct, if often obscure, references to other media texts. As Katz noted in *The Nation* shortly after the show first premiered, Parker and Stone's "points of reference are appealingly diverse, reaching all the way back to a classic short about a rebellious little Jazz Age boy who only wants to 'sing-a, about the moon-a and the June-a and the spring-a'" (35). To critics, such gestures are known as "intertextuality," which, in the most basic sense, describes "The way texts refer to other texts" (Ward 214). But as Ott and Walter have demonstrated, the ways in which one text can "refer" to another text are actually quite diverse, ranging from parodic allusion to self-reflexive reference. What unites the various modes of intertextuality is pleasure. The pleasure of watching Timmy and Jimmy fight is not limited simply to the hilarity of two crippled children beating each other senseless, although that is amusing. It is also pleasurable because it fosters a sense of in-group superiority among those viewers who possess the special pop cultural literacy to recognize or "get" the allusion to *They Live*.

My concern with intertextuality in *South Park*, however, has less to do with the nature and function of its specific extratextual gestures, such as the reference to *They Live*, and more to do with the ways in which the viewing or "reading" of texts is altered by repeated exposure to such references. Intertextual gestures are a fundamental feature of *South Park*'s textuality; they are a feature that privileges fragments and gaps over narrative and continuity by routinely encouraging viewers to process information associatively as opposed to linearly. Simply stated, *South Park*'s underlying intertextual form promotes a spatial, rather than a temporal, logic. The claim that repeated exposure to a particular textual form trains our consciousness to work in specific ways will, no doubt, strike some as nothing more than gross technological determinism. But I am not advancing a cause-effect argument. Whereas intertextual form certainly does not cause nonlinear thinking, it does foster it.

In his book *Lateral Thinking*, Edward de Bono outlines two principle ways of processing information: vertical thinking, which is analytical and proceeds step-by-step, and lateral thinking, which is provocative and operates side-by-side. Vertical thinking is closely linked to story and narrative, progressing in a temporal, sequential way. Lateral thinking, by contrast, is closely tied to intertextual form, radiating in a spatial, fragmentary way. By privileging shocking images and sound bites, *South Park* invites viewers to read or view it "askew" rather than to "follow" it. In continuously prompting viewers to make extratextual connections and associations as well as to "jump" from one iconic image to the next, *South Park* teaches a particular mode of viewing and information processing. Once viewers master this mode, they need not recognize *South Park*'s conscious intertextual references to derive pleasure because they will create their own references and hence their own pleasures. This is what it means to read intertextually.

Reading intertextually, according to Roland Barthes in *Image, Music, Text*, is a form of writing and of active textual production. To consume a "work" is, for Barthes, a very different activity than to *produce* a "Text." Whereas consumption involves a unified and stable work (161)—the finished product of an Author—textual production begins with the "removal of the Author" (145). Once the Author (and authorized reading) is removed, reading (intertextually) becomes of type of browsing, or in Barthes's words, "drifting."[10] Because browsing or drifting is an act of textual production rather than consumption, it privileges the openness of the signifier over the finality of the signified. One can "drift" either by scanning the images of a specific episode or by surfing the vast televisual landscape itself. The latter is how I typically watch television; I flip from channel to channel, pausing only briefly on those images that entice me before moving on again.[11] *South Park's* short catchphrases and outrageous images are ideal for drifters, as they offer quick flashes of excitement. Drifting is governed by the body and its desires, rather than by narrative form, so the pleasure associated with it is scandalous, atopic, and revolutionary (Barthes, *The Pleasure* 23). Indeed, Barthes contends that production of the Text, which occurs through drifting, is bound to a radical, disruptive pleasure (*Image, Music, Text* 164).

The Ironic

South Park clearly revels in controversy. Each week, the creators seek politically incorrect and culturally taboo social issues, which they then explore and exploit. This section concerns not the specific social issues that the show addresses, but its attitude toward those issues. To illuminate this attitude, I turn to one of my favorite moments in the first season. In the episode "Death," Stan's grandfather, who is celebrating his 102nd birthday and has lost his will to live, repeatedly attempts to trick Stan, Kyle, Cartman, and Kenny into killing him. Over the course of the episode, the boys struggle with the ethics of euthanasia, wondering whether assisting someone with suicide is "right." Searching for an answer, the boys first put this question to their teacher, Mr. Garrison, and then to their most trusted adult friend, Chef. Both individuals defer, Mr. Garrison saying, "I'm not touching that with a 20-foot pole," and Chef responding, "I'm not touching that with a 40-foot pole." Frustrated, the boys phone into a local television talk show, *Jesus and Pals*, to put the question to Jesus. Jesus, who has demonstrated that he is all-knowing in response to previous phone calls, pauses momentarily before confidently retorting, "I'm not touching that with a 60-foot pole." This is among my favorite moments in the first season because it so clearly captures the show's central attitude toward social controversy—that of irony.

Admittedly, I am not the first person to observe that *South Park* is ironic. A year after its premier on Comedy Central, David Klinghoffer, a critic for the *National Review*, identified *South Park's* ironic "sensibility" as one of its key sources of amusement (51). But whereas Klinghoffer laments this fact as an "aggravating quality of the Nineties" (51), I see it as a significant element of postmodern textuality. Irony is a challenging concept—one made even more challenging by the fact that irony is used in two senses. In the first sense, irony is a message whose essential or underlying meaning contradicts its superficial or literal meaning. This, the classical version of irony, is a rhetorical trope authors and speakers use when they mean the opposite of, or something different than, what they actually say. In this version, the ironist is advancing a point of view, taking a stand, and therefore believes he or she has access to the truth. In the second version of irony, the ironist's message is devoid of certainty because he or she is aware that there are no universal truths, no truths that exists outside of language. In this version of irony, which Candace Lang refers to as "humor" to avoid confusion with the first version, the ironist realizes that anything can be made to look good or bad through redescription and thus never takes himself or herself too seriously (Rorty 73–74). Humor, or "postmodern irony," stresses humility over superiority (Burke 513–14); the ironist's aim is not to provide the "correct" view, but to demystify prevailing views—to show how prevailing discourses imprison thinking.

This is precisely the perspective on euthanasia articulated in the episode "Death." Even Jesus, who is supposed to represent the Law, the Father, and the Truth, is unwilling to take a position in this debate. Indeed, all of the town's centers of knowledge are unwilling to say whether assisted suicide is "right" or "wrong." The aim of the episode, then, is not to promote a liberal or conservative message, but to present a third, metadiscourse on the controversy itself. Nor is this episode unique. As S. Clarke has noted, each episode "tackles a cutting-edge moral dilemma in its own twisted way" (quoted in Quigley 51). The show has addressed everything from cloning and homosexuality to environmentalism and sexual harassment. Often, *South Park* does not "take sides," opting instead to demonstrate the fallibility of all perspectives. This mode should not be confused with strategic ambiguity, which deliberately aims to appeal to a diverse audience by adopting an ambiguous attitude. Unlike the ambiguous attitude, which is vague, the ironic attitude is positively neutral. Because both sides of a paradigm are bound to one another—*doxa* or opinion and *paradoxa* or counteropinion (Barthes, *The Pleasure* 18, 55)—"the Neutral," according to Barthes, is "that which outplays [*déjoue*] the paradigm, or rather [. . .] everything that baffles the paradigm" (*The Neutral* 6).

Although the ironic attitude is neutral, it is not indifferent or disinterested. On the contrary, "The Neutral," adds Barthes, "can refer to intense, strong, unprecedented states. 'To outplay the paradigm' is an ardent, burning activity" (*The Neutral* 7). The ironic attitude, therefore, is often a source of intense, rapturous pleasure. Like the disruptive character of the Neutral, ecstatic or erotic pleasure dissolves classification (Smyth 281–86). In the case of two lovers, the moment of ecstasy is that moment of total expenditure, of loss and the dissolution of individual subjectivity. As Judith Butler notes, "To be ecstatic means, literally, to be outside oneself" (*Undoing Gender* 20) or to come undone. *South Park*'s ironic perspective on hotly debated and deeply bifurcated social issues is similarly ecstatic, literally exploding the paradigm.

The Liminal

South Park has a strange fascination with death. Not only does the show regularly address the topic of death, but one of the central characters, Kenny McCormick, repeatedly dies on the show. Kenny is no doubt one of the most unusual characters ever to inhabit the world of television. Despite a particularly gruesome, as well as creative, death each week, he inexplicably (re)appears episode after episode. Thus, Kenny exists in a state of perpetual transition between the living and the dead. That Kenny exists on the margin or limen between life and death may explain why his friends appear to be neither troubled by his countless deaths, nor surprised by his unexplained returns. Although Kenny's continual "crossing-over" is usually expedient, on one occasion he spends nearly the entire episode *between* life and death. In the episode "Best Friends Forever," an ironic retelling of the highly publicized Terri Schiavo case, Kenny is struck and killed by a truck. But not long after reaching heaven, Kenny's body is revived in the hospital, where severe brain damage has left him in a persistent vegetative state.

"Best Friends Forever" thus concerns a liminal entity, personae, or "threshold person." "Liminal entities," explains Victor Turner, "are neither here nor there; they are betwixt and between the positions assigned and arrayed by law, custom, convention, and ceremonial" (*The Ritual* 95). Kenny's persistent vegetative state is a liminal one between life and death. He is neither fully alive (for he is brain dead) nor fully dead (for he is physically alive). Unlike abject images and representations, which violate cultural hierarchies, and carnivalesque representations, which invert them, representations of liminality implode cultural hierarchies. Rather than simply breaching, transgressing, or turning social structures upside down, liminal phenomena call the structures themselves into question. Liminality "dissolves the norms that govern structured and institutionalized relationships and is accompanied by experiences of unprecedented potency"—by the liberation or release of "instinctual energies" (Turner, *The Ritual* 128). Although Turner does not specifically mention pleasure in relation to liminality, it is suggested by his use of the phrase "instinctual energies," which are rooted in bodily drives and innate desires.

The pleasure that accompanies liminality, then, is a material one experienced on an extra- or presymbolic level. Because social hegemony is sustained by willing consent to cultural norms and conventions, liminal images and their corresponding rejection/dissolution of the social operate as ideological ruptures in which the body and mind are momentarily set free. "The essence of liminality," according to Turner, "is to be found in the release from normal constraints [. . . on] the free play of mankind's [sic] cognitive and imaginative capabilities" (*On the Edge* 161). To appreciate fully the revolutionary potential and pleasure of the liminal, considering Julia Kristeva's distinction between the "semiotic" and the "symbolic" is helpful (*Revolution* 25–29). For Kristeva, the semiotic is the material base of the symbolic; it names the drive energies and rhythms that precede the symbolic in all signifying practices. It can be likened to the prelinguistic noises of a baby or to vocal modulations that have no (symbolic) meaning, but are meaningful. The semiotic dimension of signifying practices is located in the *chora*—a mobile, provisional space in which energy flows and charges are principally located. The semiotic is revolutionary precisely to the extent that it is outside of the Law.

The image of Kenny "between" life and death registers on an instinctual (semiotic) as opposed to a cultural (symbolic) level. It reverberates (like sound waves), rather than reifies (like language). Much like the *chora*, the space of the liminal is a "pulverization of language" and meaning (Kristeva, *Revolution* 88). The liminal does not represent instinctual energies and flows; it discharges them. This discharge of energy is analogous to the discharge of fluids that accompanies the orgasmic moment, as both are an unbounded release.

The Depthless

I have saved one of my favorite *South Park* scenes for last. Despite having seen it many times, it still evokes a chuckle. In the scene, my favorite character, Cartman, is a guest on an episode of *The Maury Show* titled, "Please Help My Out of Control Child." In the hopes of winning a prize for being the most outlandish guest, Cartman has convinced his mother to lie about his behavior. Dressed like a young female prostitute, Cartman is introduced to the studio audience by a prerecorded video, in which he proclaims, "Maury, I am out of control. Yeah, I use drugs. I can do what I want, bitch! Yeah, I have sex, and I don't use protection! It's my hot body; I'll do what I want! I don't go to school, and I kill people! Whatever! I'll do what I want!" When Vanity, the other child guest on Maury's show, tells Cartman, "Oh, whatever. You ain't tough, ho! I roam with gangs!" he quickly retorts, "Oh yeah? I roam with twelve gangs! And we only commit hate crimes! Whatever! I'll do what I want!"

In this scene, Cartman is performing for the television cameras. He seems acutely aware that identity is a matter of image and style, and that by tapping into cultural images he can alter how he is perceived. Just as Cartman's rebellious image draws on culturally created images of rebellion, *The Maury Show* is an image of the image manufactured by daytime talk shows through their celebration of surface and spectacle. Thus, the images on *South Park* cease to signify; they do not refer to some external referent, but simply to other culturally constructed images. To appreciate the significance of this claim, as well as to illustrate the ways it is linked to pleasure, considering the changing nature and function of images in the postmodern condition is useful. In *Postmodernism, or, The Cultural Logic of Late Capitalism*, Fredric Jameson notes that postmodern culture constitutes a new kind of flatness, superficiality, or depthlessness in which pastiche has replaced parody (9). Images mimic idiosyncratic styles, but they are absent the satiric impulse common to parody (Fiske, "Postmodernism" 59). The result is simulacrum, or "the generation by models of a real without original or reality" (Baudrillard, *Simulations* 2).

Simulation is a consequence of the rise of the new information technologies and their endless (re)circulation of images. For Baudrillard, our current cultural landscape is marked by radical semiurgy—an overabundance of images and information whose ever-increasing velocity and proliferation has collapsed the subject-object dichotomy, leaving "the tele-spectator [. . .] lost forever in a fragmentary fun house of mirrors [and] the infinite play of superfluous, meaningless images" (Kellner 237). This state of affairs is not all bad according to Baudrillard, however, because it means that viewers "can consume images without consuming their meanings, whether referential or ideological" (Fiske, "Postmodernism" 60). By refusing or "imploding" meaning, postmodern images escape both referentiality and ideology. Thus, the T-shirts sporting the slogan, "It's my hot body. I'll do what I want!" that immediately circulated following the episode, "Freak Strike," were, like the very characters on the show, devoid of a political or ideological message. The only message communicated by wearing one of these T-shirts is, "I watch *South Park*."

Although Baudrillard probes the relationship between a postmodern image culture and resistance (*In the Shadow* 107–8), he largely avoids the matter of pleasure. The remainder of this chapter explores the character of pleasure that often accompanies the new depthlessness of the postmodern image. If postmodern images reject deep meaning and organizing structures (Fiske, "Postmodernism" 59), then how is it that they appeal to or move viewers? The answer, according to postmodernists, is that their sensual surfaces appeal directly to affective desire and the body. "In this account of audience reception," according to Harms and Dickens, "images and other communications are not rationally interpreted for their meaning, but received somatically as bodily intensities" (222). In an image-saturated landscape, where waves of images crash on consumers in a never-ending tidal flow, sensation and signifiers are privileged over sense making and signifieds. The cartoon simplicity and obvious two-dimensionality of the *South Park*'s characters is ready-made for a material, visual pleasure. That the town's lone black child is named Token erases the need for any interpretive depth. He, like his image, is an admitted stereotype. Instead of being invited to engage in continual hermeneutic analysis of its characters, *South Park*'s viewers are encouraged to locate pleasure in surface and spectacle. This denial of the signified functions as a resistive pleasure not because it challenges a particular ideology, but because it challenges ideology itself (Fiske, *Reading* 87).

On Media Erotics and Criticism

In the *Pleasure of the Text*, Roland Barthes distinguishes between two types of pleasure, *plaisir* and *jouissance*. For Barthes, *plaisir* is a conformist, disciplining pleasure that "comes from culture and does not break with it, is linked to a *comfortable* practice of reading" (14). *Plaisir*, elaborates Fiske, is typically a hegemonic pleasure that conforms to "the dominant ideology and the subjectivity it proposes" (*Understanding* 54). *Jouissance*, by contrast, is on the order of bliss or ecstasy, a radically disruptive pleasure that "unsettles the reader's historical, cultural, psychological assumptions, the consistency of his tastes, values, memories, brings to a crisis his relation with language" (Barthes, *Pleasure* 14). Like the eroticism associated with orgasm and death (Bataille), *jouissance* is the pleasure of momentary loss, when the "self" dissolves and thus escapes the control of culture (Fiske, *Understanding* 50; Moriarty 149). Simply put, *jouissance* is the pleasure of temporarily evading the social order and escaping ideology. As a corporeal pleasure, however, *jouissance* is both transient and personal. My *jouissance* cannot be yours. That said, the modes of pleasure I have identified in *South Park* all hold the potential of yielding *jouissance* for viewers.

The abject and the carnivalesque, for instance, both can be experienced as stirring bodily pleasures, although admittedly they do not so much constitute a break with culture as a rewriting of it. Unlike other disruptive pleasures, abjection and carnival do not destroy the social. Rather, they challenge its naturalization through a series of boundary crossings. The intertextual and the ironic operate on a different register. They create a space of pleasure by decentering the Author-God and approaching texts as open, fluid, and unfinished. The deconstruction of authorizing voices and final signifieds allows viewers to become textual producers. Textual production, like orgasmic production, is a moment of total expenditure and loss in which culture splinters and breaks down. The liminal and depthless constitute a third type of transgressive pleasure in which binaries are collapsed in on one another. Another way of distinguishing among these modes of pleasure, then, would be to say that the abject and carnivalesque reorder signs (demonstrating their arbitrariness), that the intertextual and ironic explode signs (demonstrating their infinite plurality), and that the liminal and the depthless implode signs (demonstrating their emptiness). But regardless of classification, each one suggests the possibility of nonhegemonic pleasure. The six pleasures I have identified are far from a complete list, and others should be explored and charted because viewers take their pleasures differently and no two viewers are likely to share the same pleasures.

So, why bother identifying the pleasures of *South Park* at all? What is the critical reason for doing so? To answer these questions, we need first to contextualize them. Over the past thirty years, modernity has steadily, if reluctantly, given way to postmodernity. The transition to a new historical epoch was fueled by fundamental changes in both our technologies of communication and our economic system. Whereas many of the consequences of this shift are not yet self-evident, others are simply too noticeable to deny. One such consequence is the dramatic proliferation of signs and information. So boundless has been the multiplication of signs that it has, according to John Fiske, "produce[d] a categorical difference, rather than one of degree, between our age and previous ones" ("Postmodernism" 58). This sea of signs has, in turn, forever altered the nature of textuality, authorship, writing, and the circuit of production, circulation, and reception. We can no longer treat cultural artifacts or "texts" as if they speak with a unified voice, reflecting a homogeneous ideology. The great metanarratives of modernity (Marxism, structuralism, and psychoanalysis) can no longer be used to discover and explicate the foundational structures that organize our social experience because such structures do not exist.

Some are reluctant, even loath, to admit to this new state of affairs because they fear that it renders the cultural critic obsolete. They are partially correct. If no absolute, universal, unchanging structures exist beneath texts, then the project of hermeneutics may have run its course. But this does not mean nothing is to be done. If no singular and unified meaning or ideology exists to uncover in texts, then perhaps critics are pursuing the wrong thing. Instead of chasing psychic apparitions in texts, critics should pursue material experiences instead. In this model, the aim of criticism would not be to tell viewers what experiences they have had, but to illustrate the types of experiences that are possible. This would entail reconceptualizing the critic's role in society. It would involve critics acting not as "cultural workers," who do the hard work of getting to the bottom of things, but as "cultural teachers," who do the invaluable work of assisting individuals to live more meaningful and fulfilling lives within a media culture. As Barry Brummett argues, we need to implement a critical practice in which "theory and criticism's ultimate goal and justification is pedagogical: *to teach people how to experience their rhetorical environments more richly*" (103).

Media erotics provide one avenue for pursuing this aim and for transforming the practice of criticism from conquest (an attempt to master the text) into enjoyment (a desire to experience it). As an analysis of *South Park* illustrates, the material pleasures of media are numerous and diverse. By examining the various ways in which texts arouse viewers, critics both illuminate why some texts resonate with viewers and others do not in an image-saturated culture, as well as expand the repertoire of pleasures available to viewers. This latter benefit is of particular social value, especially when the pleasures being charted are transgressive. If ideology is an inescapable aspect of the human condition, then teaching viewers to locate its almost imperceptible fissures, those moments when the polished veneer of ideology is momentarily cracked, is essential for critics. To learn to experience the cracks is also to learn how to live more humanely outside them.

Notes

1. For a sustained discussion of postmodern textuality on television, see Campbell and Freed.

2. For deconstructionists "texts are not to be read according to a hermeneutical or exegetical method which would seek out a finished signified beneath a textual surface" (Derrida, *Positions* 63). Deconstruction is one of two variants of poststructuralism in the tradition of American criticism. The other, which is closer to my own sensibilities, is pragmatism. For a discussion of these two variants, see Todorov 183–84.

3. Derrida uses the term "dissemination" to explain the idea that meaning is constantly being "seeded" and therefore can never be exhausted (*Dissemination*). Deconstruction should not be confused with destruction, however. As Barbara Johnson notes, "The de-construction of a text does not proceed by random doubt or arbitrary subversion, but by a careful teasing out of warring forces of signification within the text itself. If anything is destroyed in a deconstructive reading, it is not the text, but the claim to unequivocal domination of one mode of signifying over another" (5).

4. By "nihilism" I am referring to the philosophy of "questioning" (principally language), which derives from the Heideggerian belief—reflected in philosophers such as Derrida—that there are no ultimate (that is, ahistorical, transcultural) grounds for making universal validity claims. Although pragmatists share deconstructionists' antifoundationalism, they embrace (rather than reject) rhetoric, regarding it as an opportunity to build better, and in the case of Rorty, more democratic societies.

5. In *Against Interpretation*, Susan Sontag, who has been called the "sensuous intellectual" (Lacayo 72), writes, "In place of a hermeneutics we need an erotics of art" (14). Similarly, in *The Grain of the Voice*, Barthes, often referred to as the Professor of Desire, argues, "It seemed to me that the almost wild and uncontrolled development of ideological criticism called for a certain corrective adjustment, because it threatened to impose on the text, on textual theory, a kind of father-figure whose vigilant function would be to forbid blissful enjoyment. [. . .] I'm too Brechtian not to believe in the need to make criticism and pleasure coexist" (174). Significance, according to Barthes, concerns sensual, material experiences, rather than rational, symbolic ones (*The Pleasure* 61).

6. This perspective, of course, draws heavily on Mikhail Bakhtin's study of Rabelais. According to Bakhtin, "We find at the basis of grotesque imagery a special concept of the body as a whole and of the limits of this whole. [. . .] Next to the bow-

els and the genital organs is the mouth, through which enters the world to be swallowed up. And next is the anus. All these convexities and orifices have a common characteristic: it is within them that the confines between bodies and between the body and the world are overcome" (315, 317). "The 'abject,'" writes Butler, "designates that which has been expelled from the body, discharged as excrement, literally rendered 'Other.' This appears as an expulsion of alien elements, but the alien is effectively established through this expulsion" (*Gender Trouble* 133; see also 168–70).

7. For more on the carnivalesque, see Halsall's contribution to this volume.

8. I am not claiming that *South Park* episodes lack structure. On the contrary, episodes are rigidly formulaic. But, as indicated at the outset of this chapter, I am interested in how postmodern textuality fosters material pleasures, and one of those pleasures is a "feeling" or "sense" of escape from social structure.

9. Thus, part of the carnivalesque pleasure of *South Park* is the sense of unity it invites among viewers who are collectively taking part in *play*. "Although carnival embraces and welcomes eroticism, mere orgasm is not its telos; its goal," explains Robert Stam, "is playfulness in the broadest sense, a collective *jouissance*, a felt unity with community" (170). *South Park*'s appeal to a collective sense of play is perhaps most evident in its extensive online fan community (see Ott, "'Oh My God'").

10. In *The Pleasure of the Text*, Barthes writes, "*Drifting occurs whenever I do not respect the whole*" (18). Barthes also occasionally uses the term "cruising" to describe textual production, noting that, "Cruising is the voyage of desire. The body is in a state on alert, on the lookout for its own desire" (*The Grain* 231). Although these terms appear to be closely related, I understand cruising to be a bit more active, focused, and conscious than drifting. While drifting is a random and casual movement, cruising involves directed searching. For more on approaching texts in this fashion, see O'Brien's *The Browser's Ecstasy* and Rojek and Turner's *Forget Baudrillard?*, especially pages 153–55.

11. For an extended discussion of the relationship between television surfing and pleasure, see Ott, "Television as Lover, Part I" and Ott, "Television as Lover, Part II."

Works Cited

Bakhtin, Mikhail. *Rabelais and His World*. Trans. Helene Iswolsky. Cambridge, MA: MIT Press. 1968.

Barthes, Roland. *The Grain of the Voice: Interviews 1962–1980*. Trans. Linda Coverdale. Berkeley: University of California Press, 1985.

———. *Image, Music, Text*. Trans. Stephen Heath. New York: Hill and Wang, 1977.

———. *The Neutral: Lecture Course at the Collège de France (1977–1978)*. Trans. R. Krauss and D. Hollier. New York: Columbia University Press, 2005.

———. *The Pleasure of the Text*. Trans. Richard Miller. New York: Hill and Wang, 1975.

———. *S/Z*. Trans. Richard Miller. New York: Hill and Wang, 1974.

Bataille, Georges. *Eroticism: Death and Sensuality*. Trans. Mary Dalwood. San Francisco, CA: City Lights Books, 1986.

Baudrillard, Jean. *In the Shadow of the Silent Majorities, or, The End of the Social and Other Essays*. Trans. Paul Foss, John Johnston, and Paul Patton. New York: Semiotext(e), 1983.

———. *Simulations*. Trans. Paul Foss, Paul Patton, and Philip Beitchman. New York: Semiotext(e), 1983.

Brummett, Barry. "Rhetorical Theory as Heuristic and Moral: A Pedagogical Justification." *Communication Education* 33 (1984): 97–107.

Burke, Kenneth. *A Grammar of Motives*. Berkeley: University of California Press, 1969.

Butler, Judith. *Gender Trouble: Feminism and the Subversion of Identity*. New York: Routledge, 1999.

———. *Undoing Gender*. New York: Routledge, 2004.

Campbell, Richard, and Rosanne Freed. "'We Know It When We See It': Postmodernism and Television." *Television Quarterly* 26 (1993): 75–87.

De Bono, Edward. *Lateral Thinking: Creativity Step by Step*. New York: Harper Row, 1970.

Derrida, Jacques. *Positions*. Trans. Alan Bass. Chicago: University of Chicago Press, 1981.

———. *Dissemination*. Trans. Barbara Johnson. Chicago: University of Chicago Press, 1981.

Douglas, Mary. *Purity and Danger: An Analysis of Concept of Pollution and Taboo*. New York: Routledge, 2002.

Eagleton, Terry. *The Illusions of Postmodernism*. Malden, MA: Blackwell, 1996.

Fiske, John. "Postmodernism and Television." *Mass Media and Society*. Ed. James Curran and Michael Gurevitch. New York: Arnold, 1992. 55–67.

———. *Reading the Popular*. New York: Routledge, 1989.

———. *Television Culture*. London: Methuen, 1987.

———. *Understanding Popular Culture*. Boston: Unwin Hyman, 1989.

Freud, Sigmund. *The Freud Reader*. Ed. Peter Gay. New York: Norton, 1989.

Harms, John B., and David R. Dickens. "Postmodern Media Studies: Analysis or Symptom?" *Critical Studies in Mass Communication* 13 (1996): 210–27.

Hartley, John. *Tele-Ology: Studies in Television*. New York: Routledge, 1992.

Jameson, Fredric. *Postmodernism, or, The Cultural Logic of Late Capitalism*. Durham, NC: Duke University Press, 1991.

Johnson, Barbara. *The Critical Difference: Essays in the Contemporary Rhetoric of Reading*. Baltimore, MD: Johns Hopkins University Press, 1980.

Katz, Alyssa. "Those %#$@^*# Kids." *The Nation* 16 Feb. 1998: 35–36.

Kellner, Douglas. *Media Culture: Cultural Studies, Identity and Politics between the Modern and the Postmodern.* New York: Routledge, 1995.

Klinghoffer, David. "Dirty Joke." *National Review* 9 Mar. 1998: 48, 51.

Kristeva, Julia. *Powers of Horror: An Essay on Abjection.* Trans. Leon S. Roudiez. New York: Columbia University Press, 1982.

———. *Revolution in Poetic Language.* Trans. Margaret Waller. New York: Columbia University Press, 1984.

Lacayo, Richard. "The Sensuous Intellectual: Susan Sontag 1933–2004." *Time* 10 Jan. 2005: 72.

Lang, Candace D. *Irony/Humor.* Baltimore, MD: Johns Hopkins University Press, 1988.

Marcuse, Herbert. *Eros and Civilization: A Philosophical Inquiry into Freud.* Boston, MA: Beacon Press, 1974.

Moriarty, Michael. *Roland Barthes.* Stanford, CA: Stanford University Press, 1991.

O'Brien, Geoffrey. *The Browser's Ecstasy: A Meditation on Reading.* Washington, DC: Counterpoint, 2000.

O'Day, Marc. "Postmodernism and Television." *The Routledge Critical Dictionary of Postmodern Thought.* Ed. Stuart Sim. New York: Routledge, 1999. 112–20.

Ott, Brian L. "'Oh My God, They Digitized Kenny!' Travels in the *South Park* Cybercommunity V4.0." *Prime Time Animation: Television Animation and American Culture.* Ed. Carole A. Stabile and Mark Harrison. New York: Routledge, 2003. 220–42.

———. "(Re)Locating Pleasure in Media Studies: Toward an Erotics of Reading." *Communication and Critical/Cultural Studies* 1 (2004): 194–212.

———. "Television as Lover, Part I: Writing Dirty Theory." *Cultural Studies <=> Critical Methodologies* (forthcoming).

———. "Television as Lover, Part II: Doing Auto[Erotic]Ethnography." *Cultural Studies <=> Critical Methodologies* (forthcoming).

———, and Cameron Walter. "Intertextuality: Interpretive Strategy and Textual Practice." *Critical Studies in Media Communication* 17 (2000): 429–46.

Quigley, Marian. "The Politics of Animation: *South Park.*" *Metro Magazine: Media and Education Magazine* 124/125 (2000): 48–53.

Rojek, Chris, and Bryan S. Turner, eds. *Forget Baudrillard?* New York: Routledge, 1993.

Rorty, Richard. *Contingency, Irony, and Solidarity.* New York: Cambridge University Press, 1989.

Sontag, Susan. *Against Interpretation and Other Essays.* New York: Picador, 2001.

Smyth, John Vignaux. *A Question of Eros: Irony in Sterne, Kierkegaard, and Barthes.* Tallahassee: Florida State University Press, 1986.

Stam, Robert. *Subversive Pleasures: Bakhtin, Cultural Criticism, and Film.* Baltimore, MD: Johns Hopkins University Press, 1989.

Suleiman, Susan Rubin. *Subversive Intent: Gender, Politics, and the Avant-Garde*. Cambridge, MA: Harvard University Press, 1990.

Sutton-Smith, Brian. *The Ambiguity of Play*. Cambridge, MA: Harvard University Press, 1997.

Todorov, Tzvetan. *Literature and Its Theorists: A Personal View of Twentieth-Century Criticism*. Trans. Catherine Porter. Ithaca, NY: Cornell University Press, 1987.

Turner, Victor. *On the Edge of the Bush: Anthropology as Experience*. Tucson: University of Arizona Press, 1985.

———. *The Ritual Process: Structure and Anti-Structure*. Ithaca, NY: Cornell University Press, 1977.

Ward, Glenn. *Teach Yourself Postmodernism*. Chicago, IL: McGraw-Hill, 2003.

CHAPTER 3

Orphic Persuasions and Siren Seductions

Vocal Music in *South Park*

JASON BOYD and MARC R. PLAMONDON

In *South Park: Bigger Longer & Uncut* (1999), Saddam Hussein convinces Satan, the Lord of Hell, that he must return to the land of the living. To achieve this, Saddam takes his cue from Orpheus, whose song so moved Hades, God of the Underworld, that he allowed Orpheus's wife Eurydice to return with him to earth—an allegory of song's power of persuasion. In *South Park*, both the television show and the movie, songs are often employed by characters who are trying to persuade other characters to adopt a particular point of view or course of action; for example, in the movie Mrs. Broflovski tries to persuade the town to take action against Canada in the war against potty mouth; Cartman persuades his classmates (at least temporarily) that life was better in the third grade than in the fourth ("4th Grade"). Not only do these songs affect other characters, but the soothing charms of music also enable viewers to suspend their disbelief that these farcical ideas and causes could be persuasive to these characters. Listening to Kyle's mother or Cartman, viewers can almost believe in the possibility of a grassroots organization such as Mothers Against Canada or in the yawning gulf between the idyllic time that was the third grade and stark reality of the fourth. By normalizing the often bizarre situations and improbable cause and effect in *South Park*'s plots through the conventions of Orphic song—a technique that has served opera and musicals so well—the satiric messages expressed through the music are driven home to viewers who would otherwise see *South Park* as only absurd.

But the power of song can be deployed in a more beguiling way: As Orphic songs are put to use in more extreme situations in which the satire or the absurdity of a *South Park* episode pushes the limits of what viewers think they comprehend as sophisticated viewers of television, the music functions as a seductive force operating directly on the viewers. The seductive quality, as opposed to the persuasive quality, of music is epitomized in the mythic Sirens, whose singing was so enchanting resisting it was impossible, regardless how compromising or deadly the purpose behind the message. Saddam's Orphic song compromises Satan's intent to stand up to Saddam by persuading Satan that he can change. *South Park*'s Siren songs, more powerful than the Orphic songs, musically lull the viewers into morally ambiguous positions and complicate the complacency many viewers have about the certainty of their convictions and about where their sympathies lie.

Did the Devil Make Us Do It?

South Park: Bigger Longer & Uncut uses Orphic and Siren songs to enable the movie's satiric message. This sophistication of the movie's use of song to enhance satire is highlighted when compared with an earlier musical film project involving Parker and Stone—*Alferd Packer: The Musical* (1993)— released on DVD by Troma Studios in 1996 as *Cannibal! The Musical*. The film's plot adheres faithfully to the broad outlines of the historical record regarding Alferd Packer, and recounts this history without significant alteration or elaboration.[1] However, the viewer comes to realize, as the movie progresses, that the deadly Packer-guided 1874 expedition from Utah to Colorado (in which the members resorted to cannibalism) and the resulting trial of Packer for murder is merely the backdrop against which is enacted the narrative core and emotional impetus of this film—in keeping with the traditional mainstay of the musical, a love story: Packer's horse, Liane, abandons him for another man, the trapper Frenchy Cabazon, (the originating cause of the tragedy that befalls the expedition), but Packer and the woman who saves him—the *Denver Post*'s sob sister, Polly Pry—learn how to love again through their budding affections for each other.

This love story constitutes the film's creative departure from history. In spite of the implication of its title, *Cannibal! The Musical* is not an unconventional musical about cannibalism, but is rather a conventional musical about love betrayed and about learning to love again. The love songs, if taken out of the context of the movie, are practically indistinguishable from conventional pop love songs: When Liane disappears, Packer sings a lament worthy of a boy band star, "When I Was on Top Of You,"[2] replete with Vaseline-on-the-lens flashbacks to their happy times together since boyhood: "Your eyes, your smile / Made my little life worthwhile. / There's was nothing I couldn't do / When I was on top of you,"[3] and Pry expresses her feelings for Packer in the reflective song, "This Side of Me": "Safe as an island, / Far off to sea. / I'd almost forgotten / This side of me." (The comic dimension of this scene emerges not from the music or lyrics, but from the extra who tries to figure what Polly, staring into the middle distance as she soliloquizes in song, is looking at.) Despite one of the leads in the musical's romantic triangle being a horse, the humor of this plot is not derived from a parody of the romantic conventions of the musical, but rather resides in the incongruity between this convention being played out more or less straightforwardly within the history of an accused cannibal who is about to be hanged for murder. Unlike *South Park: Bigger Longer & Uncut*, the plot of *Cannibal! The Musical*, perhaps because it is based on an affectionately regarded figure of Colorado history, is not satiric. Ultimately, this is the film's weakness because, lacking a satiric target to focus and sharpen the film's humor, it appeals either as a goofy, sophomoric comedy or as an excessively subtle parody of the musical genre.

South Park: Bigger Longer & Uncut tells a story about the dangerous consequences of censorship and the importance of free speech (even if it is only profanity), dramatically and hilariously heightening the stakes by intersecting this cautionary tale with a parody of the Apocalypse. (Who knew the Seventh Sign was the murder of two foul-mouthed, flatulent Canadians? Not St. John the Divine, obviously.) As Kyle points out to his mother after the Apocalypse has been averted: "You see, mom? After all that, it was Cartman's filthy fucking mouth that saved us all." The satire of the movie and much of the music is concentrated on excoriating that pervasive social behavior known familiarly as the "blame game" and this practice's concomitant refusal of responsibility—by individuals, parents, and human beings. Although parodies of musical theater can be found—the big song and dance hoedown "Uncle Fucka" from Terrance and Phillip's movie *Asses of Fire* and Big Gay Al's "little song I wrote about the war," "I'm Super" (the type of escapist musical number that would find a home at a United Service Organization [USO] show, the point of which is to distract the troops from the realities of war, and distract it does)—the musical format of the film is to a large extent deployed as a means not of making fun of the musical, but highlighting the satire of the plot. Several songs in the movie satirize the practice of blaming one's individual failings on movies, parents, government, society, foreigners, and the ultimate scapegoat, Satan. The movie's lesson—besides the one imparted to Stan by The Clitoris—is summed up by Kyle's comment to his mother at the end of the movie, "Whenever I get in trouble, you go off and blame everybody else. But I'm the one to blame. Deal with me."

"Blame Canada" satirizes parents who fail to take responsibility for monitoring their children's consumption of popular culture and shows a song's Orphic potential to gild the didactic pill. "Blame Canada" starts at a South Park parent-teacher meeting at which Mothers Against Canada is founded.

When someone at the meeting asks, "But what is the source [of the dirty language the kids are using]?" Kyle's mother replies "Oh, that's easy": "Times have changed. / Our kids are getting worse. / They won't obey their parents; / They just want to fart and curse!":

STAN'S MOTHER: Should we blame the government?

CARTMAN'S MOTHER: Or blame society?

THE FATHERS: Or should we blame the images on TV?

KYLE'S MOTHER: NO! Blame Canada!

The Orphic power of Kyle's mother's scapegoating lyrics is demonstrated by the lyrics of the other mothers, who, similarly, are more than willing to get on the bandwagon and thus avoid taking responsibility in favor of blaming an external influence. They embroider on Mrs. Broflovski's opening move in the blame game: Stan's mother sings, "Don't blame me / For my son Stan. / He saw the darned cartoon / And now he's off to join the Klan!" followed by Cartman's mother, who adds, "And my boy Eric once / Had my picture on his shelf, / But now when I see him he tells me to fuck myself!" This is followed by Kenny's mother who claims, "My son could've been a doctor or a lawyer, rich and true. / Instead he burned up like a piggy on a barbecue."

In the same way the cherished adult fantasy about the natural innocence of children expressed in "Mountain Town" is debunked by the alacrity with which the boys take up the profanities of *Asses of Fire*—which, although in some cases they are clearly innocent of their meanings, they recognize and value as "dirty"—the viewer knows that the boys are no worse than they ever were: that Stan has not joined the Klan, that Cartman (who is never actually heard telling his mother to fuck herself) has always been rude to his mother, and that Kenny's death did not rob his mother of a son who was likely to become a doctor or a lawyer. All these claims are clearly false, and the idea of blaming the corruption of America's youth on another country (especially Canada, long under the cultural dominance of the United States) is comically absurd, but the Orphic power of "Blame Canada," which charts Mothers Against Canada's rapid development into a nationwide movement that results in a massive march on the Capitol in Washington, D.C., lies in the ability of the song to impress on the viewer (despite the silliness of the idea of Mothers Against Canada) the dangerous efficacy of xenophobic pressure groups whose causes are sparked by knee-jerk ignorance and hate mongering (a couple is so entranced by the song that they abandon their baby and carriage on the sidewalk to join the marching crowd led by Kyle's mother). The final lyrics of both these songs expose the real culprits—not Terrance and Phillip or their country—but parents and their lazy child rearing: In the finale of "Mountain Town," the boys, marching in unison, sing (with a *rallentando con majestoso* providing an additional emphasis): "Off to the movies we shall go, / Where we learn everything that we know, / 'Cause the movies teach us what our parents don't have time to say!" The finale of "Blame Canada" confirms the boys' insight, with the parents themselves admitting at the end of the song that the sensationalized anecdotes the mothers recount are to preempt and deflect attention from their failure of responsibility as parents: "We must blame them and cause a fuss / Before somebody thinks of blaming us!"

Like Mrs. Broflovski in "Blame Canada," other characters in the movie exploit the Orphic potential of song. Given the satire on the refusal of responsibility, we should not be surprised that the villain of the movie—Saddam Hussein—plays the blame game most explicitly when he pleads with Satan: "It's not my fault that I'm so evil. / It's society. Society. / You see, my parents were sometimes abusive, / And it made a prick of me" in the song "I Can Change." (The satire of this empty promise—he does not sing "I *will* change"—is reinforced by Saddam's claim that, in performing his dance, he is changing before our eyes: "Just watch, just watch me change. / Here I go! I'm changing!") The idea that fundamental personal change can be effortless or just happen naturally—"Any minute now, I will be born again," sings Saddam, sporting a phony halo—is also satirized in Mr. Mackey's self-help song "It's Easy, M'Kay." Besides once again showing parents abrogating their responsibilities by having the school counselor deal with solving the profanity problem, this song satirizes simplistic addiction and self-help programs that fail truly to challenge the individual to change substantively in favor of an easy fix by having Mr. Mackey's four-step program deal not with eliminating the problem (that is, swearing as an unacceptable social behavior) but with substituting graphic expletives with more genteel variants ("Instead of 'shit' say 'poo,' / As in . . ./. . . 'This poo is cold'"). His blithe assurance at the conclusion of the song—"Now you're cured!"—echoes Saddam's at the end of "I Can Change": "You see? I've really matured." The fleeting insubstantiality of Mr. Mackey's cure and Saddam's turning over a new leaf is emphasized by the songs being explicitly foregrounded as songs, as artificial performances: Mr. Mackey accompanies himself on the piano, and Saddam strikes a pose in front of a theater curtain before he razzle-dazzles Satan with his song. In both songs, the musical theater conventions in evidence—Mr. Mackey's donning of a vaudevillian boater and cane, the dramatic pulling back of a curtain to reveal Saddam's backup dancers, the significant role "choreography" plays in both songs—are not present to make fun of musical theater, but to highlight and satirize the insincerity of Saddam's promises and the superficiality of Mackey's program. Both songs, despite this, have an Orphic impact on the characters who hear them: The kids are (momentarily) swayed into singing and dancing along with Mr. Mackey, and Satan rediscovers his love for Saddam as the latter's serpent-tongued suasions climax in serpentine undulations.[4]

Satan's song "Up There," which has been characterized as a "Mariah Carey–style inspirational ballad" (Holden), runs the risk of being dismissed at first glance as a simple parody and, consequently, of having its satiric function overlooked. Reinforced by the brief shot of Satan standing, arms out-stretched, at the prow of the ship à la Kate Winslett in *Titanic* (1997), the song suggests a parodic mimicking of the blockbuster movie's love song, "My Heart Will Go On," sung by Céline Dion. And while "Up There" and Ariel's song "Part of that World" from *The Little Mermaid* (1989) share similarities, the idea that Satan's song is meant to be understood by the viewer as a par-ody of Ariel's song is to overlook the function of "Up There" in *South Park: Bigger Longer & Uncut*.[5] Regardless what allusions to previous musical exam-ples may have been intended, the function of the song in the movie clearly is not parodic: If the intention were to make the viewer laugh derisively at Satan's trite romantic *Titanic*-inspired fantasies, Saddam would have been, like Leonardo DiCaprio in *Titanic*, standing behind Satan hugging and kiss-ing him—or doing other things to him from behind. Both the composition and deployment of this song in the movie harken back to the use of the love songs in *Cannibal! The Musical*. These songs, such as "Up There," closely imi-tate familiar styles of music rather than being patterned on specific songs, and the faithfulness with which these musical styles are replicated militates against them being defined as parodic. But whereas the nonparodic songs in *Cannibal!* fail to have any real function or effect beyond incongruity, Satan's "Up There," because it neither parodies a musical genre nor, consequently, the character singing it or the situation in which it is sung, leads the sympa-thies of the viewer for Satan into an unusual detour, and therefore becomes a Siren song.

When "Blame Canada" was nominated for an Academy Award, the rumor circulated that this song was chosen because it had the fewest profan-ities: Some pointed out, however, that "Up There" had none, but that the problem with this song was that it controversially portrays Satan in a positive light.[6] In the movie, Satan emerges as a sensitive, easily manipulated guy trapped in a toxic relationship and tied to a dead-end job with no upward mobility (unless strict conditions—the Seven Signs—have been met). His personal character is not based on his job description: When Satan first encounters Kenny, he plays up his role as the Lord of Hell, but this tough guy persona is almost immediately dissipated by the appearance of Saddam, who crassly blows Satan's diabolical front by asking Satan to rub his nipples while *he* tortures Kenny. Satan introduces Saddam Hussein as his "partner in evil," although "evil partner" would be a more appropriate characterization: The point *South Park: Bigger Longer & Uncut* makes about the partnership between Satan and Saddam is that the origins of evil do not reside in some otherworldly personification of evil such as the Devil, but lie within our-selves—that evil is an all-too-human trait. The all-too-human Saddam has evil designs on earth; not only is it his face that appears in the viewer during the military briefing, telling the world "I'm comin' to getcha! I'm comin' to getcha!" but also the war and all its attendant evil has come about solely due to human actions. The populist fascism exemplified by Kyle's mother, who, as "Minister of Offense," has become the Himmler of America's Final Solution to the Canadian Problem, has been instrumental in creating hell on earth with no help from Satan. When Mrs. Broflovski, after having brought about the fulfillment of the Seventh Sign by shooting Terrance and Phillip dead, says in justification, "I was just trying to make the world a better place for children," Saddam tauntingly retorts: "Yeah! And you brought enough intolerance to the world to allow my coming!"

"Up There" defeats the conventional expectation that it will demonize Satan through ridicule, thereby alienating his character from the viewer's sympathies; instead, it reinforces Satan's depiction as a big softie. Contrary to biblical propaganda, Satan's interest in coming to earth is not infernal in nature, but rather stems from his being "so lonely down here" and "there's such a big world up there, / I'd like to give it a try":

> Up there, there is so much room,
> Where babies burp and flowers bloom.
> Everyone dreams; I can dream, too.
> Up there, up where the skies are ocean-blue,
> I could be safe and live without a care,
> If only I could live up there!
> I wanna live, I wanna live up oooo hoo!
> Baby, oooo! I want to live up there!

Like his terrestrial fantasies—mountain climbing, hang gliding, sipping martinis on the deck of the gay cruise ship the *S. S. Manhandler*—Satan's cherished visions of what life is like "up there" are not of pain and torture and evil, but cloyingly conventional: a couple embracing in a flower-filled meadow, bright-eyed babies, the flight of dandelion seed and seagulls, a shooting star. The song cements the building sympathy the viewer feels for Satan, a sympathy that is not a covert Satanist public relations ploy, but one intended to satirize the ultimate move in the blame game—making the Devil, the *ne plus ultra* Other, responsible for the evils of the world—by redirecting attention from stereotypical villains to real, human villains such as Saddam Hussein (who, significantly, does not feature in any of Satan's "Up There" fantasies). "Up There" is a ballad of yearning that Satan sings alone after a lover's tiff with Saddam. Overheard only by the viewer, Satan's song is a Siren appeal intended to lure the viewer into assenting to a crucial proposition in the movie's message that would otherwise be seen as counterintuitive—that the personification of evil is instead the poster boy of likeability, that the true face of evil is not red, horned, and fanged but uncomfortably mundane (significantly, Saddam's face is distinguished by being animated from real images). The crucial Siren song of the movie, "Up There," by seducing the viewer into sympathizing with rather than making a scapegoat of Satan, produces *South Park: Bigger Longer & Uncut's* most definitive statement in the film's satire of the blame game and the failure to take responsibility. And by cutting short Saddam's coming by casting him off, Satan ironically enables the movie's heavenly ending. That this satire on blaming others and avoiding responsibilities should end with Kenny—granted a wish by Satan for helping Satan see that Saddam was no good for him—selflessly taking responsibility for fixing the mess the United States has got itself into by wishing things back to the way they were before things had gotten so out of hand is fitting. The again imitative but not parodic "grand finale" music that accompanies the cometlike apotheosis of the long-suffering and continually unlucky Kenny makes for a genuinely uplifting conclusion that leaves the viewer in no doubt that Kenny deserves his halo and wings for, Christlike, not passing the cup.[7]

Seductive Music in an Absurd World

The variety of the television episodes allows for a greater variety of music than in the movie. Chef's songs are prominent: Ostensibly used to teach the young boy protagonists about life and love, they invariably become songs about sex and relationships whose satiric humor is beyond the full comprehension of the boys (except perhaps Kenny). Apart from Chef's songs, the original music in the television episodes falls into two broad categories: parody and seduction. The television show features music by real rock bands and, more interestingly, songs that parody real musical trends and styles. Cartman's song "Fingerbang!" parodies boy-band songs, while the episode, "Something You Can Do with Your Finger," parodies the entire boy-band culture. Similarly, Cartman's music group *Faith + 1* satirizes the culture of Christian rock, and the songs Cartman writes for the band are very thinly veiled parodies of a particular style of Christian rock. The show's other vocal music, music that is not parody and not obviously an element of the humorous satire typical of *South Park*, is, like the songs in the movie, often a powerful expression of seduction, at times used by one character to seduce others into believing something to which they are resistant, and at times used to seduce the viewer directly into the absurdity of the world of *South Park*.

An example of the powerful hold music has over people, and perhaps the most clear example of an Orphic song in *South Park*, is in "The Succubus." Chef has quit his job in the lunchroom at school because Veronica, a woman he has recently met, has persuaded him to do so. The four boys go to ask Chef

FIGURE 3
The boy's boy band, "Fingerbang."

about this, and they realize that something is wrong when Chef tells them how he talked with Veronica all night about the "power of the Goddess," rather than making "sweet love to her down by the fire." And if this is not enough to indicate to the boys and to the viewer that normalcy has been severely upset, Chef suggests that Veronica sing a song to the boys to make them feel better, rather than singing one himself. She sings the song, accompanying herself on an acoustic guitar, and Chef joins in for the third line of the song. Not only does the song not conform to Chef's typical songs, but both Veronica and Chef adopt a quasi-British accent and a singing voice that is more from the diaphragm with a relaxed throat, which is more typical of operatic than popular singing.[8] Kyle's comment, as the duo start on the second verse of the song, sums up what the boys and the viewer must be thinking, "This—is insane." The boys discover, with Mr. Garrison's misplaced help, that Veronica is a succubus: She has seduced Chef and is able to keep him under her power through her song. They manage to defeat the succubus by singing her song backward in her presence. The power of her song is countered, Chef is saved from marriage to a demon woman, and the boys get their friend back.

Although Veronica's song is used for its Orphic powers of persuasion over Chef, it has a secondary seductive effect on Cartman. The boys learn about defeating the succubus by spending all night in Cartman's room looking through books of lore and magic. At six in the morning, after Kyle finds the answer, written in a pseudo-medieval style—"Succubus, enchants its victim with eerie melody This is succubi power. Only playing this melody backward can vanquish the succubus power"—he asks, "What's that song she always sings?" He then proceeds to sing the first line of the song. Cartman takes up the song, singing the next two lines, even though he is trying to get to sleep after having rejected their efforts ("You know what? Screw Chef. There, I said it. Screw him. Let him marry a succubus. I wanna go to sleep."). The implication is that Cartman cannot control himself: He must sing the song that Kyle started. While the song itself might be to blame, the succubus song being so powerful that Cartman loses control of his mind (much like the "brown noise" in a later episode causes people to lose control of their bowels), it is more probable that music itself has a strong hold over Cartman's life. The song seduces Chef into agreeing to marry Veronica, but music in general seduces Cartman: He cannot help but sing.

That Cartman is seduced by music, even though he was not the target of the succubus's song, suggests that *South Park* uses music for indirect seduction. The episode "The Death Camp of Tolerance" attempts this type of indirect musical seduction, but does so to complicate the seduction techniques of the episode: It attempts to teach social tolerance to the boys and uses music to undermine its own attempts. The boys are forced to finger paint pictures by a Hitleresque man in Devitzen's Tolerance Camp: "You will make a painting that shows people of different races and sexual orientations getting along. Fingerpaint! Fingerpaint! You will not make any distinction between people of different color, people with different sexual preferences. You will accept everyone!" The boys and their classmates are forced to learn tolerance to accept the homosexual identity of their new fourth-grade teacher, Mr. Garrison. But unknown to their parents, Mr. Garrison has been overstepping the bounds of acceptable behavior in the hopes of being fired from his position and winning a legal battle and a large monetary settlement. When Mr. Garrison inserts the class gerbil, Lemmiwinks, into the rectum of Mr. Slave, his new teacher's assistant (known as Teacher's Ass, for short), both the schoolchildren and the viewers know that he has gone too far. The viewers only (not any of the characters) are treated to the adventures of Lemmiwinks as he journeys through Mr. Slave's innards. Any semblance of realism is put aside as Lemmiwinks is given a quest by the ghost of a Frog King: The gerbil must journey to the opening of the large intestine where he will encounter the Sparrow Prince. He also encounters the Catatafish in the stomach and eventually makes his way out of Mr. Slave, to be crowned the Gerbil King. Accompanying the absurd images of the gerbil traveling through Mr. Slave's bowels is a song in the style of English renaissance or medieval ballads. "The Ballad of Lemmiwinks" is not, however, meant to satirize its own style of music, in the manner of "Fingerbang!" but instead comes across as good (though amateurish) imitation.[9] The lyrics are somewhat ironic—for example, "Freedom from the Ass of Doom / Is the treasure you will win"—but neither the song nor the situation are satiric: There is no real criticism of the practice, real or fabled, of inserting small rodents into the rectum. The song, instead, ennobles the practice by aligning it with medieval quests, real or fabled, such as the quest for the Holy Grail. The "Ballad of Lemmiwinks" reinforces the quest nature of the gerbil's predicament in Mr. Slave's ass, but also highlights the absurdity of what is being portrayed as the viewer realizes that the absurdity of the quest is being aligned with the attempts on the part of Devitzen's camp to force tolerance on people. The song seduces the viewer into believing that romanticizing the adventures of the gerbil is an effective means for teaching tolerance, but the viewer realizes that neither the song nor the Tolerance Camp can have any lasting effect; few viewers will regard gerbiling as a noble practice as a result of this episode. At an even deeper level, the absurdity of Lemmiwinks's adventures points to the absurdity of thinking that a lesson in tolerance for what is more urban legend than common practice among gay men is even necessary.

"The Ballad of Lemmiwinks" is a Siren song used to lull the viewer into a world of absurdity. Although it points to various levels of absurdity in the episode, other Siren songs are used in other episodes to lull the viewer into their absurd worlds without playing up the absurdity. A good example of this is the episode "Here Comes the Neighborhood." Token comes to believe, partly as a result of being "ripped on" by his classmates, that he does not fit in because he is from a rich family. After buying $5 pants at J-mart, Token realizes that even such acts of extreme desperation will not allow him to fit in. He is left alone to sing his song, "Why Can't I Be Like All the Other Kids?" The primary effect of the song is to allow the viewer to sympathize with Token. We do see a hint of satire: The viewer is asked to sympathize with a child who feels he does not fit in because he is from an affluent family. But because the singer is a child and has been until recently blissfully ignorant that his parents are rich and that no one else in town has a DVD player, the viewer allows the pathos of the song to have its effect. The song's reinforcement of the viewer's sympathy with Token is what allows the episode its absurd turn: After thinking he can be friends neither with his classmates nor with the children of the rich Hollywood families who move to South Park, he decides to live with the lions at the zoo. The episode has prepared us for this development: We can assume that Token's favorite movie is *The Lion King* because that is the DVD he brings to watch with his friends. But when Token is introduced to Aslan, the leader of the lions in the zoo, and when Aslan turns out to be more juvenile than his classmates (Aslan seems almost more obsessed with fart jokes than even Terrance and Phillip, and he speaks to Token imitating the formal style of address a Jedi Master uses with his apprentice in the *Star Wars* movies), the episode takes the viewer even deeper into the realm of the absurd. The absurdity of the scene runs parallel to the absurdity of Token's inability to fit in with the poorer children and the absurdity of the townspeople wanting to get rid of the "richies" that move in. The world of the talking lions is not present for the sake of satire or parody, as with the other levels of absurdity in the episode; instead, it is present as an exercise in viewer sympathy: The show tests how far it can push the limits of reality and still maintain the viewer's interest. Without Token's song solidifying that sympathy, the absurdity of the scene with the lions would fail.

The absurd world of the talking lions in the zoo parallels the absurdity of the way the residents of South Park treat the rich Hollywood families that have recently moved to town. The South Park residents try to force or scare off the newly arrived families, all of which are of African-American background, because the established residents are afraid, among other things, of being forced out of town as a result of "inflated real estate costs." The viewer quickly comes to understand the show's humorous parody of the more usual U.S. race-relation tensions. The absurdity is heightened when the townspeople decide to dress as ghosts by covering themselves in white sheets to frighten the rich families away and to burn wooden, lowercase letter *t*'s on their lawns to convey the message, "time to leave." The viewer, having been seduced into sympathizing with the lonely (African American) rich kid and having been exposed to the world of the adolescent zoo lions, is all the more able to recognize the parody of race relations and will probably look on the episode as predominantly farcical. Everything is undermined by Mr. Garrison's final comment about "niggers," which is the first indication that, for him at least, the rich Hollywood families were really not welcome in South Park because of the color of their skin. Token's song functions to introduce the complex satire, seducing the viewer into accepting the absurdity of the episode while allowing the viewer to recognize it as such. Mr. Garrison's comment, which is actually partially censored by the episode, pulls the rug out from under the viewer, and the episode forces us to question the boundaries between absurdity and reality. Just as the viewer rejects the absurd world of the talking lions, the viewer is asked to view the world of dressing in white sheets and cross-burning as absurd.

The parallel song to Token's, although with a different effect, is Kyle's "A Lonely Jew on Christmas" in "Mr. Hankey, the Christmas Poo." The music itself is not a parody of any particular style of music. The use of the song, however, is satiric in that one would not expect to encounter such a song within a *South Park* episode: It counters normative expectations. The song is highly successful within its context for several reasons. Most of its humor results from the innocence of the Jewish boy trying to understand why he cannot partake of the Christmas activities that his friends share:

And I can't sing Christmas songs or decorate a Christmas tree
Or leave water out for Rudolph, 'cause there's something wrong
    with me:
My people don't believe in Jesus Christ's divinity.

The song acts to increase the viewer's sympathy for Kyle. In singing this song about feeling sorry for himself, a song that aptly exemplifies his child-hood innocence of more sophisticated spiritual matters, a song that expresses his feelings of exclusion from the enjoyable experiences of his friends, Kyle becomes the locus for the viewer's own anxieties of not being able to fit in with others, not being allowed to enjoy what others are enjoying. This process of identification with Kyle is vital to the episode. When the mayor asks the townspeople for an idea for a new icon for Christmas, Kyle suggests Mr. Hankey, the Christmas Poo. With his explanation, Kyle sings the Mr. Hankey song. The suggestion is ridiculous, and the song (or, at least, its ren-dition) is terrible. The viewer is faced with an important conflict: Should I continue identifying with the Jewish boy who feels so alienated by Christmas and accept his ludicrous and somewhat disgusting notion of the Christmas feces, or should I reject my identification with the boy who places such importance in Mr. Hankey, agreeing with Cartman who says, "Don't mind him: He's a very disturbed little boy," thereby invalidating my previous iden-tification with him? The viewer is more likely to continue to identify with Kyle, based perhaps on previous knowledge of how the television show func-tions, but also based strongly on the seductive nature of his song. This episode arguably pushes the boundaries of what is acceptable, both for Christmas spe-cials and for television in general, farther than any previous one. It includes, as part of the final commercial break, a fake commercial advertisement for the Mr. Hankey Construction Set: Two children are bored and their mother comes in with the construction set game—which includes a "special fecal fishing net" with which to select "your best Mr. Hankey"—as a remedy. The fake advertisement includes a scene where a baby is eating the leftovers of something that has smeared brown all over her high-chair tray. The implica-tion is that the baby has eaten one of the older children's Mr. Hankey. This idea and the image used to convey it are at the center of the absurd world the episode has created, and the viewer has been lead into this world through the seduction of Kyle's "A Lonely Jew on Christmas." The Siren song allows the episode to challenge the viewer's sympathies: It helps counter the viewer's instincts to agree with Cartman, who leaves for home, saying, "Talking poo is where I draw the line."

While the viewer is usually delighted with Cartman as a character, he is rarely the locus for viewer sympathy. On one level, he can be aligned with Shelly, who is an almost incessant source of oppression and aggression for her brother Stan. However, Cartman is the center of musical production in the show. When Shelly attempts to sing one of the oldest of English Christmas songs, "I Saw Three Ships" (in "Mr. Hankey's Christmas Classics"), Stan and Kyle giggle and make faces in the background, resulting in Shelly's rendition of the song being reduced to smashing her brother and his best friend with the piano. Just as she is unable to seduce Stan, Kyle, and the viewer into a state of sympathy, Shelly's music fails. Cartman's music, on the other hand, enjoys success every time. His identity as a foul-mouthed, culturally insensitive, right-wing, maladjusted little boy is compromised by his interest in music. We get frequent glimpses of the sensitive side of Cartman, mainly when alone or with his mother. A good example is his tea party with his stuffed animals in "Cartman's Mom Is a Dirty Slut," where he plays out his anxieties about his self-image and his friends, watching unnoticed, believe he has serious psychological problems. But the importance of music in his life reveals Cartman's softer side. His apparent compulsion to sing the song of the succubus is matched by his frequent outbursts into popular song, such as "I Don't Want to Wait," "In the Ghetto," and the parody song "Stinky Britches." In "Cartman's Mom Is Still a Dirty Slut," Cartman reveals his compulsive need to finish Styx's "Come Sail Away" whenever he hears the first part of the song ("Yeah, I can't do anything until it's done," he confesses). "Cat Orgy" opens with Cartman playing with his stuffed animals and dolls in his bedroom. After his mother interrupts and asks him to come meet the babysitter (Shelly), he breaks out into a rap song inspired by Will Smith's "Wild, Wild West." His claim that he is a "bad-ass cowboy" is seriously undermined by his choice of sidekick, Artemis Clyde Frog, and his attempts to reproduce vocally the LP-record scratching noise of standard rap songs. Cartman's songs in general act to increase the viewer's identification with Cartman, the chubby kid who is not well understood by his friends. In "*Simpsons* Already Did It," Cartman has a musical dream of living underwater in a world of Sea People. The song reveals his vulnerable side: He wants to escape to a world of "free and clean" living where his companions "don't ever complain" and "they don't call me fat." The song allows us to sympathize with this boy by revealing a side of him we rarely see. The song's effect is seriously undermined when, after waking from his dream, Cartman says, "Wow! Only three more hours, Sea People! Only three more hours and you can take me away from this crappy, goddamned planet full of hippies." The right-wing statement against hippies ("hippies" is of course Cartman's term for the enemy and essentially refers to anyone whose views and desires do not correspond with his own) jars the viewer who has until that point been seduced by Cartman's plight and innocent desire to escape into a fantasy world. That the show is able to create sympathy for Cartman and then immediately undermine it demonstrates the show's powerful use of the seduction of Siren songs, forcing viewers to question their sympathies for such a usually nonsympathetic character.

Cartman, of all the characters, seems to have the greatest insight into music's ability to create sympathy, and he is not above using it for his own purposes. In the episode where Cartman creates a Jennifer Lopez hand puppet, "Fat Butt and Pancake Head," Cartman is able to fool everyone, including Ben Affleck, that his hand is a real, second Jennifer Lopez. He does this not through the poor ventriloquism, but through the music he has his hand sing. The music is supposedly in the style of Latin American pop music, the style of the real Jennifer Lopez's music, but it is really just a parody, in the manner of "Fingerbang!" and other similar parodies. The first song she sings is simplistic: Its repetition of the words "taco" and "burrito" emphasizes the triviality and the stereotyping of the musical style. When Cartman's hand lands a recording contract, Cartman must write more songs for his Jennifer Lopez to sing. The satire becomes clear when, after working on songs for a short while, Cartman tells his hand: "That's three more songs we've written already! Your style of music is so easy: It doesn't require any thought at all!" But because the music is so close to the style of music expected from the original Jennifer Lopez, Cartman is able to hoodwink almost everyone. The fact that everyone—except Kyle, who is usually the most reluctant person to believe anything Cartman says—has been seduced by Cartman's music becomes all the more clear when Cartman's Jennifer Lopez reveals that she is an impostor: She is really Mitch Connor, a con man, who, in a moment of remorse, takes a cyanide pill and leaves Cartman's hand forever. Kyle admits the possibility that Cartman's hand might have really been possessed by Mitch Connor (who successfully posed as Jennifer Lopez), and Cartman's triumph comes when he is able to exclaim to Kyle, "I got you kinda!" But while the viewers are not taken in, the episode shows Cartman's understanding of and ability to use music's Orphic power of seduction.

In "4th Grade" Cartman shows a more sophisticated use of song. After the boys' first class in fourth grade, they believe they have now to leave behind their youthful innocence and Cartman sings a song about how life was better in the third grade. The song is delivered without irony: It is perhaps not worked seamlessly into the situation, but the fourth graders listen to it in all seriousness and its heartstring tugs even make one boy cry. We find a hint of parody, mainly resulting from Cartman's delivery of the song. In the last line of both the first and second stanzas, "But that sense seems to slowly fade after third grade" and "Just to go back one minute to the third grade," Cartman reverts to a spoken voice for the phrases, "sense seems to slowly" and "one minute." In doing so, Cartman imitates a style of singing directly descended from the style of Rex Harrison in My Fair Lady (1964) that makes use of spoken moments in song to achieve heightened emotional effects. Cartman displays considerable insight into and mastery over popular singing styles.

More important, Cartman's emphasis on "one minute" through a de-lyricization technique, heightened by the fact that it is the second use of the technique and comes a beat later than its counterpart in the first verse, exemplifies his and, by extension, his creators' cunning. At the end of the episode, after Mrs. Choksondik makes the boys realize the importance of facing the new challenges of life, Stan and Kyle come to a realization and Stan says, "Third grade sucked! Cartman, why the hell did you try to make us think third grade was so great?" This draws attention to the fact that some ulterior motive might have prompted Cartman's song. The song initially seems innocent enough, but understood from a different perspective, it becomes an example of powerful seduction through an Orphic song. Cartman's real reasons for wanting to return to third grade are not revealed in the episode, but the viewer can piece together the possibility that he feels he has already jeopardized any chances he has of letting his new teacher think he is anything but a troublemaker. His relationship with the teacher is destroyed at 8:35 A.M. on the first day when he alone stands on his desk, pulls down his pants, and tells the teacher, "Kiss my ass!"—when the class had agreed moments before to perform this act of defiance en masse. Cartman's song, "Remember How It Used to Be in the Third Grade," becomes his means of convincing his classmates that they must invent a method of returning to the third grade. When, immediately after the song, Kyle remarks that he had already forgotten about how great third grade was, we hear the following exchange:

CARTMAN (almost as an aside): Wish I was still there.

STAN: Hey, that's it. We got to go back to third grade.

KYLE: How?

STAN: We travel back in time!

CARTMAN: Oh, yeah! Time travel.

Cartman's innocent-seeming comment, "Wish I was still there," spurs Stan into coming up with the idea of traveling back in time. Cartman's reaction is on the surface one of wonder at Stan's idea, but is delivered in the manner of one who is really thinking that he himself already came up with the idea, and he vocalizes this thought through an ironic delivery of his line, "Oh, yeah! Time travel," as if he were saying with an undertone of sarcasm, "Why didn't I think of that?" Cartman's song helps confirm that he did think of it: His emphasis on "one minute" in the last line of the song ("Just to go back one minute to the third grade") is what plants the germ of the idea of time travel into Stan's mind. Cartman's song becomes a song of Orphic seduction, convincing his classmates that they too must want to return to third grade. Cartman becomes a young, "big-boned" Machiavelli in his ability to instill in others his own desires, come up with a plan to fulfill his desires, and allow others to believe that they came up with the idea on their own. Cartman achieves his desires through song.

In "The Innocence of Children: Effects of Vulgarity in *South Park*," Emily Ravenwood maintains that because the vulgarity of the show's regular characters "is so overwhelming, those few characters who are not parodies stand out in high relief. The issues those characters represent are assured of the audience's sympathies because there is, literally, nowhere else for those sympathies to alight" (7). Ravenwood suggests that none of the four main characters—Kyle, Stan, Cartman, and Kenny—is able to win the viewer's sympathies. An examination of the music surrounding Cartman shows that he, the least sympathetic of the boys, is at least at times a sympathetic character.[10] Just as the show occasionally exposes the dark side hidden behind Cartman's mother's bright and sunny midwestern demeanor, Cartman's music betrays his complex, emotionally vulnerable inner self, usually hidden by his crass exterior. Although the show does not necessarily want to make the viewers identify with Cartman and adopt his attitudes and points of view, it does want to challenge the viewers' beliefs, allowing for a multiplicity of perspectives, attitudes, and sympathies. Song is the enabling force.

Absurdity and the Real World

In *South Park*, the movie and television series, song is used not solely for the sake of a few chuckles, not solely as a parody of music or attitudes often associated with music, but as a powerful tool for satire, a means to lure viewers into foreign worlds and unexpected mental paradigms. The function of song goes well beyond the gilding of the philosophic pill: It helps *South Park* challenge the viewer's otherwise comfortable perspective on life and community. As the show has evolved over time, so has its use of music, and the show continues to explore the boundaries of acceptable television and acceptable use of song. This study cannot explicate fully the varied and complex role assigned to song in *South Park*, but the Orphic and Siren songs represent the most powerful and original uses of music in the first seven seasons.

A consistent feature of the use of song in these earlier seasons of *South Park* and the movie is a lack of self-consciousness: Characters often burst into song without drawing attention to the fact that they are singing. A departure from this earlier use of music occurs in the ninth season where this lack of self-consciousness is reversed. In "Follow That Egg," Mrs. Garrison sings a song about Mr. Slave, "Love, Love Lost Long Ago." The song starts as a song in her head, but becomes one she sings out loud to the class. What is remarkable is not that she is singing, but that the students stare at her in astonishment as she sings. It is as if the children have finally realized, after eight seasons, that a spontaneous eruption into song is not standard social behavior. Another episode in the ninth season shows another development of the use of music: It interestingly reverses the use of music to seduce the viewer into an absurd world. Wing, from the episode "Wing," is the wife of the owner of City Wok, recently brought over from China by the Chinese mafia. Her remarkable singing abilities are what bring her husband hopes of fame and riches. Because her attempts to sing within the Western popular music idiom are poor at best, the episode seems at first to be a satire of the television sensation of *American Idol*, especially the California university student, William Hung, who enjoyed 15 minutes of fame (well, perhaps more than 15 minutes) as a result of his attempt to get on the show. The viewer is lulled into the absurd world where Wing's renditions of such songs as Abba's "Dancing Queen" and "Fernando" could result in one character saying, "My God, her voice is sooo beautiful!" However, the fictional realm of the absurd is undermined by the revelation at the end of the show that Wing in the episode is a representation of a real person: Wing, a Hong Kong emigrant to New Zealand, whose singing was used for the episode. *South Park* manages to seduce the viewer with her music into thinking that Wing's singing is a parody; once the seduction is complete, the show reveals that reality is actually more absurd than the fictional world of *South Park*.

Notes

1. See "The Real Story" page on *Cannibal! The Musical: The Official Website* for more information about Packer's history.

2. Parker had previous experience in this song genre: When he was 15 he, with David Goodman, recorded the album *Immature: A Collection of Love Ballads for the '80's Man* ("Trey Parker and Matt Stone").

3. All lyrics from the musical are quoted from the versions on the Songs/Lyrics page ("*Cannibal! The Musical* Songs, Lyric and Tabs") on *Cannibal! The Musical: The Official Website*.

4. Satan's susceptibility to the blandishments of song (no matter how despicable the singer might be) is earlier revealed in "Mr. Hankey's Christmas Classics": Satan is so moved by the pathos of Hitler, who is overcome singing "O Tannenbaum" while kneeling over an empty Christmas tree stand, that he presents Hitler with a tree while singing "It's Christmastime in Hell." Perhaps as a sly acknowledgment of this Orphic similarity with Hitler, Saddam is seen kissing and packing in his suitcase a little Hitler doll just before singing, "I Can Change."

5. The context of each song is completely different; in addition, the function of "Part of That World" is to set up the complication that will drive the movie's plot by providing Ariel's motivation (pure curiosity fueled by teenage rebellion) for wanting to explore life on land, whereas "Up There" functions not to advance the plot or provide Satan's motivations for wanting to come to earth, but to establish the viewer's affinity with Satan.

6. See the *Wikipedia* entry on the movie for a reference to this.

7. Given that Kenny is greeted and awarded his halo and wings by a host of naked, large-breasted women, he seems to have gone to the Muslim Paradise because, as we later learn in "Probably," the Christian Heaven is the exclusive domain of Mormons who "make things out of egg cartons," stage plays "about how alcohol can ruin family life," and sing "songs about how much it hurts to lie." This makes it a fitting hell for Saddam Hussein, when Satan wants to prevent him from continually returning to hell to harass him.

8. The style of singing they adopt is even a marked departure from the style the song is sung in the movie, *The Poseidon Adventure* (1972), where it first appears. In the movie, "There's Got To Be a Morning After" is sung by a naïve, young, hippy-ish woman with a soft, unembellished voice.

9. The music is modeled directly on the ballad music from two television animated movies that center on quests: *The Hobbit* (1977) and *The Return of the King* (1980). In both movies, part of the narrative is conveyed by similar, medieval ballad-style songs. Parts of "The Ballad of Lemmiwinks" are remarkably similar to "The Greatest Adventure" from *The Hobbit.*

10. We argue that all four boys and even some of the peripheral characters are able, at least at times, to win the viewer's sympathies.

Works Cited

Cannibal! The Musical: The Official Website. 1998–2006. 3 Mar. 2006 <http://www.cannibalthemusical.net/>.

Holden, Stephen. "Making a Point with Smut and Laughs." Review of *BLU. New York Times* (30 June 1999) <http://movies2.nytimes.com/mem/movies/review.html>.

Ravenwood, Emily. "The Innocence of Children: Effects of Vulgarity in *South Park.*" *Comparative Literature and Culture: A WWWeb Journal* 1.2 (June 1999) <http://clcwebjournal.lib.purdue.edu/clcweb99–2/ravenwood99.html>.

"South Park: Bigger Longer & Uncut." *Wikipedia.* 3 Mar. 2006. <http://www.wikipedia.org>.

The South Park Scriptorium. 1998–2005. 3 Mar. 2006. <http://www.spscriptorium.com/>.

"Trey Parker and Matt Stone." *The South Park Scriptorium.* 3 Mar. 2006. <http://www.spscriptorium.com/SPinfo/ParkerAndStone.htm>.

CHAPTER 4

"*Simpsons* Did It!"

South Park as Differential Signifier

JEFFREY ANDREW WEINSTOCK

In attempting to appreciate *South Park*'s cultural significance, one needs to acknowledge that the program did not simply emerge out of nowhere. Rather, it developed out of and participates in the tradition of television animation. Standing on the shoulders of giants (not to mention mice, rabbits, dogs, and dinosaurs), *South Park*'s horizon of possibility—what it dares to attempt—as well as both its aesthetics (the way it looks and sounds) and its content (its dialogue and plotlines) all have been influenced by its animated predecessors and respond to the changing dynamics of the television marketplace. Of course, every television program—animated and otherwise—participates to varying extents in a particular generic tradition and simultaneously attempts to distinguish itself both within that tradition and from its contemporary competitors. However, part of the fun of *South Park* is its self-consciousness of itself as an animated program within a tradition of television animation and its hyperawareness of itself as a "differential signifier"—that is, as an animated program whose meaning is precisely dependent on the fact that it is both similar to and different from other animated programs.

This chapter focuses on two things: *South Park*'s indebtedness to the traditions of prime-time animation and Saturday morning cartoons and *South Park*'s self-conscious positioning of itself within the contemporary marketplace of animated programming. In connection with the former, I will attend briefly to the importance of programs including *The Flintstones*, *Scooby-Doo*, *Ren & Stimpy*, and *Beavis and Butt-head*, to *South Park*'s aesthetics and narratives. In connection with the latter, I will look at the ways in which *South Park* engages directly with the animated programs *The*

Simpsons and *Family Guy*. My argument in this chapter has two components to it. The first part is that to understand *South Park*'s cultural significance, one needs to appreciate the tradition in which it participates and the program's relationship to other similar programs; the second component is that part of the enjoyment viewers derive from the program is related precisely to the ways in which *South Park* plays on the viewer's "televisual literacy"—that is, part of the fun is recognizing *South Park*'s similarities to and differences from other animated programs, its allusions to cherished childhood programs, and its at times favorable and at other times mocking assessments of other contemporary programs.

Prime Time Animation

LIMITED ANIMATION: *THE FLINTSTONES*

Prime-time (the programming slot between 8 P.M. and 10 P.M.) animation dates back to 1960 when the then newly launched ABC premiered *The Flintstones* opposite CBS's *Route 66* and NBC's *The Westerner*.[1] The program received mixed reviews but high ratings (its pilot even beat NBC's success, *Bonanza* [Farley 149]), and *The Flintstones* retained its prime-time slot for a very respectable six years. Noting the success of *The Flintstones*, NBC and CBS followed suit and developed their own prime-time animated programs. In 1961, CBS introduced *The Alvin Show* featuring a trio of animated singing chipmunks and put it up against ABC's *The New Steve Allen Show* and NBC's *Wagon Train*. Also in 1961, NBC brought out *The Bullwinkle Show* and matched it up against *Lassie*, which was on CBS, on Sunday evenings. (*Bullwinkle* had the advantage of being in color; *Lassie* was in black and white.)

As Hilton-Morrow and McMahan detail, ABC really found its niche with prime-time animation and broadcast five prime-time animated series in 1961: *The Flintstones*, *Calvin and the Colonel*, *Matty's Funday Funnies*, *Top Cat*, and *The Bugs Bunny Show* (76). This initial wave of prime-time animation subsided for the 1962–1963 season, with only *The Flintstones* returning, but ABC retained an interest in animated programs and premiered *The Jetsons* in 1962, which lasted one season before moving to Saturday mornings, and then *Jonny Quest* in 1964, which also lasted in prime time for only one season. *The Flintstones*' run on prime time ended in 1966 and, with only two exceptions, animated programming disappeared from prime time until the premiere of *The Simpsons* on FOX in 1989—23 years later.[2]

The importance of *The Flintstones* to the development of television animation and to *South Park* in particular cannot be overstated. Although Fred and Wilma (not to mention the Great Gazoo) have yet to make an appearance on *South Park*, one aspect of *The Flintstones* clearly appropriated by *South*

Park is what Farley refers to as *The Flintstones'* "animatedness" or "audiovisuality"—its visual style, the simplicity of its animation, and the relationship of image to sound. The visual style employed by *The Flintstones'* creators Hanna-Barbera called "limited animation" made use of rudimentary drawings and shallow perspective and the program was produced using saturated, unmodulated colors (Farley 153). The movement of the characters on the program was also crude and jerky—Hanna-Barbera reduced the number of drawings per second, as well as the number of moving parts. According to Farley, "Discarding the prevailing smooth animation aesthetic, *The Flintstones'* rudimentary movements signified that Hanna-Barbera was starting—literally from scratch—a new mode of production" (154). Related to the simplification of visual style and animation was a correspondingly increased emphasis on soundtrack and dialogue.

The result of these aesthetic decisions, according to Farley, was a "spectacularizing effect" that called attention precisely to the mechanics of television production and the limits of the animated format (155). She argues that part of the appeal of *The Flintstones* was—and perhaps remains—the program's high degree of self-reflexivity, which is apparent both in its rough form and in its preoccupation with Hollywood and the entertainment industry. (With regard to the latter, Farley mentions Fred's stint as a rock star, Wilma's several television careers, Pebbles and Bamm-Bamm's "discovery," and the occasional incorporation of guest stars culminating in a visit by Samantha and Darrin from *Bewitched* to Bedrock [155]). Farley concludes that *The Flintstones* thus functioned as a form of "stretch TV" that "transgressed and broadened the boundaries of what TV animation could do" (155).

Clearly, much of the preceding conversation also applies to *South Park*. Visually, *South Park* borrows a good deal from the "limited animation" approach *The Flintstones* pioneered—*South Park* shares *The Flintstones'* saturated, unmodulated color palette and "lowers the bar" even further, as it were, in relation to the rudimentarity of visual form and animation.[3] And, as with *The Flintstones*, this simplification of visual representation is accompanied by a corresponding increase in emphasis on dialogue and sound effects, as well as heightened self-reflexivity. With regard to the former, dialogue plays a central role in each *South Park* episode and is the primary means of furthering the narrative. With regard to the latter, *South Park*'s crude visual aesthetic foregrounds its own constructedness and differentiates it from other animated programs (and movies) with smoother animation aesthetics. Indeed, as Savage observes, *South Park*'s opening credits in which human hands assemble cardboard cutouts at an accelerated pace overtly thematize the program's own artifice and call attention to the program's mechanics of production from its very first moments (213).[4]

Part of the fun of *South Park* is the tension established between its relatively sophisticated dialogue and involved narratives and its extremely limited animation—an ironic disjunction between the program's visual style and its content that arguably is descended from *The Flintstones*. Importantly, however, *South Park*'s aesthetic participates in furthering one of the program's fundamental themes: the sophistication of children. One of the hallmarks of *South Park* is its presentation of children not as innocent little angels, but as foul-mouthed "little bastards."[5] The "deliberate immaturity" (Gardiner 53) of *South Park*'s visual aesthetic accentuates the ironic contrast between culturally enshrined ideals concerning children's simplicity and innocence and their actual willfulness, perversity, and sadism. In essence, the program looks like it was made by children about children for children, and this perception structures a humorous ironic contrast when the children actually swear like sailors and are placed in very adult situations.

Intriguingly, as concerns self-reflexivity, *South Park* also shares *The Flintstones*' preoccupation with the entertainment industry and its own status within that field of production. As with *The Flintstones*, a significant source of humor on *South Park* derives from its depictions of and commentary on contemporary celebrities.[6] Celebrities regularly visit South Park or are visited by the boys. Beyond this, when not watching television (*Terrance and Phillip*, *Fighting 'Round the World with Russell Crowe*—to get to *Terrance and Phillip*), the boys occasionally appear on television shows, on television show sets, or at television studios.[7]

In addition, like Fred, Pebbles, and Bamm-Bamm, the children on *South Park* pursue musical careers on several occasions.[8] Indeed, almost every episode of *South Park* in one way or another engages with some aspect of the entertainment industry and the program's tongue-in-cheek fascination with its own Hollywood origins participates in highlighting both the possibilities and limitations of the animation format.

GROSSNESS AND STUPIDITY: *REN & STIMPY* AND *BEAVIS AND BUTT-HEAD*

If *The Flintstones* constitutes a sort of spiritual progenitor for *South Park*, the animated programs *Ren & Stimpy* and *Beavis and Butt-head* can be considered as older brothers that share certain important family traits and have influenced just how much *South Park* can get away with. Like *The Flintstones*, *Ren & Stimpy* was strategically slotted into prime time to woo viewers away from rival networks. Canadian animator John Kricfalusi created the program and his animation team Spümcø produced it for the children's cable network Nickelodeon. The pilot was finished in 1990 and the first episode aired in August 1991. However, from the very start, Nickelodeon was uncomfortable with the program's vulgarity and violence, and it was subject to network censorship on numerous occasions. In September 1992, Nickelodeon fired Kricfalusi and one of Kricfalusi's friends, Bob Camp, took over writing and directing the episodes. Spümcø artists, upset by the firing of Kricfalusi, began to leave and Nickelodeon eventually formed Games Animation to take over production. As a result of declining ratings, Nickelodeon eventually cancelled the show in 1995 and its final episodes aired in 1996.

Parker and Stone occasionally acknowledge their appreciation for Kricfalusi and *Ren & Stimpy*.[9] However, as with *The Flintstones*, *South Park*'s debt to the program cannot be overstated. While *Ren & Stimpy*, like *The Flintstones*, strove for a deliberately crude look and was self-referentially preoccupied with television and the mechanics of its own production, what *South Park* arguably gleaned most explicitly from *Ren & Stimpy* was the latter's exuberant pursuit of grossness and vulgarity. The cartoon famously was committed to transgressing all limits of propriety and taste and this led to "its infamous, seemingly endless displays of bodily effluvia, including brains, blood vessels, nerve endings, hair balls, scabies, spit, 'nose goblins,' 'private moments' in the kitty litter tray, and (years before *South Park*'s Mr. Hanky [sic]) a living fart named Stinky" (Farley 158). According to Barrier, "Kricfalusi—like most 10-year-old boys—never met a bodily function, a rude noise, or a television commercial that wasn't a rich source of comic inspiration" (83).

As Farley's parenthetical aside concerning Mr. Hankey, the Christmas Poo, suggests, when *Ren & Stimpy* went off the air in 1996, it bequeathed to *South Park*, which premiered the following year, the title of gross-out king. Along with *The Flintstones*, Farley also considers *Ren & Stimpy* a form of "stretch TV"—that is, as a program that gleefully transgressed established animation conventions and thereby both altered and extended the medium's possibilities. What characterizes both programs, according to Farley, is a sense of *play*, "a mode of communication emphasizing disruption, imagination, expressivity and (above all) fun" (160). Both *The Flintstones* and *Ren & Stimpy* retained viewers during their prime-time runs by "engaging in a play mode which spectacularized television, making a novelty of familiar formats, poking fun at convention, [and] transgressing established boundaries" (161). *South Park* clearly is cut from the same cloth.

Beavis and Butt-head, which more or less paralleled *Ren & Stimpy* in terms of series life, shared with *Ren & Stimpy* the preoccupation with stupidity and vulgarity, while lowering the bar even further in terms of animation rudimentarity. The characters, which animator Mike Judge created, made their debut in a 1990 low-budget short film entitled succinctly, *Huh?* The 40-second long short was featured in *Spike and Mike's Sick and Twisted Festival of Animation* that same year. In 1991, MTV hired Judge to produce animated segments for its series *Liquid Television*. Judge produced two *Beavis and Butt-head* shorts that aired in 1992 and these led to the television series that premiered on MTV in 1993. The program ended in 1997 (the same year *South Park* premiered) after having produced 199 episodes.

In several respects, *Beavis and Butt-head* should be acknowledged as the most immediate forbearer of *South Park*. Visually, the program's "degraded aesthetic" (Farley 159) offers perhaps the closest parallel to *South Park*'s own two-dimensionality, flatness of color, and minimization of movement. Although *Beavis and Butt-head* does not present itself as constructed out of paper cutouts, it clearly shares with *South Park* an intentionally crude visual aesthetic that de-emphasizes moving parts. In addition, the *Beavis and Butt-head* narratives regularly are interrupted by sequences in which the two sit on their couch and critique music videos—yet another manifestation of contemporary animation's self-referential obsession with the entertainment industry. These sequences feature the incorporation of nonanimated segments from videos and juxtapose them with scenes of cartoon characters in a way suggestive of *South Park*'s distinctive representations of celebrities in which nonanimated representations of celebrity heads are affixed to animated bodies.

Of course, *Beavis and Butt-head* shares with *Ren & Stimpy* and bequeathed unto *South Park* an emphasis on crude, lowbrow humor that is especially preoccupied with body parts and bodily functions—a detail apparent even in the name of the series. "Butt-head" in fact seems to be the character's given name; fart jokes constitute a significant percentage of the series' humor; and the duo were responsible for expanding Western culture's discursive possibilities substantially by popularizing a variety of colorful terms, including "assmunch," "asswipe," "dumbass," "dil-weed," and the ever popular "butt burglar." When not commenting on music videos or insulting each other, the two get into trouble at school; enrage their neighbor, Tom Anderson (an early version of the character who would become Hank Hill on Judge's next series, *King of the Hill*); and wreak havoc in their place of employment, Burger World, where they demonstrate a fondness for frying various objects, including mice, earth worms, and their own fingers. Occasionally, when he has consumed too much caffeine and sugar, Beavis transforms into his alter ego, "The Great Cornholio," with his trademark catchphrase, "I need TP for my bunghole!"

While none of the characters on *South Park* is quite as dumb as Beavis or Butt-head, one important thematic issue both programs share is the ineptitude of parents and educators. If anything can be said to be poignant about *Beavis and Butt-head*, it is the utter lack of any parental supervision in the lives of the main characters. Much of the action takes place on the couch in Beavis's run-down living room. None of the children's parents is ever in evidence—not even as an off-screen *Charlie Brown*-esque unintelligible voice. It seldom appears that they have much to eat. The adults featured on the program, for the most part, are ridiculed as inept or naïve. Principal McVicker at the duo's high school, for example, shakes and stammers as he plots ways to get rid of Beavis and Butt-head that never work out. Gym teacher Bradley

Buzzcut, a former Marine, is aggressive and unsympathetic. Butt-head's good-natured neighbor, Tom Anderson, is almost blind and seems slightly senile. And even the pair's kindly teacher, the hippie David Van Driessen—who seems to be the only person who cares about the children—is utterly unable to reach the two.

One aspect of *Beavis and Butt-head* that *South Park* seems to have appropriated is this parodic attitude toward traditional authority figures. *South Park*, we should note, is not nearly as dark as *Beavis and Butt-head* in that parents are present in the lives of all the children to varying degrees, but all the adults in *South Park*, as in *Beavis and Butt-head*, are incompetent, dysfunctional or, in various ways, just plain ridiculous. For example, Cartman's mother can be cajoled into doing anything (even entering her son into the Special Olympics) if Cartman pesters her vigorously enough; the town's policeman, Officer Barbrady, approximates Tom Anderson in his blindness and senility; the children's teacher, Mr. Garrison, provides inaccurate, inappropriate, or useless information in his lectures and appears to have a split personality; and all the adults (with the possible exception of Stan's mother, Sharon Marsh), to varying degrees attempt to manipulate or use the children to achieve their own ends.

Not surprisingly given *Beavis and Butt-head*'s crude humor and ridiculing of authority figures, the program was subject to the same sort of media scrutiny and scathing invective later directed at *South Park*. Social conservatives, such as Michael Medved, described the program as "the epitome of mindless and amoral entertainment" ("Beavis"), while Democratic senator Fritz Hollings, in the process of deriding the program, erroneously referred to it as "Buffcoat and Beaver," and thereby initiated a running gag on the program of adults mispronouncing the pair's names. However, what really focused media attention on the program were two incidents in which children were harmed or harmed others allegedly after having been influenced by *Beavis and Butt-head*. In 1993 the show was blamed after a 5-year-old boy set fire to his mother's mobile home killing his 2-year-old sister (both boys on *Beavis and Butt-head* have an obsession with fire), and then in 1994 the media watchdog group Morality in Media blamed the death of an 8-year-old girl who was struck by a bowling ball thrown from an overpass onto a New Jersey highway on an episode in which Beavis and Butt-head load a bowling ball with explosives and drop it from a rooftop.

From its very first season, *Beavis and Butt-head* had carried a humorous disclaimer, similar to *South Park*'s, stating:

> Beavis and Butt-head are not real. They are stupid cartoon people completly [sic] made up by this Texas guy who we hardly even know. Beavis and Butt-head are dumb, crude, ugly, thoughtless, sexist self-destructive fools. But for some reason the little wienerheads make us laugh.

Following these two incidents, MTV responded by broadcasting the program only after 11 P.M. and by changing the original disclaimer to a new one:

> Beavis and Butt-head are not role models. They're not even human, they're cartoons. Some of the things they do could cause a person to get hurt, expelled, arrested . . . possibly deported. To put it another way, don't try this at home.

In contrast, *South Park*'s disclaimer emphasizes the program's satirization of celebrities and vulgarity:

> All characters and events in this show—even those based on real people— are entirely fictional. All celebrity voices are impersonated . . . poorly. The following program contains coarse language and due to its content it should not be viewed by anyone.

Whereas *South Park*'s disclaimer is less concerned with viewers attempting to copy onscreen action, the presence of the disclaimer, as well as its humorous tone, seem designed to stem the sorts of legal difficulties *Beavis and Butt-head* encountered.

Saturday Morning Cartoons

The other main branch of television animation to which *South Park* is indebted for its form and content is the tradition of Saturday morning cartoons for children. As Hilton-Morrow and McMahan summarize, Saturday morning programming had received little attention prior to hiring Fred Silverman as director of daytime programming at CBS in 1964 (77). Silverman developed "Superhero Saturday" by placing cartoons including *Superman*, *Space Ghost*, *The Lone Ranger*, and *Jonny Quest* into the lineup. The format was successful and advertising rates skyrocketed.

South Park creators Parker and Stone are part of the generation that grew up with Saturday morning cartoons (Parker was born in 1969; Stone was born in 1971) and the team occasionally acknowledges the influence of these much-beloved childhood programs through direct allusion and parody. For example, as noted in the book's introduction, the episode "Korn's Groovy Pirate Ghost Mystery" not only parodies a typical *Scooby-Doo* narrative in which apparent ghosts turn out to be just smoke and mirrors, but also imitates the animation techniques of *Scooby-Doo*. Another episode, "The Super Best Friends," parodies the Hanna-Barbera animated program, *The Super Friends*, which aired from 1973 to 1985. In the *South Park* version, the superheroes of the original animated program are recast as a coalition of deities including

Buddha, Mohammad, Krishna, Joseph Smith, Lao Tzu, and the anomalous Sea Man (included purely for off-color double entendres).[10] And in the episode "Osama Bin Laden Has Farty Pants," the animation style shifts toward the end from the limited animation aesthetic of *South Park* to the smooth animation style of Loony Toons as Cartman torments Osama Bin Laden in a manner paralleling Bugs Bunny's persecution of Elmer Fudd.

For the viewer conversant with the Saturday morning programs being both celebrated and gently ridiculed, these episodes are especially funny because of *South Park*'s parodic approach to children's programming. In each of these episodes, *South Park* recasts familiar themes and even in some cases alters its production style to approximate the look of the program being parodied, but then infuses the episodes with crude humor, dark themes, and social commentary not generally considered appropriate for children. Thus, in "Korn's Groovy Pirate Ghost Mystery," to scare the fifth graders that are harassing them, Stan, Kyle, Kenny, and Cartman decide to use the corpse of Kyle's recently deceased grandmother; Cartman becomes convinced that a life-size anatomically correct Antonio Banderas blow-up doll his mother has ordered is his Christmas present; the band Korn performs an extremely aggressive song; and, of course, Kenny dies. In "The Super Best Friends," the deities based in the Hall of Super Best Friends are called on to combat the evil David Blaine and his cult of brainwashed "Blaine-tologists" who are preparing to commit mass suicide by drowning themselves in the reflecting pool by the Lincoln Memorial in Washington, D.C. When Lincoln's statue comes to life as a result of Blaine's magic and, Godzilla-like, goes on a rampage, it is only stopped by being assassinated by a giant John Wilkes Booth statue created and animated by the Super Best Friends. And in "Osama Bin Laden Has Farty Pants" (which aired on November 7, 2001, less than two months after the 9/11 attacks), the children visit Afghanistan to return a goat and to try to understand why they are hated by their Afghani counterparts. After being taken hostage by Osama Bin Laden, the boys are rescued and Cartman remains behind to torment Bin Laden. As the episode shifts into Loony Toons mode, Cartman characterizes his quarry through a series of visual placards, including one depicting a rooster and a lollipop—which the viewer mentally translates into "cocksucker."

What these parodies of children's programs reveal is both how much the tradition of Saturday morning cartoons have influenced Parker and Stone and how bland most of those cartoons actually are. As is the case with *South Park* in general, much of the humor involved in these episodes is produced by the ironic disjunction between the program's mature themes and language and its fourth-grade protagonists and crude animation style. However, the parodies of beloved children's cartoons "up the humor ante" for the viewer in the know by overlaying and transgressing an additional set of conditioned expectations—there are never, for example, any corpses in *Scooby-Doo* or swear words in Loony Toons and no one ever contemplates or attempts suicide on *The*

Super Friends. By appropriating aspects of children's cartoons and redeploying them with a marked difference, *South Park* simultaneously pays homage to the lost delights of Saturday morning viewing, points out how banal such programs actually are when considered from an adult perspective, and, in the process, distinguishes itself from such banality through its deployment of off-color and political humor targeted at adults.

The Differential Signifier:
The Simpsons and *Family Guy*

South Park's visual aesthetic, as well as its content, clearly has been influenced by the tradition of television animation in which it participates and within which it works to define itself. As noted herein, much of the terrain that *South Park* now occupies as a prime-time cartoon for adults initially was surveyed by pioneering programs such as *The Flintstones* and settled by more recent cartoons including *Ren & Stimpy* and *Beavis and Butt-head*. In addition, the program's possibilities also have been structured by the subtradition of Saturday morning cartoons for children to which *South Park* occasionally pays homage, even as it pokes fun at it.

In appreciating *South Park*'s cultural significance, one thus needs to bear in mind that *South Park*'s success is a historical phenomenon related to the ways in which previous programming has opened particular spaces for *South Park* to colonize. *South Park*'s animation aesthetic can be traced back to *The Flintstones*, while its irreverent playfulness and "no-brow humor" clearly is linked to more immediate predecessors, *Ren & Stimpy* and *Beavis and Butt-head*. On the most basic level, whether *South Park* would exist at all had these previous programs not existed and done well is questionable. In addition, the program's capability to provoke an amused response often turns on, to varying extents, the viewer's "televisual literacy"—his or her familiarity with the subtraditions of prime-time animation and Saturday morning cartoons.

At the same time, however, that *South Park* has both benefited and works to differentiate itself from animated programming that has preceded it, it also seeks to distinguish itself from its contemporary competitors. Part of *South Park*'s curious self-referentiality—its hyperawareness of itself as an animated program—is the frequency with which it alludes or refers to other animated programs, both past and present. *South Park* thus evidences an awareness of itself as a "differential signifier," that is, as a program whose meaning is dependent on the ways in which it compares to and, importantly, contrasts with other animated programs. The two contemporary programs with which *South Park* most explicitly associates with and tries to define itself against are that inescapable monolith of television animation, *The Simpsons*, and the more recent series, *Family Guy*.

That *South Park*'s creators would feel themselves to be operating in the shadow of *The Simpsons* is unavoidable. After all, *The Simpsons*, which debuted in 1989, has now become not just American television's longest running animated program, but its longest running sitcom to date. The program has so far won 23 Emmys and its influence on American culture has been substantial. *South Park*'s attempt to wrestle with this formidable opponent is most apparent in the episode entitled "*Simpsons* Already Did It." In this episode, Butters, who has been dismissed by Stan, Kyle, and Cartman as their replacement for Kenny in favor of Tweek, decides to seek his revenge on the cruel world that rejected him in the guise of his alter ego, Professor Chaos. The difficulty he encounters, however, is that he is unable to hatch an original plan. Every time he comes up with something he likes—including a plan to block out the sun—his sidekick, General Disarray, informs him that *The Simpsons* "already did it." Finally, Professor Chaos thinks he has arrived at something completely novel—he is going to replace the cherries in chocolate-covered cherries with mayonnaise—only to learn that this will be the premise of a *Simpsons* episode to air that evening. This news shatters Butters's evil plan and initiates a "break with reality" that causes Butters to see the world through "*Simpsons* vision"—his

FIGURE 4
Butters sees the world through *Simpsons* vision.

world becomes animated after the fashion of *The Simpsons* and the people he sees approximate characters from the program.

A parallel plot of this episode—one that clearly distinguishes *South Park* from its major network rival—is one in which Cartman, Kyle, Stan, and Kenny mistakenly believe that the brine shrimp they slipped into Ms. Choksondik's coffee have resulted in her demise. They conclude that they must break into the morgue and retrieve their Sea Men from her stomach. In danger of being discovered in the act, the boys hide, and with nowhere else to turn, Cartman climbs into the corpse. Having evaded detection, the boys are successful in their mission and return home where a retrieved semen sample combines with Cartman's brine shrimp to form a new life form: Sea People. (In Cartman's "mathematical" equation: "Sea People + Sea Men = Sea Ciety.") Cartman decides to expand his experiment and negotiates with South Park's sperm bank for as much semen as they can supply, which he then supplements with a donation from "this guy Ralph in an alley" who Cartman (illustrating the extent of *South Park*'s difference from *The Simpsons*) characterizes as a sucker because "this stupid asshole didn't even charge me money for it [semen]. He just made me close my eyes and suck it out of a hose!" Cartman then combines more brine shrimp with his new batch of semen and goes to sleep dreaming of the harmonious underwater world that will welcome him in the morning.

The Professor Chaos's revenge and Cartman's sea people plots then merge when Cartman awakes to find that, indeed, his experiment has been successful and his new Sea Ciety worships him as a god. Everyone is invited over to see the results, and Butters denounces the Cartman's experiment as a *Simpsons'* knockoff:

CARTMAN: I'm gonna' send a message to my people and tell 'em to develop a great machine that will shrink me down to their size, so I can live amongst them forever. [Butters laughs at him] What the hell is wrong with you, Butters?

BUTTERS: They did that on *The Simpsons*! Ha! "Treehouse of Horror," Episode 4F02, "The Genesis Tub." Lisa loses a tooth, and the bacteria on it start to grow, and makes a little society, and they build a statue of her thinking she's God! [laughs more]

CARTMAN: So?

KYLE: Yeah. So?

CARTMAN: Dude, *The Simpsons* have done everything already. Who cares?

STAN: Yeah, and they've been on the air for like, 13 years. Of course they've done everything.

MR. GARRISON: Every idea's been done, Butters, even before *The Simpsons*.

CHEF: Yeah. In fact, that episode was a rip-off of a *Twilight Zone* episode.

BUTTERS: Really? So I shouldn't care if I come up with an idea, and *The Simpsons* already did it? It doesn't matter!

A "trivia" note included on the TV.com summation of this episode asserts that Butters's reaction when he learns that *The Simpsons* already did it mimics "Matt and Treys [sic] own reaction when they think of a good idea, then realize that [*The Simpsons*] did it already, leaving them with random ideas." Although this assertion is subject to verification, it certainly is not much of a stretch to think that there is at least some truth to it. "*Simpsons* Already Did It" makes clear that the *South Park* creators are aware of their position vis-à-vis *The Simpsons* and some real anxiety is expressed about the ability to innovate in light of *The Simpsons* record-setting run. The conclusion to the episode—in keeping with the general tenor of the episode as a whole—maintains a respectful attitude toward *The Simpsons*, while suggesting that innovation is not the primary determinant of quality or value with regard to animated programming. Whether this sentiment is sincere or a case of sour grapes is debatable.

Interestingly, while the "*Simpsons* Already Did It" episode decries originality as a primary determinant of quality, even as it offers a highly original (if off-color) variation on a theme *The Simpsons* uses, as well as an original approach to the latter series itself), *South Park*'s most explicit engagement with its competition, the two-part "Cartoon Wars" episode, stridently insists that narrative coherence and humor derived from the narrative arc are hallmarks of comedic integrity. In contrast to the generally respectful attitude expressed toward *The Simpsons* in "*Simpsons* Already Did It," this episode targets the program *Family Guy*'s "relentless pursuit of non sequiturs" (Stabile and Harrison 10, note 7) for scorn and ridicule. In the process, *South Park* not only clearly strives to define itself against its competition, but also offers a pithy statement of its narrative philosophy.

Family Guy is an animated program animator Seth MacFarlane created for FOX in 1999. The show was cancelled once in 2000 and again in 2002, but strong DVD sales and reruns on Cartoon Network's *Adult Swim* led FOX to resume production of the show in 2005. The title character, Peter Griffin, is nicely described on Wikipedia as "an inept blue-collar head of a lower-middle-class family frequently beset by the consequences of his foolish antics" ("*Family Guy*"). Most notable about the program is *Family Guy*'s brief, frequently nonsensical cutaways suffused with obscure pop culture references.

The "Cartoon Wars" double episode of *South Park* begins with panic in South Park over the announcement that *Family Guy* will air an image of the Muslim prophet Mohammed and the expectation that "terrorists" will launch a spectacular counterattack—the clear historical referent here is the publication of twelve caricatures depicting the prophet Mohammed by the Danish daily newspaper *Jyllands-Posten* in September 2005 and the ensuing contro-versy. Within *South Park*, although this image of Mohammed is censored, *Family Guy* then announces that the representation will air uncensored in the next episode. In response to this, Cartman uncharacteristically appears to adopt a position of religious sensitivity and decides to lead a crusade to pull the episode from the air. He sets off on his Big Wheel for Hollywood accom-panied by Kyle to try to convince the network executives not to broadcast the offensive program.

What is revealed during the context of the cross-country journey is that Cartman really has other motivations—in keeping with what we know about Cartman, he does not care at all about offending Muslims; however, he hates *Family Guy* and believes that if one episode is pulled off the air, it will start a domino effect eventually resulting in the series' cancellation. Although Cart-man seldom serves as the voice of the program's creators, we can easily hear Parker and Stone in Cartman's passionate declamation to Kyle:

> Do you have any idea what it's like? Everywhere I go: Hey Cartman, you must like *Family Guy*, right? Hey, your sense of humor reminds me of *Fam-ily Guy*, Cartman! I am nothing like *Family Guy*! When I make jokes they are inherent to a story! Deep situational and emotional jokes based on what is relevant and has a point, not just one random interchangeable joke after another!

Cartman's speech here lifts *South Park*'s self-reflexivity to new heights. Cartman, foregrounding his own status as animated character, reveals that he is tired of being compared to a character in a different animated program because the program of which he is a part possesses an entirely different phi-losophy with regard to the place and function of humor. Later, in the second part of the episode, when Kyle becomes mad at Cartman for having trapped him in a net, Cartman responds, "Good, Kyle! That's good anger you're show-ing there! See that? That's emotional character development based on what's happening in the storyline! Not at all like *Family Guy*." What is discovered in the second part of "Cartoon Wars" is that Cartman's assessment of *Family Guy*'s structure is wholly correct when it is revealed that the writing staff of *Family Guy* is actually composed of manatees that generate episodes by com-bining "idea balls" seemingly at random. When the "Mohammed" ball is removed from their tank, they refuse to work.

And, as if this scenario wasn't metatextual enough on its own, Bart Simpson is then thrown into the mix. When Cartman arrives at the FOX stu-dios to meet with the network president, he finds that Bart is already in line for the same purpose. The two debate who is best suited to persuade the net-work to yank *Family Guy* and each offers testimony regarding his qualifica-tions. In response to Bart's putting forward that he once cut the head off of a statue (which itself is an allusion to the "*Simpsons* Already Did It" episode in which Butters contemplates doing the same), Cartman nonchalantly volunteers that he once killed a boy's parents (Scott Tenorman) and fed them to him as chili. Bart prudently steps aside.

In the end, the episode moves beyond its caustic assessment of *Family Guy* and becomes a homily on free speech. (In an ironic inversion, the President himself is shown explaining the First Amendment to reporters, which they seem to find an entirely foreign concept.) Despite Cartman's persuasive machinations, which ultimately morph into threats, Kyle is able to convince network executives that freedom of speech is paramount and—in perhaps the clearest statement of *South Park*'s general philosophy—that either everything is available as a potential topic for humor or nothing is. The episode of *Family Guy* is broadcast. However, at the moment that Mohammed is supposed to appear, the viewer's screen goes black and, breaking the frame of the narrative, the following message appears on the home viewer's screen: "In this shot, Mohammed hands a football helmet to Family Guy. Comedy Central has refused to broadcast an image of Mohammed on their network." And then, to make the hypocrisy of U.S. media abundantly clear, the "terrorists" retaliate for the image of Mohammed we as viewers of *South Park* never see by pirating the airwaves and airing their own animated segment featuring President Bush and Jesus defecating on the U.S. flag, the point being that Americans have been intimidated by the threat of terrorism into sacrificing freedom of speech.

A great deal can be said about *South Park*'s "all or nothing" mentality and its political engagement in the "Cartoon Wars" episode with the issue of free speech.[11] However, for the purposes of this chapter, what is most fascinating about both "*Simpsons* Already Did It" and "Cartoon Wars" is *South Park*'s explicit engagement with and critique of other animated programs and its corresponding statement of narrative philosophy. These two episodes clearly demonstrate the ways in which *South Park* is hyperaware of itself as a differential signifier, as an animated program competing with and attempting to distinguish itself from other animated programs.

Beyond this, what one ultimately finds embedded in these metatextual episodes in which *South Park* foregrounds its own status as animated program is the program's articulation of its own narrative philosophy and even an implicit response to its many critics. *South Park* assuages its "anxiety of influence" with regard to *The Simpsons* by maintaining that "there's nothing new under the sun," that innovation is not necessarily the primary virtue of any program, and that even *The Simpsons* borrows themes and ideas from previous programs. Rather than innovation, what *South Park* identifies as primary criteria of quality are narrative coherence and situationally derived humor. Articulating these values allows the program to identify itself with *The Simpsons* and to distinguish itself from *Family Guy*. Furthermore, it offers an implicit response to its many vocal critics by establishing standards for assessment of value that highlight what *South Park's* creators obviously feel are its virtues. *South Park* thereby constructs its own identity through the process of comparing itself with and contrasting itself against other animated programs and part of the pleasure of watching *South Park* is appreciating the program precisely as a differential signifier: as an animated program that participates in and self-consciously refers to specific aspects of the tradition of animated television even as it attempts to distinguish itself within that tradition.

Notes

1. Although *The Flintstones* is generally considered the first cartoon to air in prime time, it was preceded by *CBS Cartoon Theater*, which was hosted by Dick Van Dyke and aired reruns of Terrytoons theatrical shorts (which included Mighty Mouse, Heckle and Jeckle, and Deputy Dawg) for 3 months in 1956. In addition, *The Gerald McBoing-Boing Show*, a cartoon based on a Dr. Seuss character, was produced for one season in 1956 and then repeated in 1957 on CBS. Both shows, however, were designed to showcase theatrical cartoon shorts. Therefore, *The Flintstones* remains the first animated series comprising all original programming to air in prime time.

2. The exceptions are a program called *Where's Huddles?* that aired briefly on CBS in 1970 as a summer replacement series (Hilton-Morrow and McMahan 77) and a program inspired by *All in the Family* called *Wait Till Your Father Gets Home* which was produced from 1972 through 1974.

3. *South Park* animation director Eric Stough explains in a 2002 interview that the program is animated at twelve frames per second and that they are able to use and reuse files from previous shows (Interview). Digital animation means that there is also no need for an ink-and-paint department. In a separate interview with *Melody Maker's* Danny Wallace, Parker and Stone delightedly reveal that when they incorporate an establishing shot of a house, it's always the same house, no matter who is supposed to live there (*South Park*).

4. One should note that although the show continues to emulate stop motion cutout animation, which was the original form of animation for the show, computer animation has since replaced this form of production.

5. Parker and Stone delight in overturning the stereotype of young children as innocent and refer to them instead as "nasty bastards" or "little bastards" at every opportunity. See, for example, McConnell 6; Wallace, "*South Park*"; and Wallace, "Kick Xmas" 14. In an interview with James Poniewozik in *Time*, the two add that they believe that "people are born bad and are made good by society, rather than the opposite" (8).

6. See Damion Sturm's contribution to this volume.

7. See, among others, "The Mexican Staring Frog of Sri Lanka" in which Jimbo and Ned's cable hunting program squares off against *Jesus and Friends*; "It Hits the Fan" in which television profanity threatens to end the world; "Freak Strike" in which both Butters and Cartman appear on talk shows; "The Biggest Douche in the Universe" in which Stan launches his own program about talking with the dead; "South Park Is Gay" in which the *Queer Eye for the Straight Guy* team are revealed to be "crab people"; and "Quest for Ratings" in which the boys host their own news program.

8. See, among others, "Timmy! 2000" in which Timmy performs with a rock band; "Something You Can Do with Your Finger" in which Cartman tries to fulfill his dream of performing with a boy band; "Fat Butt and Pancake Head" in which Cartman's hand takes on a life of its own and starts its own musical career; and "Christian Rock Hard" in which Cartman creates a Christian rock band.

9. In a 1998 interview with David Wild in *Rolling Stone*, they note that *Ren & Stimpy* had "some funny stuff," and an article by Stef McDonald notes in passing that Parker and Stone's production studio walls are "plastered with *Ren & Stimpy* posters" (30).

10. This pre–9/11 rendering of Mohammed has recently received new scrutiny given the violent response to Danish representations of Mohammed.

11. On *South Park*'s "all or nothing" premise, see Samuels and Coleman in this volume.

Works Cited

Barrier, Michael. "Master of the Cult Cartoon." *Nation's Business* June 1998: 83.

"*Beavis and Butt-head*." <www.answers.com/topic/beavis-and-butt-head>. 17 Sept. 2006.

"*Family Guy*." <en.wikipedia.org/wiki/Family_guy> 17 Sept. 2006.

Farley, Rebecca. "From Fred and Wilma to Ren and Stimpy: What Makes a Cartoon 'Prime Time'"? In Stabile and Harrison, 147–64.

Gardiner, Judith Kegan. "Why Saddam Is Gay: Masculinity Politics in *South Park—Bigger Longer & Uncut*." *Quarterly Review of Film and Video* 22 (2005): 51–62.

Hilton-Morrow, Wendy, and David T. McMahan. "*The Flintstones* to *Futurama*: Networks and Prime Time Animation." In Stabile and Harrison, 74–88.

Interview with Eric Stough, animation director. *Animation Magazine* 16.7 (26 July 2002). Available online at <www.spscriptorium.com/SPinfo/MakingOfSouthPark.htm>.

McConnell, Bill. "*South Park*: Sliding Into Success." *Broadcasting & Cable* 129.5 (1999): 35–36.

McDonald, Stef. "Tales from the Park Side." *TV Guide* 18 Oct. 1997: 28–30.

Poniewozik, James. "10 Questions for Matt Stone and Trey Parker." *Time* 13 Mar. 2006: 8.

Savage, William J., Jr. "'So Television's Responsible!': Oppositionality and the Interpretive Logic of Satire and Censorship in *The Simpsons* and *South Park*." *Leaving Springfield: The Simpsons and the Possibility of Oppositional Culture*. Ed. John Alberti. Detroit: Wayne State University Press, 2004. 197–224.

"*Simpsons* Already Did It." <www.tv.com/south-park/simpsons-already-didit/episode/ 170460/summary.html>. 17 Sept. 2006.

Stabile, Carol A., and Mark Harrison, eds. *Prime Time Animation: Television Animation and American Culture*. London: Routledge, 2003.

Wallace, Danny. "*South Park*." *Melody Maker* 75.28 (11 July 1998): 11.

———. "Kick Xmas, Dude!" *Melody Maker* 75.51 (Dec. 1998): 14–15.

Wild, David. "South Park's Evil Geniuses and the Triumph of No-Brow Culture." *Rolling Stone* 19 Feb. 1998: 32–37.

PART TWO

Identity Politics

Freud Goes to South Park

Teaching against Postmodern Prejudices and Equal Opportunity Hatred

ROBERT SAMUELS

Like many other television shows and movies, *South Park* gains a great deal of its popularity by proclaiming itself to be politically incorrect and intolerant of all forms of tolerance. Moreover, through a common rhetorical reversal, the creators of this show often present themselves as being tolerant of intolerance; in other words, as my students often report, its humor is generated by "saying what you are not supposed to say." This chapter argues that this rhetorical reversal, where one is taught to be intolerant of tolerance and tolerant of intolerance, is part of a larger social effort to challenge and reverse progressive efforts to fight stereotypes and prejudices in American culture. Furthermore, this rhetorical reversal can also be seen in the political and cultural process of undermining the popular support for the welfare state while calling for tax breaks for the wealthy. In this upside-down world, minorities are now often seen as victimizers and abusers of the welfare system, whereas the wealthy majority is positioned to be the victim of excessive taxes and reversed racism.

Knowingly or unknowingly, shows such as *South Park* feed this rhetorical reversal that influences so many students and makes teaching about critical thinking and social change in higher education even more difficult. One reason why pop culture humor plays such a major role in this attempt to reverse the cultural representation of minorities and dominant groups is that comedy itself often works by reversing values and social positions. Thus, in the classic structure of humor, a man acts like a woman or a pauper acts like a king. Moreover, much of popular comedy today is based on the use of ethnic stereotypes and prejudices that are allowed to be recycled because the victims of these negative depictions are the ones making these destructive self-representations. In fact, this chapter argues that the very structure of cultural assimilation and immigration calls for the internalization of negative self-representations.

Assimilated Stereotypes in *South Park*

The assimilation and internalization of self-hatred in the film *South Park: Bigger Longer & Uncut* (1999) is represented through the character of Kyle Broslovski who is attacked in a humorous way for being Jewish.[1] Furthermore, the representation of his character and his family play off of the most basic stereotypes concerning Jewish people. Importantly, one of the two main writers of this show is Jewish and thus we are forced to ask the question of why Jews in our culture often participate in the recirculation of anti-Semitic stereotypes.

This question of internalized anti-Semitism offers us one of the keys to understanding contemporary prejudices. Most systems of prejudice go through three major stages. At first, prejudices are brutally applied through real acts of dehumanization and enslavement. The next stage of prejudice often involves legal segregation and state-sponsored discrimination. Finally, in a third stage, the objects of prejudice internalize the stereotypes by which they have been victimized.[2] In this postmodern stage, negative and positive stereotypes provide a ground for self-recognition and identity.[3] Moreover, the mass culture industry reinforces these negative self-representations by basing characters on the largest available cultural generalizations. Internalized anti-Semitism thus plays into this logic by basing Jewish identity on cultural assimilation, victimhood, and self-deprecating humor.

However, when the various stereotypes and prejudices in the show and movie are pointed out, some students are quick to argue that every group is equally attacked and no one takes the attacks seriously. Here, we see strong examples of the rhetoric of reversal and universalization: From a globalizing perspective, these students claim that equal opportunity hatred is not intolerance and that popular culture has no meaning or effect anyway. In fact, students often feel that the teacher who points to prejudice in culture and society is really the one with the problem. In this version of "shooting the messenger," the teacher who tries to get students to become aware of the destructive nature of prejudice in our society is seen as a highly sensitive person who does not know how to take a joke and does not accept the universalized notion of equal opportunity intolerance.

Teachers must recognize this cultural reversal and not try to challenge directly these deeply held unconscious social beliefs. However, students can learn how to detect and move beyond the various rhetorical mechanisms that our culture uses to reinforce and recirculate prejudices and stereotypes. The trick is to analyze destructive rhetorical figures in a safe transitional place that is neither too personal nor too alien. Popular culture comedies such as *South Park* can offer us this transitional space, but providing students with the critical tools and concepts that can be employed to stop the flow of information and examine the specific cultural elements used to construct humor and identity in our society is important.

One rhetorical strategy that popular culture employs is the use of extreme exaggeration both to circulate prejudices and to deny the import of these negative self-representations. For example, in the *South Park* movie, one of the main stereotypes is the relationship between the aggressive Jewish mother and the oppressed Jewish son. In fact, the main plot of the movie is that Kyle's Jewish and politically correct mother wants to attack Canada because two Canadian filmmakers have made a foul-mouthed film that has affected her son and his friends. In this narrative, the stereotype of the overly protective Jewish mother is exaggerated to the point that this maternal super-ego threatens to cause an international war. Furthermore, this extreme depiction of a Jewish mother is presented along with a series of de-contextualized references to the Holocaust and World War II: There is a Canadian Death Camp, children join La Resistance, there are charges of "crimes against humanity," and various representations of concentration camps.

An important idea in this pop culture example is the notion that what in part links the internalization of anti-Semitic stereotypes to the subtle and not-so-subtle reminders of the Holocaust is the strategy of taking serious issues concerning prejudice and trying to empty them of their initial meaning and value. For instance, in one scene that takes place in Hell, we see a morphing between images of Gandhi, George Burns, Hitler, Saddam Hussein, and Satan. From the postmodern perspective of the filmmakers, little difference exists between someone who played God in a movie (George Burns), someone who was a leader of his people (Gandhi), a former totalitarian leader (Hitler), a hated former leader (Hussein), and the Christian representation of Evil (Satan). Because these figures are only images without any historical and cultural context, they seem to have lost all inherent value or significance. In fact, these images have become secondary texts that can be assimilated into new contexts for our humor and entertainment. Furthermore, the fate of these de-contextualized images parallels the fate of immigrating people who must assimilate to a new cultural context by shedding the value of their previous cultural and historical traditions and beliefs.[4]

We can find a strong incidence of this logic of assimilation and internalized anti-Semitism in the title of the movie: *South Park: Bigger Longer & Uncut.* This title combines allusions to censorship, the uncircumcised penis, and a sense of phallic power. Moreover, because the Jewish mother becomes

the main proponent of politically correct censorship in the movie, we discover an interesting equation between the circumcision of the Jewish male,
the dominance of the Jewish mother, and the censorship of free speech. Here,
the Jewish ritual of circumcision is blamed on the mother and attached to a
loss of freedom. In fact, what is idealized is the non-Jewish, uncircumcised
exercise of phallic power and free speech.[5] The assimilation and internalization of anti-Semitism thus results in the idea that the root of all evil in the
world is derived from the Jewish tradition of circumcising men and cutting
them off from their free and manly expression of aggression and sexuality.[6]

Because the movie declares itself to be bigger, longer, and uncut, we
can assume that true phallic power comes from the ability to deny circumcision and censorship by identifying with the idealized free and non-Jewish male member.[7] The movie therefore subtly plays on the standard
stereotypical opposition between the powerful Christian male and the
feminized Jew. In turn, this opposition is projected onto a political fight
where the Jewish mother becomes the source for feminizing and censoring
the victimized Jewish male. Furthermore, this demonization of the Jewish
mother and the feminized Jewish male is hidden behind the general
rhetorical defensive strategy of mocking the idea that the media influences
children in a negative way. According to the film's logic, the problems
with our children do not stem from the fact that they copy the obscene
and prejudicial representations that they see in the media; rather, the
problem is that the Jewish maternal superego wants to censor and castrate
the naughty boys for expressing their true desires. Importantly, some students are often quick to buy this conservative rhetoric positing that the
true cause of intolerance in our society is the politically correct people
who are trying to fight intolerance.

One reason why some students may equate political correctness with
intolerance and prejudicial intolerance with tolerance is that that they have
grown up in a culture shaped by a successful conservative campaign to reverse
our understandings of prejudice and tolerance. A key aspect of this rhetorical
reversal is the universalized notion that our society no longer has any prejudices and therefore anyone who points out prejudices must be the cause of
prejudice. In the case of teaching about prejudices, this reversed rhetoric cannot help but to enter into the room, and teachers can deal with this conservative ideology in an indirect way. Because a direct attack on the conservative effort to reverse racism may serve to reinforce students' political
ideologies and investments, examining this rhetoric in a nonpolarizing way is
important. Furthermore, the first step in this process of educating against the
rhetorical reversal is to critique the notion of universal tolerance and then
show examples of intolerance in popular culture. Teachers can also work to
change the popular view of political correctness by critiquing its excesses and
affirming the positive aspects of treating others with respect.

Although many students will claim that *South Park* is a liberal, anticonservative show, for the writers of the film and television program, political correctness is clearly the primary evil they fight against.[8] Like the incorrigible children that they portray and like many contemporary Americans, Matt Stone and Trey Parker feel strongly that censorship is worse than hate speech and that free speech is the ultimate good that should be celebrated. This desire to endorse a universal message of free speech coupled with their idealization of the unrestrained individual is apparent in the many interviews in which they defend their usage of bathroom humor and politically incorrect stereotypes. For instance, in response to the question of why he stresses the Jewishness of the character Kyle, Stone, whose mother is Jewish, proclaims, "It just creates more opportunity for comedy. It gives us more things to make fun of and we just think it's funny."[9] What Stone does not say is why Kyle's Jewish identity is funny and how this humor relates to Stone's own secular upbringing in Texas and Colorado.

Why Do We Laugh?

To help my students think about the culture of political incorrectness and internalized racism, getting them to reflect on how humor and comedy function is important. One of the first ideas I posit is the notion that humor often derives its source from real feelings of pain and anxiety that are then turned into a "positive" experience by entertaining others. In fact, in Freud's highly misunderstood work, *Jokes and Their Relation to the Unconscious*, he posits the true goal of a joke is to bond with a third party and to bribe this social other not to analyze or criticize one's humor (119). Thus, jokes not only release repressed urges and desires, but they also constitute a social act of bonding.

Importantly, Freud's theory of humor is dominated by references to Jewish jokes.[10] One reason Freud gives for this choice is the debatable idea that Jews are more self-critical than other people and thus they make better comics (133). However, as many people insist, in our culture, all types of social groups are the target of humor and, in most cases, the comic is from the same group that is being attacked. Central to this structure of in-group comedy is the idea that attacking someone in your own group is okay, but someone from another group cannot attack your group. In many cases, I have found this logic of the inner group attacking itself functions to circulate prejudice under a safe cover. Furthermore, one of Freud's central ideas about humor is his notion that the ethnic group member performs an act of self-mockery for a neutral party and, therefore, even when a person of an in-group mocks his or her own group, that presentation of intolerance is performed for the social and cultural other.

In this structure of humor, we find the basic process of assimilation as the appeal of the minority to the dominant culture's definitions and values.

Furthermore, Freud insists that the object and second party of the joke plays the role of the social censor who must be avoided (116). In fact, for Freud, the primary example of humor is a dirty joke that is meant to seduce a woman, but due to her high moral standing, the joke must be redirected toward a male third party. In this structure, the third party becomes the ally of the first party joke teller against the second party female object and social censor. If we now apply this structure to the general framework of the film *South Park*, we see that the Jewish mother represents the object of the joke and the source of social censorship.[11] To overcome the Jewish mother's resistance to the pure expression of sexual aggression (the desire of the joke teller), the mother must be attacked for the benefit and the enjoyment of the third party or audience. The joke teller and the audience thus bond over the attack on the Jewish mother.

Through this theory, we can begin to see how so much of our popular culture is often centered on a process of male bonding through the tragic or comedic stigmatization of minority groups. Even if the audience is not comprised entirely of men, this theory argues that the viewer is placed in the third-party position of being the one who accepts or rejects the presentations of the first-party joke teller. Here, the third party represents the dominant culture that must be bribed by the first party's victimization of the second party. In the case of *South Park*, we can say that Matt Stone (a Jew) victimizes his Jewish mother and identity to bond with his audience. Internalized anti-Semitism thus serves the processes of assimilation by sacrificing a part of the subject's own ethnic identity in the goal of bonding with the dominant culture.

The Myth of Free Speech

In response to this theory of assimilation and prejudice in popular culture, some may argue that we have a society built on tolerance and equal opportunity prejudice and, therefore, no one group is ever really being singled out. Although I would not deny aspects of this argument, I respond by pointing out that the rhetoric of universal equality can work to veil important inequalities in our society. In fact, teachers can reveal to students how the agenda of conservative politics helps to explode the myth of the neutral realm of universal free speech and tolerance. As Stanley Fish argues in his book *There's No Such Thing as Free Speech*, the claim for a universal tolerance of all expression is always grounded on a hidden agenda of particular vested interests (7). Moreover, Fish posits that all universal claims are invalid because they do not take into account the context and history of their own formulations (viii). Therefore, Fish affirms that we must always contextualize every universal claim to see what interests lie behind it. In the case of *South Park*, the universal claim of free speech relies on the unstated idea that words have no real effect on people and thus they should never be constrained. However, this idea is itself challenged by the notion that the words of the politically correct do actively constrain the freedoms of the politically incorrect. Yet the way out of this conflict is to argue that, unlike the words and actions of the proponents of political correctness, the politically incorrect makers of this movie do not believe that their representations have any meaning or context.

With regard to *South Park*, by making references to the Holocaust without any concern for the original context of these representations, the writers are able to claim that these depictions are not harmful to any particular group. Likewise, the representation of Kyle's Jewishness is seen as being purely entertaining and not anti-Semitic because the writers believe that their representations have no value or effect. One reason they can make this claim is that they do not believe that ethnic identity itself has any value or meaning other than its ability to make people stand out from the dominant crowd and be laughed at. Within the context of *South Park* and the ideologies affecting student subjectivities, this strategy of denying the value or import of ethnic identity and other cultural influences is a key to the idea that popular culture is really about nothing. In this sense, what Americans seem to value the most is the idea that our culture is meaningless and our words and representations have no real effect. From this perspective, there is no such thing as hate speech and what is really wrong about politically correct people and teachers in general is that they take words and representations too seriously. In this way the United States uncannily is the most Zen-like culture around because what we value the most is our ability to spend a great deal of time experiencing nothingness and nonmeaning.

It's Only a Joke

In the teaching of popular culture, this Zen-like philosophy represents one of the strongest convictions of the audience.[12] Students often steadfastly cling to their right to meaningless entertainment and interpret any attempt to contextualize or interpret popular culture as a horrible act threatening to rob them of their most cherished value. How do we then reconcile these two opposing claims? On one side, we have the argument that popular culture has no meaning or value and, on the other side, we find the argument that nothing has more value than the defense of popular culture and the freedom of expression.

Freud's theory of jokes helps us to reconcile this conflict by positing that the main function of jokes is to present serious issues in a manner that shields them from any type of criticism and analysis. As with free speech, humor thus creates a responsibility-free zone where people are given the opportunity to state anything they like without fear of censor or restraint. Yet humor itself needs restraint because it is generated out of the conflict between infantile desires (pure sex and aggression) and social norms. To hide this conflict, the first-person joke teller must rely on the third-party audience's ability to process the information of the joke while denying the value of the same information. For example, ethnic jokes rely on cultural stereotypes that the audience must recognize and understand but not acknowledge as being meaningful or valuable.

This Freudian theory of humor helps to define the relations among assimilation, popular culture, and internalized prejudices. In the context of assimilation, one first reduces one's ethnic identity to the level of a stereotype, and then one tells the dominant culture that this representation means nothing. Thus, Matt Stone says that people like to laugh at the stereotypical representations of Jewish characters and, at the same time, he claims that these representations are only entertainment and have no real meaning. Freud is able to account for this contradiction between the value and the meaninglessness of stereotypes through his notion of preconscious representations. This theory is one of the most misunderstood and neglected aspects of his work because it breaks down the simple opposition between unconscious and conscious ideas. By saying that stereotypes are preconscious, Freud indicates that we use them without our conscious awareness of them, and so they take on an automatic quality as if they were coming from some foreign place. Therefore, we feel that we are not responsible for these preconscious representations because we are barely aware of them and we do not use them intentionally. Yet in popular culture these types of preconscious prejudices are the most prevalent because people assimilate and circulate ideas that they claim are not their own and have no meaning. Furthermore, saying that people have no prejudices because our culture itself is predicated on the ability of a mass audience to recognize generalized traits of characters and ethnic groups is ridiculous. What we often assimilate in our culture are serious preconscious representations and generalizations that are placed in an unserious responsibility-free zone.

The Rhetoric of Denial

One reason why a film like *South Park* is such an effective pedagogical tool is that it helps to reveal the popular rhetorical methods employed for both assimilating stereotypes and denying their value and responsibility. The way that the writers accomplish this task of removing themselves from any responsibility for their representation of prejudices is to make the scapegoating process itself a ridiculous aspect of the film. Thus, the movie includes a song that openly anticipates the critics of the movie and the movie within the movie:

Off to the movie we shall go
Where we learn everything that we know
'cause the movies teach us
What our parents don't have time to say
And this movie's gonna make our lives complete

Although these lyrics indicate that children are highly influenced by the media, the words present this argument in such a stupid-sounding song that people are signaled not to take this idea seriously. In fact, this blaming of the media is then transformed into the humorous technique of using Canada as a scapegoat:

Blame Canada
Shame on Canada for—
The smut we must cut
The trash we must smash
The laughter and fun
Must all be undone
We must blame them and cause a fuss
Before somebody thinks of blaming us

Like the song about the influence of the media, this song posits that parents blame other people, such as Canadians, to avoid their own responsibilities. The film sends important messages, but it then undercuts these same messages by placing them in contexts where the audience is told not to take them seriously. Therefore, by making fun of the way that people blame the media and other people for their own problems, the movie is able to remove all responsibility from its own representations.

Within this context of scapegoating and the denying of responsibility in the movie, we find several references to the Holocaust. For example, as the war between the United States and Canada heats up, we see a news anchor deliver the following address:

A full-scale attack has been launched on Toronto, after the Canadians' last bombing, which took a horrible toll on the Arquette family. For security measures, our great American government is rounding up all citizens that have any Canadian blood, and putting them into camps. All Canadian-American citizens are to report to one of these Death Camps right away. Did I say, "Death Camps"? I meant, "Happy Camps," where you will eat the finest meals, have access to fabulous doctors, and be able to exercise regularly. Meanwhile, the war criminals, Terrance and Phillip, are prepped for their execution. Their execution will take place during a fabulous USO show, with special guest celebrities.

The mention here of "Death Camps," "fabulous doctors," and the execution of "war criminals" refers to and mocks aspects of the Holocaust. Once again, we must ask why would these writers do this? Are these references made because they are so recognizable, or does the humor set out to make light of the true traumatic nature of the Holocaust?

One possible way of responding to these questions is to look at the way the Holocaust is tied to Jewish identity in our culture and the way that this identity is both affirmed and denied in the film. In the case of the Jewish boy, Kyle, one of the running jokes on the show and in the movie is that it is not his fault for being Jewish. We find this sentiment stated in one of the final scenes of the movie where Kyle's friend Cartman tries to bond with Kyle as they face potential death:

CARTMAN: [hunkering down, with Kyle, in the trench] Kyle? All those times I said you were a big, dumb Jew? I didn't mean it. You're not a Jew.

KYLE: Yes, I am. I am a Jew, Cartman!

CARTMAN: No, no, Kyle. Don't be so hard on yourself.

The anxiety that causes this joke to be funny is the idea that being Jewish is inherently bad and a constant source of self-hatred; thus, Cartman can only bond with his friend by trying to tell him not to take his Jewish self-hatred so seriously. What may tie this question of Jewish self-hatred to the Holocaust is the idea that Jews hate themselves for being victims and their victim status comes from the Holocaust.

This topic of ethnic self-hatred is one of the most difficult issues for students. Because so much of popular culture seems to be about self-love, thinking about the roles self-negation plays in our society does not make sense to many students. Yet this type of self-conflict is exactly what needs to be explored in a class dedicated to positive social change because the inability of people to acknowledge the multiple parts of their own identities results in limiting self-knowledge and demonizing others who are connected with the rejected parts of the self.

On Jewish Self-Hatred

To explore further this question of ethnic self-hatred, I look to Sandor Gilman's work on anti-Semitism. In his book, *Jewish Self-Hatred*, Gilman argues that a central driving force behind internalized anti-Semitism is the Jewish desire to assimilate into the dominant culture. He claims that for Jewish people to fit into the society in which they live, they must not only accept the values and mores of the dominant reference group, but they must also accept that group's fantasies about Jews (2). Yet the dominant group sends a double message to Jews: You should be like us, and thus lose all of your ethnic differences, and you will never be like us because of the differences that we have attached to you (2). Assimilation therefore offers a double bind for the Jewish person and all other minority groups, and Gilman posits that this double bind is then internalized (2–3). Self-hatred is in this sense based on the minority group's identification with the dominant group's hatred of any type of ethnic difference.

Gilman adds to this argument the idea that the assimilated person always knows that he or she has not completely assimilated, and thus a lingering sense of failure and rejection is always either internalized or projected onto other members of one's own group. For instance, Gilman argues that most of Freud's Jewish jokes that he discusses in his theory of humor are based on demonizing Eastern European Jews (264). Gilman posits that Freud makes fun of these other Jews so that he can split off the good Jew from the bad Jew and differentiate between his own assimilation as a good German scientist and the failure of other (Eastern European) Jews to assimilate. Moreover, Gilman thinks that one reason Freud wanted to conduct a scientific study of Jewish jokes was that Freud believed science offered a universal non-Jewish language (268). Freud's turn to "objective science" is therefore itself an attempt at assimilating into a universalizing discourse; however, this act of assimilation constantly fails, and so he must perpetually return to the question of Jewish identity.

The irony of Freud's attempt to create a non-Jewish universal science of the mind was made apparent when the Nazis and other people labeled psychoanalysis the "Jewish Science." From one perspective, this term is accurate because the question of Jewish identity has often haunted the ability of psychoanalysis to be considered a modern universal science of the mind; Judaism has always represented a challenge to universalizing discourses, be it the universalizing discourse of Christianity, American assimilation, modern science, or Fascism. Not only do the Jewish people often consider themselves to be God's chosen people, but they have also been labeled as different from the dominant cultures in which they live. Jewish particularity has therefore often come into conflict with the universalizing tendencies of Western culture. Yet, in this age of identity politics, one would think that this particularizing ethnic identity formation would be a source of power and self-affirmation. However, as my analysis of *South Park* shows, ethnic identity has become a major form of debasement and entertainment for the general public.

To understand why Jewishness and other forms of ethnic identity represent sources of humiliation and self-hatred in culture today, we can take into account the link between the universalizing global economy and the popular culture of assimilation. Because capitalism, like modern science, is ideally a universal discourse that treats every participant in the same way, it tends to take on an air of being tolerant of everyone and everything. As Jean-Paul Sartre argues, a price theoretically does not change when a Jew or a Muslim approaches the price tag, just like a scientific experiment does not change if a Jew or a non-Jew does it.[13] Jews and other minority groups thus turn to science and capitalism to escape their own particular identities and to enter into a discourse where they can be treated as equals. This equality is the ideal of modern universal tolerance: Everyone should be treated equally regardless of race, creed, or gender. However, postmodern culture turns this modern ideology on its head and, instead of preaching universal tolerance, it often preaches universal intolerance. Thus, what becomes circulated and distributed is not some purely abstract science experiment or price tag but a system of prejudices and generalizations in the form of the mass media.

In revealing and critiquing the use of prejudice in the movie *South Park*, I have shown how popular culture often circulates the intolerance of ethnic difference under the safe protection of meaningless humor and equal opportunity racism. However, humor is never completely meaningless and racism and intolerance are never universal or equal. In fact, we can affirm that pop culture representations have helped to provide the rhetorical foundation for a political reversal of victims and victimizers. In this cultural context, revealing these reversals and teaching against equal opportunity hatred becomes important.

Notes

1. This chapter deals with the movie *South Park: Bigger Longer & Uncut* (1999) and not with the television show. However, I hope that the reader and avid watcher of the television program will be able to see connections and differences between the movie and the show.

2. Elisabeth Young-Bruehl's *The Anatomy of Prejudice* offers a broad analysis of the history of prejudice in Western culture.

3. Although Jewish people have often internalized stereotypes, this mode of self-representation only begins to dominate the use of prejudices in contemporary culture.

4. This chapter uses the notion of assimilation to account for the central defining process of postmodern culture. Assimilation not only refers to the ways that minority cultures are asked to fit into the dominant cultures, but also the technological methods that allow for the reconstruction of history and narrative discourses.

5. For a discussion of the multiple meanings of circumcision in Western culture and Judaism, see Daniel Boyarin's A *Radical Jew: Paul and the Politics of Identity* (67–68, 230–31, 112–13, 225–26).

6. Sandor Gilman's *Jewish Self-Hatred* provides a detailed discussion of the history of internalized anti-Semitism.

7. In the movie, one of the young characters confuses Jesus with the clitoris as the key to making a female happy.

8. While political correctness is often associated in popular culture with the supposedly oppressive power of minority groups and academic liberals, this film reveals some of the hidden anti-Semitic sources for the condemnation of these groups.

9. This interview with Matt Stone and Trey Parker can be found on the online version of the Jewish Student Press Service, at http://www.jsps.com/stories/southpark.shtml.

10. For an extended analysis of the Jewish aspects of Freud's jokes, see Sandor Gilman's *Jewish Self-Hatred* (261–69).

11. Whereas Freud distinguishes among the first, second, and third parties of the joke, he does not differentiate between the object of the joke and the object's relation to the social censor.

12. Most teachers shy away from being critical of students; however, the ways that students and other people resist interpreting many aspects of popular culture is necessary to note.

13. See Sartre's *Anti-Semite and Jew* (110–11).

Works Cited

Boyarin, Daniel. *A Radical Jew: Paul and the Politics of Identity*. Berkeley: University of California Press, 1994.

Fish, Stanley. *There's No Such Thing as Free Speech*. New York: Oxford University Press, 1994.

Freud, Sigmund. *Jokes and Their Relation to the Unconscious*. New York: Norton, 1960.

Gilman, Sandor. *Freud, Race, and Gender*. Princeton, NJ: Princeton University Press, 1993.

———. *Jewish Self-Hatred: Anti-Semitism and the Hidden Language of the Jews*. Baltimore, MD: Johns Hopkins University Press, 1986.

Sartre, Jean-Paul. *Anti-Semite and Jew*. New York: Shocken, 1948.

Young-Bruehl, Elisabeth. *The Anatomy of Prejudices*. Cambridge, MA: Harvard University Press, 1996.

CHAPTER 6

Cynicism and Other Postideological Half Measures in *South Park*

STEPHEN GROENING

South Park is neither politically correct nor incorrect; it's on a different, post-ideological map altogether.
—Frank Rich, "Comedy after Monica"

The first episode of *South Park*, "Cartman Gets an Anal Probe," aired on Comedy Central on August 13, 1997. Appearing amid the culture wars of the 1980s and 1990s, in which debates raged in the mainstream media over Murphy Brown's fitness as a mother, Tinky Winky's sexual preference, and whether the Waltons or the Simpsons exhibited proper family values, *South Park* quickly made a name for itself as rude, crude, vulgar, offensive, and potentially dangerous.[1] Notably, the battles over values and political correctness were staged in the arena of television: Fictional characters were recruited as champions or as villains, often both. Subsequently, detractors cast the four schoolchildren of *South Park* as negative role models even as fans drafted them as righteous defendants of free speech. The culture wars and the crisis of political correctness were partly due to the widespread belief that cultural values were becoming increasingly relativized and consequently devalued as a matter of lifestyle choice. In an era of the micropolitics of identity, seemingly everyone laid claim to being oppressed, marginalized, and dominated. Many groups labored to assemble their identities around recovered histories of oppression. Even nonmarginalized groups jumped on the bandwagon, claiming discrimination at the hands of affirmative action. These decades of micropolitics gave birth to a theorization of a horizontal network of power relations. By the time *South Park* hit television screens, this horizontal network, in which everyone is oppressed but no one oppresses, had taken on the substance of common sense.

On the geopolitical scene, the 1990s saw the beginning of a new post-Soviet era, which to some also meant the end of history and ideology. These triumphalist narratives declared victory for the West, the United States, and capitalism. The rise of a global economy rendered moot the ideological battles between free-market capitalism, Soviet-style planned economy, and a range of "third ways," which moved in and out of fashion. The pinnacle of social evolution had been reached and ideology was no longer necessary to motivate change. As Daniel Bell puts it in his book *The End of Ideology*, in a postideological society ideas no longer act as "social levers"—ideology fails to motivate and mobilize, a phenomenon Bell attributes to a general satisfaction with society (370–75). These "end-times" or postmodern times mean political ideas have been exhausted (the subtitle of Bell's book), false consciousness declared nonexistent, ideology rendered obsolete, and ideology critique unnecessary.[2] The era of postideology has arrived.

The salience of *South Park* for analyzing what has been called the postideological era lies in its satirical mode. The program ridicules a range of topical social issues in a manner approaching ideological critique that does not complete the process of critique. Cynicism, which has become the preeminent aspect of the postideological era, is marked by such half measures. If we take ideology as a set of ideas that assume material force, then to be cynical is to admit the presence of ideology but not submit to its material impact. For those with whom *South Park*'s brand of parodic social satire resonates, the appeal of the cynical attitude lies in adopting a position of safety and avoiding the tremendous obligations of ideology while acknowledging the ideological. Postideological subjects such as *South Park* viewers endeavor to adopt a kind of immateriality that avoids the commitment imposed by ideology. Lack of commitment has particular appeal in a society rhetorically dominated by the micropolitics of identity, which call attention to an overwhelming list of injustices. For *South Park* and its viewers, cynicism, manifesting as irony and ironic detachment, justifies withdrawal from political action.[3]

In *Critique of Cynical Reason*, Peter Sloterdijk suggests that cynicism may be a possible explanation for why ideology fails to have any leverage in contemporary society. Cynicism, a quality some maintain to be the special province of Generation X, *South Park*'s target demographic (see Becker, this volume), is a kind of perversion of false consciousness. As Slavoj Žižek explains in *The Sublime Object of Ideology*, cynicism is a *false* false consciousness.[4] Žižek takes as his starting place for a definition of ideology the phrase from Karl Marx's *Capital*: "they do not know, but they are doing it." Žižek observes that this Marxist definition of ideology has little purchase in the contemporary social world; in part this definition "implies a kind of basic, constitutive naïveté," which no longer can be attributed to social actors. The Marxist definition of ideology depends on misrecognition or a distortion of reality (false consciousness), indicating a distance between reality, our ideas about it, and consequent representations of reality. In this model, the corrective, ideological critique, is a two-step process. First, it attempts to demonstrate and expose ideological distortion. Second, ideological critique seeks to close the distance between reality and the ideological through political action. Cynical reason, on the other hand, turns false consciousness on its head because the cynic is not fooled and recognizes ideology when he or she encounters it. But the cynic makes no attempt at corrective or political action to close the distance between ideology and reality. The cynic knows he or she is being lied to, but also believes it is of small consequence (Žižek 28–33). *South Park* embodies this cynical mode because it engages topical issues ironically, closing off the possibility of political action.

South Park presumes its viewers are aware of stereotypes, social issues, and current events. Amid a struggle for power and meaning in what is seen as a flattened and relativized social milieu, *South Park* in particular demands a kind of radical detachment directly counter to the commitment necessary for ideology to function. The program's satire depends on its viewers' lack of motivation. *South Park* appeals to a youth demographic (regardless of calendar age), consisting of media-savvy individuals who acknowledge the distortions and misrepresentations inherent in television and other forms of mass culture and yet proceed to act as if these representations have no consequences. Indeed, according to its fan base, one of *South Park*'s chief appeals is its ability (some call it responsibility) to make fun of everyone (see Samuels, this volume). This "equal opportunity offensiveness" ignores the historical bases—such as slavery, genocide, patriarchy—mobilized for the formation of the new social movements of micropolitics of identity.

In the interest of trying to locate some specifics about a hotly contested program, this chapter examines the *South Park* episode "Big Gay Al's Big Gay Boat Ride" (hereafter referred to as "Boat Ride"), which originally aired September 3, 1997. In "Boat Ride," Stan has just adopted a dog named Sparky and discovers that Sparky is gay. Stan is also the star quarterback for the South Park elementary school football team, the Cows. The Cows are set to play the heavily favored Middle Park Cowboys in the weekend's homecoming game. When his teammates tease him about Sparky, Stan tries to find out what being gay means and how he can stop Sparky from being gay. Stan tries several "deprogramming" methods, including enticing Sparky with a female poodle. Eventually Sparky runs away and Stan chooses to look for him rather than play in the homecoming football game.

FIGURE 5
Big Gay Al and Stan.

South Park's humor relies on a symbolic world of the majority that forms identity through the continual telling of out-group jokes. Even when these jokes or stereotypes are subverted, the humor depends on knowledge of these stereotypes. When Stan wonders where his dog Sparky is, Cartman, continuing to insinuate that Sparky is gay, says, "maybe he's at the mall buying leather pants." This comment only avoids being a non sequitur if viewers know the stereotype that gay men wear leather pants. This portrayal depends on viewers ironically knowing that stereotypes are false and yet continuing to use them in their everyday interactions. *South Park* treats stereotypes as an inevitable part of everyday life, ridiculing them and yet offering no possibilities for undoing prejudice. From the outset, Stan knows that being gay is undesirable and negative, even though he does not understand what being gay entails. From the start, the episode therefore shows how stereotypes are based on ignorance. Thus, the program's exposition of stereotypes as ridiculous and founded on ignorance constitutes the first step of ideological critique but it fails to move on to the second, corrective action.

By not interrogating the utility of stereotypes, *South Park* allows viewers to feel comfortable with their own use of prejudicial remarks. The continued reiterating of out-group jokes confirms viewers' status and privilege while ostracizing those who do not find the jokes funny. For viewers, the payoff of cynicism is the comfort of feeling superior and in the know. Lack of commitment means less social risk and a greater chance of social belonging. However, the progressive potential of satire means that viewers who identify with the characters are also given the opportunity to realize that they themselves share these prejudices and stereotypes. How viewers act on this identification and possible reflection is another matter. This ambiguous satire encourages the detached and cynical viewer because it requires no commitment one way or the other. *South Park*'s satire appeals through ambiguity because it allows viewers to resolve the episodes as they see fit (within the bounds of the story world). This quality is not unique to *South Park*.[5] To be popular, *all* television programs must appeal to a wide range of viewpoints. Thus, for the television industry, garnering the widest possible audience is the payoff of cynical programming, which does not adopt a discernable position. Under the U.S. system of commercial television in which the networks generate revenue by selling spots to advertisers, ratings determine the presence and longevity of a program. Even in a multichannel, time-shifting, narrowcasting age, networks group viewers by consumerist interests, discouraging political positioning.[6] The draw of action films, cellular phones, fast food, soda pop, video games, and anything else advertised on Comedy Central transcends any single position on abortion, affirmative action, cloning, famine relief, homosexuality, immigration, plastic surgery, Scientology, transgender surgery, or any of the myriad topics *South Park* exploits. Thus, the appeal of the program's particular brand of indeterminacy and polysemy for both viewers and the television industry is in its topicality and immediacy—its ability to be timely, of the moment, and yet radically open to viewers' own worldviews.

The beginning of "Boat Ride" demonstrates the appeal of *South Park*'s ambiguous satire. As the four boys wait at the school bus stop, Stan claims his dog, Sparky, can "kick Sylvester's ass," even though Sylvester is "the toughest dog in South Park." Sparky proceeds to walk off screen toward Sylvester, an approximation of dogs whining plays on the soundtrack, and Cartman comments, "He's doing something to his ass. He's not kicking his ass. But he's definitely doing something to his ass." Kenny, whose dialogue is rendered unintelligible by the winter coat he wears with the hood pulled tightly around his head, says something that Stan does not understand. Cartman translates: "I think Kenny is right. Your dog is a gay homosexual." Cartman's redundant pairing of "gay" and "homosexual" satirizes homophobia. In *South Park*, the word "gay" is consistently used as slang to connote negativity—it is often interchangeable with "stupid." Here the word "gay" is meant as the insult, where "homosexual" is the descriptive noun. Sparky is not a "cool" homosexual but a "gay" one. Cartman's dialogue calls attention to the floating significance of the word and points out that apparent synonyms do not have the same meaning in different contexts. Even as the phrase "gay homosexual" critiques political correctness and the crucial issue of naming, this kind of relativism sets the stage for widespread cynicism. Because the same word can be offensive or empowering depending on context, this lack of clear-cut standards discourages commitment to a position in favor of the safety of social belonging.

The difference between "homosexual" and "gay" in this episode takes on further importance later in the episode when Stan asks his teacher, "What's a homosexual?" and Mr. Garrison tells him about "gay people": "Gay people . . . well, gay people are evil, evil right down to their cold black hearts which pump not blood but a thick vomitus oil which oozes through their rotten veins and clots in their pea-sized brains which becomes the cause of their Nazi-esque patterns of violence." Such rhetoric is extreme and implausible. The humor (such as it is) lies in Mr. Garrison's need to use such violent language to ensure Stan conforms to dominant sexual norms.[7] Mr. Garrison's exchange of one term, "homosexual," with another, "gay," shifts the discourse from the scientific to the populist. Mr. Garrison does not even engage in a discussion regarding what might distinguish a homosexual from a nonhomosexual. For Mr. Garrison, the criteria of homosexuality are not at issue; what is at issue are the qualities of "gay people," which apparently have nothing to do with sexual preference. Mr. Garrison's speech exemplifies the lies of ideology that are so outrageous as to be transparent. The answer does not address Stan's question at all and Mr. Garrison's reply undermines the credibility of schoolteachers in general as ideologues. This is the first step toward cynicism, recognizing that representations of the world have little correspondence to reality. The portrayal of Mr. Garrison implies that children do not form these bigoted views out of thin air, but that they are taught by adults. In this world created by adults, however, the children have little opportunity to create their own set of representations.

Stan attempts to train Sparky, first teaching him to roll over and shake hands, and ends with the command: "Okay, now . . . don't be gay. Don't be gay, Sparky. Don't be gay." Kyle asks if the training is working, and Stan replies that he does not know. Cartman retorts that Sparky still "looks like a gay homosexual to me." The pervasiveness of homophobic rhetoric is evident here because the characters believe that (1) homosexuality can be learned and unlearned, and (2) homosexuality is physically evident. Sparky runs away from home after Stan yells at his friends, "I don't want a gay dog! I want a butch dog! I want a Rin-Tin-Tin!" After Stan discovers that Sparky has run away because of these remarks, he decides he really does love the dog.

In the subsequent search for Sparky (which doubles as soul-searching), Stan discovers Big Gay Al's Big Gay Animal Sanctuary in the woods outside of town. There, a magical character named Big Gay Al, who wears a pink cravat and speaks with a lisp, shelters gay animals that have been ostracized or mistreated by their owners, including Sparky. Big Gay Al attempts to teach Stan tolerance by means of an automated boat ride reminiscent of Disneyland's "It's a Small World." The ride is a tour through a history of homosexuality, which Big Gay Al narrates utilizing animatronic props. This history is curiously flattened; the tableaux of "oppressors" includes the Nazis, Republicans, and Christians (shown as members of the Inquisition and as contemporary fundamentalists) essentially equating these historically distinct groups and their actions. Around the final curve, pairs of animatronic children of various nationalities sing that "being gay is okay" because "gay means happy and happy means gay." This multilayered scene manages to satirize Disney's ersatz "family of man" message, provide pleasure to viewers who know the Disney ride but have outgrown it, and once again call attention to the many meanings of "gay."

The boat ride transforms Stan's attitude. He tells Big Gay Al that the ride was "cool" and goes back to South Park, throws the final touchdown of the game, and proclaims to the bewildered and dubious townsfolk that "being gay is okay." The sudden resolution to this episode satirizes the modern notion of intellectual and emotional working through and working out. Stan's "hero's journey" is not a process as much as an epiphanic conversion. The absence of process in this episode critiques the modernist tenet of the pursuit of knowledge leading to liberation. In the modernist narrative of enlightenment, the truth can be reached through knowing the distance between ideology and the real. This critique of enlightenment reappears in several episodes in various forms. The depth of Stan's transformation from ignorant homophobe to enlightened progressive is open to question. The episode resolves with Stan being convinced by an entertaining diversion. Thus, *South Park* cynically replaces political commitment with amusement.

In addition to cynicism, ideology's failure to mobilize has been attributed to rising standards of living. This hypothesis, held by Bell and others, is that the post–World War II gains in living standards have lead to a general satisfaction with society.[8] In this argument, ideology that proposes a future unlike the present is obsolete precisely because a better future cannot be imagined. The future is now and now is "The Triumph of Popular Culture," to borrow the title of Matthew Henry's essay on postmodernism and *The Simpsons*. The title invokes the "end-times" mode of postmodernism and postideology, and in keeping with postmodernist tenets prematurely predicts the death of high culture. This universal present is one of the key attributes of the postmodern condition and consists of a flattened temporality in which the future is no different than the present and the past becomes merely the repository of stylistic choices for empty pastiche.[9]

The fact that *South Park* is a genre-mixing, self-referential cartoon with an ironic obsession with pop culture (both well-known and obscure) makes it emblematic of what many would call postmodern television. But calling

South Park postmodern is inadequate by itself, in part because the term has been applied to so much by so many. For instance, postmodern is often used as an umbrella term for any genre-blurring or genre-mixing cultural expression. For others, what distinguishes postmodernism is a self-reflexivity, which, according to their analysis, maintains an ironic distance between the show and its participation in capitalism: so-called postmodern irony.[10] In *The Politics of Postmodernism*, Linda Hutcheon explains that postmodernism has progressive potential because it critiques its complicity in commodity exchange. Through what Hutcheon calls the "postmodern paradox," postmodernism "manages to legitimate culture (high and mass) even as it subverts it" (15). By rushing to legitimate postmodernism, these analyses fail to realize that *postmodern irony is the figurative manifestation of cynicism*. Postmodern television reformulates Marx's definition of ideology from "they do not know, but they are doing it," to "yes, we know we're tools of the advertisers and we're doing it anyway." What appears to be postmodern and potentially progressive in *South Park* therefore should be more accurately conceived of as a consequence of cynicism.

South Park's irony rarely addresses its own role in commodity exchange and more often targets knee-jerk political correctness and the politics of identity. The episode "Here Comes the Neighborhood," for instance, displaces Token's status as the lone African-American child in South Park Elementary to Token's status as the wealthiest (supposedly only wealthy) child in South Park Elementary. Token manages to convince other wealthy people to move to South Park, who are, of course, African American, which results in current South Park residents feeling as if their quiet mountain town is, in the words of Mr. Garrison, "being overrun by *those* types." While this episode satirizes racial panic, it also manages to represent economic marginalization and oppression of African Americans as fictive. Of course, Token's name itself satirizes the entertainment industry's penchant for casting a lone African-American character in an otherwise all-white show: a postmodern ironic gesture if there ever was one because Token *is* a token in South Park Elementary.

Excusing certain representations in a television program because the program makes fun of itself is a defense through misdirection. It is the equivalent of the rhetorical opening, "I'm not racist, but . . ." which is invariably followed by a racist statement. Irony may be used as a tool to help viewers feel better about themselves and their position in society, but it does not neutralize the political consequences of representation. Postmodern irony creates the comfort of laughter in an impossible situation and excuses characterizing the situation as inevitable. The ironic satire of *South Park* enables viewers to feel superior to other social actors and vent their frustrations with political leaders, economic factors, and their own feelings of helplessness.[11] Postmodern irony is cynical irony: calling attention to injustices and proposing that nothing can be done.

Postmodern irony is an effect of the postideological era. For ideological critique to take place, one needs a relatively stable text that can be analyzed as supporting, carrying, or reproducing ideology. To locate ideology, one must be standing outside of it; that is, distance must exist between reality (however understood) and the ideological. Theorizations of ideology from the Marxist to the colloquial rely on some conception of distance between reality and ideology (hence the common distinction between an ideologue and a realist). Recognition of ideological distortions depends on leveraging this critical distance. However, because ideology has pervaded every aspect of daily life, this distance appears absent, and results in cynically ironic acknowledgements of ideology.

This becomes a particularly intractable problem in a relativized society marked by the micropolitics of identity, described in this chapter's opening. The new conception of power relations has created a society without norms against which to measure ideological distortion. Nonetheless, forms of economic oppression remain: Commodity exchange, even if ironically critiqued by postmodernism, persists unabated and perhaps is even more legitimized than before. Fredric Jameson summarizes this situation well in his periodical essay, "Postmodernism," or, the "Cultural Logic of Late Capitalism":

> If the ideas of a ruling class were once the dominant (or hegemonic) ideology of bourgeois society, the advanced capitalist countries today are now a field of stylistic and discursive heterogeneity without a norm. Faceless masters continue to inflect the economic strategies which constrain our existences, but no longer need to impose their speech [. . .]. In this situation, parody finds itself without a vocation (65).

Without a dominant class (or figure) to parody, Jameson contends, parody has transformed into pastiche: neutral mimicry as opposed to pointed satirical critique. But insipid imitation may not be the only option left for parody. *South Park* has found parody's postideological vocation and has not yet become the postsatire form of pastiche.[12] In the postideology era, parody has endless referents and no longer needs to disrupt the master's language because the accomplishments of micropolitics and political correctness have made language radically contingent: "Gay" can be an insult or a term of empowerment, depending on context. *South Park* takes advantage of the discursive heterogeneity of late capitalism through the peculiarly American version of egalitarianism: Treat everyone the same. Following this logic, and with a seemingly unlimited arsenal of jokes and targets, *South Park* sets out to make fun of everyone.

This move is celebrated by the show's fans. Contributors to a *South Park* newsgroup (alt.tv.southpark) excused objectionable language and behavior within the program as being "fair." These contributors defined fairness as "offending everyone." Here are some typical comments:

I would say that I have never been offended by our beloved Matt & Trey. I don't think offense would be the word used to describe the feelings I've had. [. . .] I find it hard myself to take offense to something that makes fun of EVERYONE and EVERYTHING.

[. . .] well, it's hard to explain how I feel about the stuff that some people might find offensive. I've always felt that Matt and Trey are "Equal Opportunity Offenders"—they poke fun at people regardless of race, gender, sexual preference, or political affiliation. And I think they do this to make us look at ourselves and how stupid various prejudices can be.

A general consensus in the news group emerged that, although the program was offensive, it was also extremely funny. Many viewers reconciled their conflicted feelings by emphasizing how the program attacked everyone; this "equal" treatment therefore absolved the viewers of racism, sexism, homophobia, and so forth. The argument can be summarized thusly: Because the program makes fun of black *and* white people it is not racist; therefore, I am not racist for laughing at the jokes. The idea that "equal opportunity" for offense can be given to all groups avoids the notion that different groups have different histories of oppression in the United States.

The creators of *South Park*, Matt Stone and Trey Parker, have stated that their mission is to make fun of everything. In an interview after their wildly successful first season, Stone remarked, "We hate the fact that there exist things that can't be made fun of" (Rich A23). The audience believes this omnivorous approach to satire is the natural result of the horizontalization and relativization of society. An example of this kind of equivalency between ethnic, racial, and sexual identities can be seen in the episode "Cartman's Mom Is a Dirty Slut." In this episode, Cartman sets out to discover his father's identity. His mother, known as Mrs. Cartman (a red herring, it turns out), recounts the hazily remembered story of the night Cartman was conceived, during which she had sexual relations with Officer Barbrady, Chief Running Water, Mr. Garrison, Chef, and "the 1989 Denver Broncos." As the story moves through these possibilities, Cartman attempts to get back to his imagined roots. When he believes his father to be Chief Running Water, Cartman dons a headdress, a bear-fetish necklace, moccasins, and a deerskin jacket. After discovering that Chef might be his father, Cartman exchanges his first costume for a high fade wig, tracksuit, a clock necklace, and gold jewelry. The humor lies partly in Cartman's parody of mass culture's stereotypes of Native Americans and African Americans.[13] But Cartman's treatment of tradition as commodified costuming is never explicitly critiqued. Thus, the episode gives a free pass to those who would relativize culture through commodification.

The logic of "equal opportunity" satire equates stereotypes of Native Americans and African Americans to stereotypes of white Americans and thus falsely renders horizontal the real histories of domination and oppression in the United States. A satire that creates a kind of "open season" on everyone and everything raises potential difficulties for the audience in distinguishing between serious criticism (the exposition of hypocrisy in U.S. social discourse) and racist, sexist, and homophobic material. If nothing can be taken seriously, then likewise any social analysis made through the satire does not need to be taken seriously either.

One of *South Park*'s many satiric devices in its mission to ridicule everything is to target ideology. The program disavows the commitment necessary for ideology to take hold, preferring a highly mobile and detached approach to satire. Stone and Parker demonstrate this kind of uncommitted mobile satire in public interviews. When asked why Kenny is killed in every episode, during an interview included on the *South Park Volume I* DVD, Matt and Trey respond, "because he's poor." This answer calls attention to economic injustice without apologies and refuses to answer the question as an inquiry into authorial choice, story motivation, or both. Their answer is reminiscent of an exchange in a document called "Matt and Trey Answer 40 Questions," available through Comedy Central:

> 26: There has been a rumor going around that one of the kids was going to move away, namely Kyle. Is this true or was true? Did you change your minds? Or were you just messing with us?
>
> TREY: Kyle would be the one to move because he's a Jew.

While clearly a setup, Parker's "wink and nod" to the Wandering Jew legend exemplifies postmodern irony and postideological cynicism: both consequences of dismissing any claim as ideology and the resulting loss of critical distance. Parker's sarcastic response could be read as a superficial critique of anti-Semitism while giving him a chance to reiterate epithets. The humor is ambiguous and could lie in the shock of Parker's remark or in his mockery of anti-Semitic stereotypes. The program and its promotional materials seem to be involved in an ideological game of dare: to name that which cannot be named. *South Park*'s commitment is to be uncommitted. In this way, ideological critique of *South Park* is somewhat impossible because the program's textual qualities give voice to ideology and ridicule ideological distortions.

We have arrived, in a sense, where we started: For a television program to appeal to postideological viewers it must itself be postideological. Given that the job of *South Park* is to recruit a particular demographic, we should not be surprised that Matt Stone and Trey Parker demonstrate a deep understanding of American cynicism. Consistently one of the highest rated programs on Comedy Central, the program now represents a revenue bonanza for the cable network. *South Park* procures the highly desirable male, age 18–34 (Generation X) demographic by fulfilling their need for validation and, in so doing, *South Park* fulfills its primary corporate mission. High ratings in this category generate revenue for the network and its corporate parents.[14] After only one season, Comedy Central's ratings climbed 30%, a total of 7 million new subscribers, and *South Park* merchandise sales topped $100 million in 1998 (La Franco).

South Park is authored and viewed by those educated in a system that supports media literacy and critical skills for combating advertising and propaganda. A media-savvy society knows that advertisements have an oblique relationship to truth and, while entertaining, should not be trusted or acted on. By already being critical, *South Park* disarms those prepared with "hermeneutics of suspicion."[15] *South Park's* postideological cynicism, like advertising, succeeds by playing on viewers' insecurities and desires. Postideological insecurities might include the inability to imagine an alternate future, widespread social change, or both. Despite the desire to mitigate or end social iniquities portrayed in *South Park* such as sexism, racism, and homophobia, these large-scale changes seem impossible and overwhelming. The desire for change turns into learned helplessness. Viewers may see themselves as participants in a society rife with injustice but with no immediately viable solutions and prefer the uncommitted cynical irony of *South Park's* parodic satire.

In the era of postideology in which the distance between culture and the economy has been erased or compressed, remembering that television programs are cultural commodities, and commodities are neither neutral nor inert, is crucial. In his 1958 book, *The Uses of Literacy*, Richard Hoggart warns of consumer culture, "This regular, increasing and almost entirely unvaried diet of sensation without commitment is surely likely to help render its consumers less capable of responding openly and responsibly to life, is likely to induce an underlying sense of purposelessness in existence outside the limited range of a few immediate appetites" (188). The idea that *South Park* does not have a political agenda because it makes fun of everything has an appeal for the alienated and cynical viewer. By flaunting its lack of commitment, *South Park* presents itself as harmless and demands nothing of the viewer except 30 minutes of his or her time. The cynic has little use for ideology because his or her awareness of ideology leads to feelings of helplessness. Those who feel separated or cut off from political life derive pleasure from the program, precisely because it cynically offers "sensation without commitment." *South Park* therefore allows viewers to avoid confronting their learned helplessness.

Herein lies the hidden danger of the cynicism affirmed by *South Park*. To have no use for ideology and declare oneself postideological is to trade the difficulties of agency for the convenience of acquiescence. Believing all things to be equally valid is tantamount to not believing in anything, leaving viewers vulnerable to those who do act. The declaration of egalitarianism is really a lack of commitment that disguises cynicism and apathy. In the era of postideology, the hermeneutics of suspicion are dismissed as inconsequential or irrelevant. Viewers become susceptible to particular types of domination that take advantage of complacency and apathy—actions under the category of faits accomplis. The invasions of Afghanistan and Iraq constitute a clear and immediate example. The invasions, which were given little to no criticism in the mainstream news coverage, appear to the cynic as inevitable and unavoidable. The cynic would act as if those who proposed the invasions and those who argued against invading were both lying and not to be trusted. Within the framework of cynical reason, investigating those lies is a useless exercise because everyone lies for political advantage and his own selfish ends. In such a scenario, adopting a position against or for war makes no sense. The inaction of the cynic, born of mistrust, apathy, and an acceptance of a lack of agency results in giving the activities of the dominant a free pass. The espousal of a cynical worldview in which nothing can be done about a flawed and corrupt political system, the presumed stupidity of others (*South Park* is full of such portrayals), and the inequalities of society merely affirms the status quo as an inevitable and immutable situation. From this, we see that the real cultural villainy of *South Park* is not its depictions of swearing schoolchildren but its espousal of an emergent cynicism that discourages its viewers from asserting political agency.

Notes

I would like to thank Lynn Thomas and Gregory Gardner for their hard work on early versions of this chapter; Keya Ganguly for giving me new direction; Eva Hudecova for her helpful feedback and commentary; and Andrea Christy for hours of proofreading and debate.

1. The culture wars even had their own talk show, *Politically Incorrect*, which first aired on HBO in 1993 and moved over to ABC the same year *South Park* premiered on Comedy Central. Importantly, *South Park* follows in a line of sketch comedy programs, primarily *In Living Color* (FOX, Keenan Ivory Wayans, 1990–1994) but also *Mad TV* (FOX, Quincy Jones, 1995–), which took the politics of identity as their object of satire, opposing them to the "humor of the everyday" that marks *Saturday Night Live* and network sitcoms.

2. I refer here to various pronouncements by Francis Fukayama and Daniel Bell. These have been carried over into the mainstream media, which characterizes the newfound centrism (or pragmatism) in parliamentary politics as postideological. See also Beasley-Murray.

3. Sociological and psychological studies offering empirical evidence of cynicism abound. However, they differ in their definitions of cynicism. Most studies defined cynicism as a symptom of a lack of social trust: Individuals believe or perceive others as malicious or dishonest. For instance, Cappella (2002) and Cappella and Jamieson

(1997) use the term "cynicism" as a form of mistrust in an interchangeable manner and demonstrate how cynicism erodes community, civic engagement, and so on. Cappella's suggestion that mainstream media act as propagators of cynicism by broadcasting and printing cynical or mistrustful stories and reports is particularly salient. Others take cynicism to be a belief that human beings are inherently selfish or self-interested by nature. Business management, organizational science, and human management typically see cynicism as a problem to be overcome in the workplace caused by dysfunctional relations between labor and management during organizational change (see in particular Feldman). Some intriguing studies of cynicism use a "locus of control" measurement. In these studies, research subjects who saw outside forces as having more power over their lives than interior motivation tended to be alienated and cynical because this was often coupled with the belief that those outside forces are unresponsive to the subject's needs. Twenge, Zhang, and Im provide a useful and informative metastudy of 40 years of research into the problem of "locus of control." Their findings support the notion that cynicism and alienation have been on the rise over the past 50 years, not only among college-age students, but also among children. The interplay between television and cynicism has borne particular scrutiny. de Vreese and Semetko studied a Danish referendum on the euro currency and found that "strategic political news coverage"—that is, coverage about how political campaigns are waged—tended to increase cynicism among voters but did not appear to have an effect on voter turnout. They concluded that cynicism and lower participation in electoral politics are not necessarily related. Baumgartner and Morris's study of *The Daily Show with Jon Stewart* demonstrates that, although the show informed those only casually interested in politics, its audience tended to be less interested in participating in elections. In addition, the study concluded that *The Daily Show* had a demonstrable effect (versus network evening news) of generally disenchanting viewers of the political process and political candidates. Because *The Daily Show with Jon Stewart* is generally considered to be an ironic take on the news (or even a postmodern news show) as opposed to the "straight" coverage de Vreese and Semetko detail, these findings buttress my argument regarding the linkage of irony to cynicism and apathy.

4. Peter Sloterdijk calls it an "enlightened false consciousness."

5. A good example of the ambiguity of satire is the 1974 study by psychologist Neil Vidmar and social psychologist Milton Rokeach analyzing the supposed impact of *All in the Family* on viewers. The subjects in the study had to fill out a questionnaire about how they would act in certain situations, the results of which caused them to be placed into categories, possessing either high prejudice or low prejudice. Vidmar and Rokeach found that people they designated highly prejudiced more often perceived the reactionary character of Archie Bunker as "winning" at the end of the episode. Those designated low prejudiced were more likely to perceive the progressive character of Mike (known as Meathead) as "winning." According to Vidmar and Rokeach, the results indicate that television programs, taken as discrete phenomenon, have little effect on viewers' ideology. They concluded, "many persons did not see the program as a satire on bigotry."

6. Some may argue that certain religious networks and FOX News Network appeal to viewers' religious or political beliefs rather than consumer habits. But even the Trinity Broadcasting Network treats viewers as consumers: The com-

modities purchased are bibles and other religious paraphernalia, or take the form of charitable donations.

7. Mr. Garrison's need for conformity has taken some curious turns throughout the show's life so far. At this early point in *South Park* many characters believe Mr. Garrison to be gay, which he vehemently denies in this episode, saying "I only act that way to get chicks." By the fourth season, Mr. Garrison has come out ("4th Grade") in a kind of "split personality" argument with himself. Indeed, Mr. Garrison often struggles with self-loathing and self-denial. During season six, in "The Death Camp of Tolerance," he tries to get fired from South Park Elementary by inserting a gerbil in his new lover, Mr. Slave. When Mr. Garrison undergoes a sex-change operation in the ninth-season episode, "Mr. Garrison's Fancy New Vagina," which includes some documentary footage of such an operation, he tells Mr. Slave that becoming a woman changes nothing between them, as long as Mr. Slave "stops being gay." By associating homosexuality with extreme sexual acts, identity confusion, and the grotesque, *South Park* affirms a visceral homophobia even as it denies the intellectual and rational justifications for heterosexism.

8. Of course, like most of Bell's work, this thesis pertains to Europe and North America, particularly the United States. But in an era of globalization, the totem of the rising middle class has been placed around the world.

9. Douglas Kellner argues that the lack of a future for the main characters in *Beavis and Butt-head* (and the show's fans) is one of its chief postmodern characteristics.

10. For discussions of irony as a marker of the postmodern see works by Hutcheon, Kellner, and Henry.

11. Simultaneously, *South Park* neutralizes any sort of long-term social unrest through the (typically modern) return to normalcy at the end of each episode. In some episodes this return to normalcy is abrupt and contrived (for example, "Chinpokomon"), a flattening process in the manner of "Boat Ride." In other ways, such as Kenny's recurrent death, the show avoids the return to normalcy, picking and choosing which plots and story lines carry over from one episode to the next.

12. In season ten's two-part episode, "Cartoon Wars," *South Park* accuses *Family Guy* of being pastiche. Through the mouthpiece of Cartman, Stone and Parker ridicule *Family Guy* as "one random interchangeable joke after another." *South Park* deepens its critique of what its creators see as empty, meaningless humor when Cartman discovers that manatees write the jokes for *Family Guy* by randomly choosing "idea balls," which are then combined by a machine to form a joke.

13. This moment in the episode also contains dialogue pertinent to my argument. When Chief Running Water tells Cartman that he last saw Mrs. Cartman with Chef, Cartman exclaims "Oh my god, I'm a black African American!" Similar to his "gay homosexual" line, this remark touches on the controversy of political correctness and its prioritization of naming and language over action.

14. *South Park*'s high ratings are discussed in Comedy Partners' "Creators of Comedy Central Ratings," "Comedy Central's 'South Park,'" "Comedy Central's Run-Away Hit," and "It May Be Winter in 'South Park.'"

15. Paul Ricoeur coined the term in *Freud and Philosophy*, referring to the interpretive techniques of Marx, Nietzsche, and Freud. Those who adopt a "hermeneutics of suspicion" do not trust texts, but suspect them of hiding their support for certain political interests. This interpretive approach, then, seeks to reveal these political interests.

Works Cited

Baumgartner, Jody, and Jonathan S. Morris. "*The Daily Show* Effect: Candidate Evaluations, Efficacy, and American Youth." *American Politics Research* 34.3 (May 2006): 341–67.

Beasley-Murray, Jon. "On Posthegemony." *Bulletin of Latin American Research* 22.1 (2003): 117–25.

Bell, Daniel. *The End of Ideology: On the Exhaustion of Political Ideas in the Fifties*. New York: Collier, 1962.

Cappella, Joseph. "Cynicism and Social Trust in the New Media Environment." *Journal of Communication* (Mar. 2002): 229–41.

Cappella, Joseph, and K. H. Jamieson. *The Spiral of Cynicism: The Press and the Public Good*. New York: Oxford University Press, 1997.

Comedy Partners. "Comedy Central's Run-Away Hit 'South Park' Honored with Primetime Emmy Nomination [News Release]." Los Angeles: Comedy Partners, July 1998.

Comedy Partners. "Comedy Central's 'South Park' Harpoons Moby Dick with a 8.2 HH Rating Making It the Highest Rated Basic Cable Entertainment Series Episode [News Release]." Los Angeles: Comedy Partners, April 1998.

Comedy Partners. "Creators of Comedy Central Ratings Phenomenon 'South Park' Win Producers Guild 'Nova' Award [News Release]." Los Angeles: Comedy Partners, March 1998.

Comedy Partners. "It May Be Winter in 'South Park' But the Boys Are Ready for Summer with All-New Episodes Beginning Wednesday, June 21, at 10:00 P.M. on Comedy Central [News Release]." Los Angeles: Comedy Partners, June 2000.

de Vreese, Claes H., and Holli A. Semetko. "Cynical and Engaged: Strategic Campaign Coverage, Public Opinion, and Mobilization in a Referendum." *Communication Research* 29.6 (Dec. 2002), 615–41.

Feldman, D. C. "The *Dilbert* Syndrome: How Employee Cynicism about Ineffective Management Is Changing the Nature of Careers in Organizations." *American Behavioural Scientist*, 43 (2000): 1286–300.

Fukuyama, Francis. *The End of History and the Last Man*. New York: Free Press, 1992.

Henry, Matthew. "The Triumph of Popular Culture: Situation Comedy, Postmodernism and *The Simpsons*." *Studies in Popular Cultures* 17.1 (Oct. 1994): 85–99.

Hoggart, Richard. *The Uses of Literacy*. New York: Transaction, 1992.

Hutcheon, Linda. *The Politics of Postmodernism*. New York: Routledge, 1989.

Jameson, Fredric. "Postmodernism, or, the Cultural Logic of Late Capitalism." *New Left Review* 46 (1984): 53–92.

Kellner, Douglas. "*Beavis and Butt-head*: No Future for Postmodern Youth." *Postmodern after Images: A Reader in Film, Television, and Video*. Ed. Peter Brooker and Will Brooker. New York: Arnold, 1997. 182–91.

La Franco, Robert. "Profits by the Gross." *Forbes* 21 Sept. 1998: 232.

Rich, Frank. "Comedy after Monica." *New York Times* 11 Mar. 1998: A23.

Ricoeur, Paul. *Freud and Philosophy: An Essay on Interpretation*. New Haven, CT: Yale University Press, 1970.

Sloterdijk, Peter. *Critique of Cynical Reason*. Minneapolis: University of Minnesota Press, 1987.

Twenge, Jean M., Liqing Zhang, and Charles Im. "It's Beyond My Control: A Cross-Temporal Meta-Analysis of Increasing Externality in Locus of Control, 1960–2002." *Personality and Social Psychology Review* 8.3 (2004): 308–19.

Vidmar, Neil, and Milton Rokeach. "Archie Bunker's Bigotry: A Study in Selective Perceptions and Exposure." *Journal of Communication* 24.1 (Winter 1974): 36–47.

Žižek, Slavoj. *The Sublime Object of Ideology*. New York: Verso, 1989.

CHAPTER 7

Shopping at J-Mart with the Williams

Race, Ethnicity, and Belonging in *South Park*

LINDSAY COLEMAN

Transgressions of social and racial etiquette have long been mainstays of many comedy forms, animated and otherwise; thus, we are hardly surprised that the *South Park* creators, Trey Parker and Matt Stone, should use common stereotypes and insults within their series to provoke responses from viewers. Ethnic and personal slurs are the stuff of even the most mundane conversations in the animated comedy *South Park*. Stan Marsh and Kyle Broflovski's school yard nickname for their friend Eric Cartman is "fatass." Cartman in turn refers derogatively to Kyle as "a Jew" and to friend Kenny McCormick as "poor," both statements of fact brutally converted into slurs by Cartman's dismissive tone. Pointedly, Cartman refers to his African-American peer Token as a "black asshole" in the episode "Christian Rock Hard." Through such intemperate rhetoric, *South Park* joins this long tradition of decidedly impolite, racially charged comedy.

However, in creating this pervasive atmosphere of social derision, Parker and Stone satirically illustrate aspects of contemporary United States' social condition and the power of prejudicial slurs to act as social dividers. Slurs in *South Park* are shown to function both as social insulators and as catalysts for neurosis for those on either side of the ethnic or religious divide. This need to label incessantly in *South Park* brings to the fore a vicious circle of marginalization and countermarginalization. Judgments based on stereotypes, particularly racial, ethnic, and religious, are shown to define social activity and individual self-perception in the town of South Park, Colorado. However, whereas essentialist assumptions underlie the bigoted slurs and epithets meted out by the town of South Park's white majority, Parker and Stone ultimately satirize the racism that still pervades American social life.

The superficiality inherent in the labels applied to South Park residents within the program, while not always commented on directly in *South Park* narratives, is obvious to the audience. Despite his clear intellectual brilliance, Cartman is always defined by his weight. Cartman's own mother laughs at the "fatass" jibe in "Korn's Groovy Pirate Ghost Mystery." So, too, is the sensitive Kyle defined by his Jewishness and its associated stereotypes. (Jimbo gambles $50 on his success in a spelling bee in "Hooked on Monkey Phonics" solely on the basis of his Jewish ethnicity.) However, although slurs are generated in relation both to body type and religion, the category of difference that Stone and Parker most consistently expose as grossly superficial is that of race.

Token Williams's name, after all, is a specific satirical comment on his place in the South Park community. Indeed, he is literally and self-consciously designated *as* a label and his primary role in the series is to embody a particular racial designation. We should note that he is by no means a major character and shares little with the series' other minor characters. He is not a key support character, such as Butters, nor does he serve the basic generic requirements of the school yard narrative, as does Stan's love interest Wendy or the anarchic Kenny. Token's purpose is to add tokenistic, or symbolic, racial diversity to the South Park playground. His blackness seems to suffice not only as his label within the town but also, for Parker and Stone's satirical purposes, his definition within the series. This becomes obvious when Token first makes a major narrative impression in "Cartman's Silly Hate Crime 2000." The four friends, hoping to beat the girls in a sled race, are practicing. Token comments, repeating a reductive label created by Kyle and Stan, that Cartman's "fat ass" will help them win the race. Cartman responds by throwing a rock at Token. Here Token's blackness defines Cartman's malicious but racially unmotivated act as a hate crime and he is sent to jail. This fact of racial identity determines the course of the episode's narrative rather than aspects of Token's personality, and thus Cartman's simple prank serves as the basis for an entire episode. Effectively, Token is only of interest to Parker and Stone on the basis of his race coupled with his social position within the town.

What is significant and potentially inflammatory about *South Park's* deployment of racial stereotypes is that, within the world of *South Park*, shallow stereotypical judgments are invariably true. In the episode "Christian Rock Hard," Cartman specifically recruits Token for his band as a bass guitar player. Token expresses confusion at this decision. "I don't have a bass guitar in my basement," he explains. "Token, of course you do, you're black," Cartman replies. And indeed there is a bass guitar in his basement. Not only this,

FIGURE 6
Token Black with bass guitar.

but it turns out that Token can play the guitar with a marked degree of proficiency, despite his lack of practice or experience—something Cartman credits to Token's blackness.

This confirmation of ethnic stereotypes also is evident with the owner of the City Wok restaurant, the series' stereotypical Chinese businessman, as well as with Kyle, the Jew. The Chinese man garbles his English, pronouncing City Wok as "Sheety Wonk," and in the episode "Child Abduction Is Not Funny," he builds a vast Great Wall around South Park, attracting with it clichéd Mongolians who attack the wall. In Kyle's case, in the episode "Fat Camp," Cartman, by hiring a double of himself, creates the impression that he has lost vast amounts of weight at Fat Camp and has now achieved the South Park physical norm for children. However, the ruse fails when his double begins to moralize, a trait completely contrary to Cartman's caricatured identity. It is however the narrative function of Kyle at the end of each episode. Significantly, Kyle discovers the ruse, ripping off the imposter's hat to uncover that, with his mass of fizzy red hair, he is in fact Kyle's own doppelgänger. Cartman's ruse fails because of his double's stereotypically Jewish penchant for moralizing, a trait Kyle shares. This, like Token's miraculous ability to play bass guitar, confirms that ethnic stereotypes have the valence of truth about them in *South Park*.

Another equally inflammatory factor in *South Park* is the ways in which minority characters are taught to embody their own stereotypes. Cartman, in "Christian Rock Hard," and the town's parents, in "Child Abduction Is Not Funny," "enlighten" ethnic minorities concerning their "true" abilities through comic stereotypical pronouncements. The Caucasian population of South Park ironically believes that to aid in a minority's gradual, conditional assimilation into South Park, the town must educate the minority member concerning his proper role on the basis of long-entrenched racist assumptions and minorities represented within the program then demonstrate or adopt essentialized racial features. This dynamic demonstrates the "dual-edge" of racism: Just as assuming a black person can play guitar by virtue of his blackness is racist, so, too, is a black person accepting this notion as intrinsically valid because it is issued by a white person. While the former presumes essential musicality in a black individual, the latter presumes a historical American precedent for intrinsic leadership in a white individual. Thus, the incidence of paternalistic racial stereotypes in *South Park* are indicative of essentialist notions on both sides of the race equation.

Yet although essentialist assumptions in *South Park* seemingly damn both creator and subject, Parker and Stone carefully satirize white assumptions about ethnic minorities and, in the process, construct what may be referred to as a "counterhegemony" in which minority members are shown to be more talented or capable than the white majority. "Hegemony" can be defined as "the process by which those in power secure the consent of the socially subordinated to the system that oppresses or subordinates them" (Dines 731). Parker and Stone have a dual agenda with their presentation of racially inflammatory stereotypes in the context of the Caucasian, middle-class hegemony of South Park (which reflects that of the United States at large). In the first place, they arguably wish to illustrate the ingrained prejudice in all aspects of American social life. Through the style of their series and their narrative decisions, they depict how central prejudice is to the structure of an American story of an American town. Having done this, they proceed to their second agenda item, which is the satirization of such prejudices and the establishment of counterhegemony that privileges racial minorities.

Despite the provocative aspects of *South Park*'s depictions of race and race relations noted earlier, Parker and Stone maintain a subtly reverential attitude toward their ethnic minorities. Token enjoys success with Cartman and Butters in the band Faith+1. It is a success denied to the band of Stan and Kyle, the two most prominent characters in *South Park*. Cartman also receives his comeuppance at the episode's end when a final racist epithet drives Token to knock down his front man. Kyle and Stan, by contrast, are the frequent victims of Cartman's schemes. So, too, does the City Wok owner diligently apply himself to defending the South Park wall from Mongolians. It is a far cry from his clear boredom and frustration taking City Wok orders and his half-hearted attempt at being an airline pilot for the boys in "It's Christmas in Canada." Indeed, while the socially-assimilated townspeople of South Park educate its racial minorities on their potential, these same minorities profit from such education. The noblesse oblige of the likes of Cartman result in a social revolution. This becomes evident through the wealth and success minority characters achieve in their careers when their talents are allowed to blossom—minorities on *South Park* inevitably achieve success in more areas than their supposed educators. Parker and Stone effectively satirize the presumptiveness of the White Man's Burden and upend its paternalistic vision of happy but servile racial minorities.

"Assimilation," according to Richard D. Alda, refers "to the long-term processes that have whittled away at the foundations for ethnic distinctions. [. . . It] is, in general, the perhaps unintended, cumulative byproduct of choices made by individuals seeking to take advantage of opportunities to improve their social situation" (211–12). The town of South Park, as the social center from which resident racial and ethnic minorities seek acceptance and involvement through assimilation, demands homogeneity from its conscripts. Even though both Token and the owner of the City Wok profit from their participation in Caucasian hegemony, their greater aim in the series is arguably assimilation. Effectively, they hope to transcend their labels, becoming as nondescript as the series' great exponent of normal, the Anglo-Saxon Stan Marsh. They wish to be perceived as average within an increasingly homogenous society.

This drive not to be noticed is clearly evident in "Here Comes the Neighborhood," a crucial episode on the theme of race relations in which Token atypically is at the center of the action. For the first time it is evident that the boys primarily associate Token, who is black, not with his race, but with his parents' wealth. He is teased at school not for the color of his skin, but for his ignorance of middle- and lower-middle-class life in rural America. Attempting to remedy this, he convinces his parents to let him shop at J-Mart. However, the trip to J-Mart backfires. The Williams parents feel uncomfortable in such a lower-middle-class setting. Token's new J-Mart clothing fails to impress his peers. He then intuits that to avoid the pressures of assimilation he must encourage other wealthy black families to move to South Park.

This is perhaps one of the most typical of *South Park*'s plot devices. When unable to achieve the social norm as a result of physical, mental, or social factors, the South Park individual or marginalized group attempts to counter-marginalize by reversing the trends of assimilation. This is achieved through the creation of a new subculture or expanded minority, which in turn grows into a political movement—an ironically essentialist project. Typically, to establish its social influence, the new subculture engages combatively with the external culture by allowing specific essentialist stereotypes to be propagated as a source of the former's intrinsic social importance. Unable to transcend the stereotypes bestowed on them, the subculture attempts to reverse their hegemonic use. This is achieved through a broad social base of advocacy accompanied by protests, which then are followed by counterprotests and counteradvocacy. Frequently, the advocacy begins in the children's school yard, percolates through their families, and eventually reaches the Mayor's office. This in turn results in a showdown between the rival representatives of the subculture and the mainstream, often with one of the four children as arbitrator of the conflict.

Token's struggle, as noted, follows this pattern clearly. First, he is rejected by his peers and precluded from assimilation, the essential American aspiration. He then attempts to involve his parents in resolving South Park's socioracial divide. Following their failure, he appeals to those with both more socioeconomic power and the ability to mobilize greater physical numbers in his support. Thus, whereas he may yet be accepted, he engages with assimilative aspects of the South Park world. He accepts the marginalize/countermarginalize dichotomy and, true to his experience in "Christian Rock Hard," uses the limitations of context to his benefit. Token again profits, at least temporarily, from South Park's existing hegemony.

Token hopes to provoke a black migration to South Park, catalyzing a change in the town's notions of social and economic norms. The arrival of the millionaires is akin to that of the "goobacks" in "Goobacks," and it provokes social anarchy. The immigration of top black celebrities such as Will Smith, Oprah Winfrey, and Snoop Dogg to South Park has unexpected results. Token, rather than fitting in, is alienated by the fabulous wealth and haughty manner of his new black peers. The townspeople meanwhile begin to find themselves disenfranchised in their own town. The sudden presence of money in this lower-middle-class town results in massive alienation and unites the Marshes and McCormicks in feelings of inadequacy. Token effectively has succeeded in creating a new normative category for the town: wealth. Seeking to reestablish notions of their own normality and social acceptability in a town full of opulent homes and multimillionaires, the townspeople ostracize the African Americans—as had been the case with Token and their own children—for their ostentation and wealth. In turn, Oprah, Will Smith, and Snoop Dogg march against the discrimination they ironically face for their success, creating a new subculture of protest, a new liberal norm that ideally will bridge the gap. Caught in the middle of these competing norms is a young black child frustrated in his search for assimilation. He shares the shock and intimidation of the townspeople, yet is unable to bond with them by virtue of his dual traits of wealth and color. Ironically, Token finds himself an army of one in "Here Comes the Neighborhood." The satirical bite of this scenario is potent: In his effort to fit in, Token experiences only trauma and, by the episode's end, further marginalization from his white peers. Despite the hope of creating a utopia for wealthy African Americans in the midwest and, with it, a new sense of his black identity, Token instead precipitates civil strife and the emergence of iconography associated with the white supremacist organization, the Ku Klux Klan.

The very presence of blacks in their community results in the reversion of the South Park natives to the visual forms of a racist past through their use of bed sheets to appear as ghosts. Yet the competition for racial dominance—the effort to turn ethnic majority to minority and vice versa—is never articulated as racist until the final moment of the episode. With Oprah, Will Smith, and their friends having left, Mr. Garrison finally emits the epithet, "Nigger," the unstated potent slur organizing the tension of the entire episode (the slur itself notably is truncated as the program cuts him off in midphrase). This brings into question the exact quality of racial tension in "Here Comes the Neighborhood." The appearance of the townspeople in hoods only has racial resonance for the viewer. The townspeople and the millionaires alike respond to the hooded figures as specters, Snoop Dogg castigating Will Smith for not informing him the town is "hainted." So, too, when the hoods are removed, the sheets are treated as theatrical props lacking entirely the reverence and secrecy of Klan gowns. New epithets are invented for the millionaires by the dependably racist Mr. Garrison who coins terms such as "cash-chucker" and "richer" as apparent substitutes for "spear-chucker" and "nigger." Yet Mr. Garrison's conscious manipulation of the townspeople's insecurities, exposed in the final moment of the episode, is ultimately revealed to rest upon a bedrock of both racism and what may be considered nativism.

"Nativism" refers to the notion of a national character intrinsic to those born within a particular geographic region (Knobel 2). American nativism is the nationalistic conception of an American ethnicity—or culture—from which immigrants are inherently excluded. The stance of the South Park residents may be typified as nativist, rather than purely racist. A South Park native, in the minds of the townspeople, cannot be excessively wealthy. It is not a part of their shared values. As such, the millionaires are unwelcome aliens in opposition to the South Park nativist concept of regional character. They are also not of their "blood." A kind of racism is here effected, inasmuch as it is based in notions of biological prerogative. This then stands as the ultimate historicist/mystical rhetoric in the marginalize/countermarginalize dichotomy. When threatened by a geographically and economically pervasive alternate assimilation movement such as that posed by the millionaires, nativists reach into the most profound depths of their identity arsenal to create a profile of the normative that verges on the mythic. Yet, despite the profound social energy behind it, it is a racist project that may easily be frustrated. This is illustrated by Parker and Stone in "The Jeffersons."

At the episode's beginning, the children come across a masked child named Blanket. He is the only son of Mr. Jefferson, a clear proxy for Michael Jackson. Unlike the arrival of the millionaires in "Here Comes the Neighborhood," no narrative point is made of his arrival to the town. He arrives unheralded and, until Blanket reveals otherwise, is presumed to be a naturalized South Park resident. Mr. Jefferson's introduction is done in very much the same way that Token is introduced to the series: He was not present in the series, and then, suddenly, he simply becomes one of series' minor characters. Token appeared as if he were a product of the town itself, a naturalized manifestation of its tokenistic interests. So, too, does Jefferson appear. Unlike Token, however, Jefferson does not immediately seem tokenistic in his appearance. While the audience of course recognizes Jefferson to be a thinly veiled parody of Michael Jackson, an African American, the townspeople have no notion of this. They are simply presented with a man of indeterminate age and of seemingly Caucasian racial background. He thus is cautiously accepted, despite the fact that his naturalization has not been a process visible to the townspeople. However, Jefferson quickly betrays his racial background through his politics. He exposes himself as being not of "common blood."

During a dinner at the Marshes, casual conversation leads to speculation on the guilt of black athlete Kobe Bryant in his rape trial. Although not focusing on Bryant's race, they do focus on his wealth and, following the historical nativist notion of "common blood," essentially intimate that he is not of their symbolic lineage. Butters's father remarks, "I think he's definitely going to jail. I just love seeing smug celebrities get their comeuppance." Jefferson is horrified. Mr. Broflovski, a religious minority in his own right, interjects, "Oh, come on, Mr. Jefferson, you're not one of those who think[s] the police go around framing rich, black people because they're jealous?" Clearly hoping to bridge the sudden lack of "common blood" evident in the discussion, the Jewish, semiassimilated lawyer hopes to aid a seeming social desirable in his further naturalization. Yet the divide is clear between the politics of the nativists and that of the invader. On the one side are the liberals, exemplified by Broflovski, believing in impartiality and due process; on the other side is the knee-jerk defensiveness of the black community, which Jefferson exemplifies. Ostentatious talent, wealth, and ethnic blood are evidently the cultural characteristics of an alien social type in an increasingly insular, nationalist United States and *South Park* highlights the disciplinary mechanisms that keep minorities "in their place."

Parker and Stone clearly point to the police as the disciplinary mechanism buffering the "common blood" nativists from polluting presence of alien others. This is demonstrated in the most intriguing direct narrative interrogation of race relations yet on *South Park*. Police detective Hicks is informed of a wealthy newcomer to South Park: Jefferson. Hicks is uninterested in Jefferson until informed that the latter is black. The combination of wealth, blackness, and presumable talent is too much for the lower-middle-class Hicks. Here, *South Park* satirically reverses the racism inherent in racial profiling by stereotyping the stereotypers. In the eyes of the stereotypically racist police, an individual's blackness is the sole evidence needed not to consider him the suspect of a crime, but make him its patsy. The officer's assessment of all wealthy black men as being dangerous to the nativist society is shown to be as reductive as a social paradigm that allows for the existence of the notion of the white lawmaker as sole protector of decency. Effectively, the police will protect nativist interests in a project that reduces their own racial profile to its most embarrassingly dated notions.

They proceed to plant evidence for a broad spectrum of potential crimes, including spattering blood from a potential murder victim and planting female pubic hair from a potential rape victim. The scenario is clearly designed to recreate the details of the O. J. Simpson murder trial. Indeed, Sergeant Hicks evokes that instance of racist police procedure almost immediately. "It seems like every time we frame a rich black guy he's out on the streets again in no time. It's just like O. J. Do you know how hard those cops worked to frame him? The tireless hours they put in, and then he gets off because somebody messed up and said the 'n' word out loud too many times," a dismayed Hicks exclaims. As noted in the PBS Frontline documentary "The O. J. Verdict—10 Years On," in the eyes of many, the Simpson case and its verdict had more to do with race than with the guilt or innocence of the specific perpetrator. A wealthy black man, within the context of that trial, came to represent the racial profiling to which many African Americans feel themselves subject. Effectively, Detective Furhman's racism in the O. J. case, his eagerness to protect nativist interests, was of greater importance to the U.S. television audience than the question of Simpson's guilt or innocence. In fact, in "The O. J. Verdict," an African-American shopowner explains, "they framed a guilty man." In the *South Park* episode, Hicks is cast in the role of Furhman, and Jefferson's wealth takes precedence in the eyes of the police and the community over his ill treatment of his son, Blanket.

The real irony is that Jefferson himself does not appear to be black. Like Jackson, his appearance and manner do not conform to any specific racial stereotypes. His speech is childlike and his visage androgynous and ageless. His accent, like Token's, is neutral and geographically unplaceable. And his skin is only a slightly darker shade of the cartoonish white of most South Park residents. On discovering that Jefferson does not physically register, Detective Hicks, who has already expressed some confusion about why he and other policemen have "such a passion for framing wealthy African Americans for crimes they didn't commit," vomits. The implication of this is simple: The functional racism instilled by nativist hegemony in its vassals, the police, is determined by three factors—blackness, talent, and wealth. Removing one of these elements not only disables the police from considering wealthy blacks as aliens, but undermines their conceptions of self and other.

Hicks remains impotent until he discovers that, whereas Jefferson may not appear black, his racial background confirms his actual status as a "blood" alien. Reinvigorated, he rushes to Jefferson's house to arrest him. But the moralistic Kyle, like his father, has attempted to form a bridge between the nativists and the alien. Jefferson, enlightened by Kyle on the loneliness of Blanket, agrees to give up his wealth. In the final moments of the episode, Hicks' racially inflected nativist project is thwarted completely. Although he manages to certify Jefferson's fulfillment of the three elements needed for police harassment, Jefferson has now renounced his wealth, and he now fails to fulfill the criteria necessary to activate Hicks' compulsive racist profiling. So too does his abdication of wealth destroy the dualistic oppression of the essentialist project. Not only does Hicks discover that he cannot execute the persecution of his office, but he also finds himself temporarily liberated from the patriarchal pressures of his profession. Both Jefferson and Hicks end the episode as men capable of reinvention and self-expression.

Jefferson virtually announces his alien aspect at the Marshes' dinner and is only saved by his renunciation of a part of this "profile." However, another naturalized alien lives in South Park: Kyle's brother Ike. He, in contrast to Jefferson, is a toddler and unable consciously to negotiate his identity. As his immediate kin, Kyle, and the rest of South Park by association, assumes Ike to be a natural-born citizen of South Park. This is not the case. Ike is adopted and of Canadian descent, as is revealed in "Ike's Wee Wee." Although the South Park children only discover Ike's national background in this episode, this feature has been signaled from the start of the series by the stylistic depiction of Ike. Unlike the ovular, smooth animation of naturalized South Park residents, Ike is depicted more symmetrically with a floating upper head bisected from the lower portion of his head. In this way, he exhibits the more grotesque characteristics found in those who are not native U.S. citizens. Jay Leno, for example, is depicted as a grotesque caricature. His chin literally reaches to his feet. Oprah also is depicted swollen like a giant balloon. However, until Kyle's parents explain Ike's original parentage, it never occurs to Kyle that his brother is of an alien physical type. This discovery plunges Kyle into his own knee-jerk nativist stance. After struggling with this fact of an alien existing in his own domestic sphere, Kyle eventually realizes that his love for his brother will conquer any assimilative demands he may make on Ike. Although the narrative for "Ike's Wee Wee" is a simple story of filial love conquering prejudice, Parker and Stone clearly wish to illustrate the highly socialized, conditioned aspects of what defines American identity. Just as Mr. Jefferson is a recluse, so Ike is a young child barely able to interact with Kyle and the others around him. Only the normative necessities of South Park society and, in turn, American society, require that either define themselves.

By virtue of their simple geographic presence in a given community and the thwarted presumption of their native character, they must justify their right to belong.

Although Parker and Stone satirize the powerful, the hypocritical, and the stridently bigoted, they do not provide solutions to society's problems or provide the keys to social harmony. However, through their characterizations and narratives, they illustrate the potential for positive outcomes to emerge from racial and ethnic tension. The Broflovskis are a kind, generous family always willing to mediate racial or ethnic disputes. Their liberalism and piety translate positively in their immediate socioracial environment and is instantiated in their adoption of Ike. Their politics make them, like the Williams, bridge builders in a fragmented society. In addition, *South Park* reveals assimilation to be a multivalent process. Factors such as political momentum and social utility can easily influence assimilation's precise tone.

Ultimately, these processes of liberal bridge building and relative assimilation will come to be of increasing importance not just in the world of *South Park*, but in the world at large as the racial and religious tensions of the War on Terror continue to mount. If the fictional realm can be seen as the first stage for social experimentation and appropriation, then the relative reception of assimilation narratives should give the viewers of *South Park* some notion of where the United States' social future lies. One can only hope that this spirit of generosity and open-mindedness will translate into the wider, real-world community.

Works Cited

Alda, Richard D. "Assimilation's Quiet Tide." *Race and Ethnicity in the United States*. Ed. Stephen Steinberg. Malden, MA: Blackwell, 2000. 211–22.

Dines, Gail, and Jean M. Humez, eds. *Gender, Race, and Class in Media: A Text-Reader*. Thousand Oaks, CA: Sage, 2002.

Knobel, Dale T. *America for Americans: The Nativist Movement in the United States*. New York: Twayne, 1997.

"The O. J. Verdict—10 Years On." *Frontline*. PBS. New York. 4 Oct. 2005.

PART THREE

South Park Conservatives?

CHAPTER 8

"I Hate Hippies"

South Park and the Politics of Generation X

MATT BECKER

In 2001 Internet blogger Andrew Sullivan suggested that *South Park* leaned to the political right when he coined the term "South Park Republicans." According to Sullivan, the cartoon series offers a new formulation of Republicanism that is particularly attractive to the show's typically younger viewers, in which traditional conservative Republican views, such as robust faith in the free market, combine with socially liberal attitudes toward certain issues, such as homosexuality (Sullivan). In his 2005 book, *South Park Conservatives: The Revolt Against Liberal Media Bias*, Brian C. Anderson expands on Sullivan's ideas to argue that the cartoon criticizes what Anderson considers the political left's hypocrisy and knee-jerk political correctness (PC). For Anderson, *South Park*'s "antiliberalism" represents a paradigm shift in which a new right-leaning media bloc that includes talk radio, cable news programs, Internet blogs, and shows such as *South Park* has emerged to challenge the dominance and influence of the mainstream left-liberal media establishment. As such, Anderson considers *South Park* a sign that the right is gaining ground in the "culture wars"—the supposed polarization of U.S. society since the 1960s into right and left camps over hot-button cultural issues such as homosexuality, racism, abortion, censorship, and television content.

No doubt *South Park* satirizes issues commonly associated with contemporary left-liberal politics. In the 1999 episode "Rainforest Schmainforest," for instance, the show's 8-year-old main characters—Stan, Kyle, Cartman, and Kenny—go on a school field trip with an environmental activist teacher to Costa Rica to learn about human threats to the rainforest. Yet by the end of the show the boys conclude that environmental activists do not really know or care about the rainforest and, instead, exploit its threatened destruction for personal gain. Along with hypocritical environmentalists, *South Park* also frequently mocks what Anderson calls "other shibboleths of Left," including celebrities associated with left-liberal politics, hate-crime laws, and sexual harassment policies (xiv). In these ways, the show can indeed be read as "antiliberal."

But *South Park* also routinely lampoons issues commonly associated with contemporary right-wing conservatives, such as zealous gun owners, Ayn Rand followers, and the Religious Right. In "Starvin' Marvin in Space," for example, American missionaries use food to bribe starving Africans into adopting Christianity. An African boy who the *South Park* kids call Marvin rejects these ploys as corrupt, and when he finds an abandoned spaceship outside his village, he searches the universe for a planet free of missionaries to relocate his people. The leader of the "600 Club" (an allusion to televangelist Pat Robertson and his "700 Club") learns that Marvin, with the aid of the *South Park* boys, has discovered such a place and shamelessly asks his followers for money to buy space travel equipment to bring Christianity to the aliens of this planet. Kyle warns the aliens, however, that their society will be destroyed if they accept the Christianity of the missionaries and the 600 Club.

South Park therefore has both antiliberal and anticonservative themes. Anderson, however, only briefly mentions that conservatives "do not escape the show's satirical sword" and presents plot summaries and dialogue solely from episodes with a more obviously antiliberal tilt to support his claim that *South Park* is "the most hostile [show] to liberalism in television history" (88). He also downplays the show's excessive vulgarity and blasphemy—two of *South Park*'s trademark qualities—which transgress the parameters of conservative political correctness and have thus raised the ire of critics such as L. Brent Bozell III, president of the right-leaning Parents Television Council, who calls the show "filth" and "toxic sewage" (Bozell). And, although *South Park* mocks all types of political correctness, it is equally critical of homophobia, sexism, and racism. Indeed, if *South Park* suggests a coming conservative triumph in the culture wars, as Anderson proposes (xv), then conservatives have ceded much of the cultural territory they once considered crucial to victory in these wars.

With roots in the cultural upheavals of the 1960s, the culture wars began to heat up in the United States during the 1980s with the ascendancy to national political power of the conservative New Right coalition with Ronald Reagan as its figurehead. Since that time, ideological worldviews have superseded older determinates of political group cohesion, such as religion, ethnicity, and social class. Increasingly, both the right and the left have held that the contours of American culture—shaped by what is taught in public schools, for instance, or who society officially sanctions to marry—are integral to the definition of U.S. nationhood and citizenship. For conservatives such as Anderson, the left has controlled a powerful medium in this shaping: the mass media. "Conservatives have long lamented the Left's near monopoly over the institutions of opinion and information," he writes, which has allowed "liberal opinion-makers to present their views as rock-solid truth and to sweep aside ideas and beliefs they don't like as unworthy of argument" (ix). The "liberal media," he continues, "have an all-but-monolithic power to set the terms of the nation's political and cultural debate" (x). *South Park*, he concludes, is thus important not only because it is supposedly part of a larger right-leaning media paradigm shift that will soon challenge this liberal media dominance, but also because the show's popularity among young audiences suggests that it reflects powerful antiliberal—and thus from Anderson's perspective pro-conservative—attitudes among a large percentage (and perhaps a majority) of new and soon-to-be voters.

To strengthen his argument, Anderson quotes *South Park*'s youthful creators, Trey Parker and Matt Stone, who were in their 20s when they began the show. At first glance, Parker and Stone do, indeed, seem right-leaning. Stone, for example, declares, "I hate conservatives, but I really fucking hate liberals" (qtd. in Anderson 75–76), while Parker contends, "we avoid extremes but we hate liberals more than conservatives, and we hate them" (Anderson 178). Yet, as with the show's vulgarity and blasphemy, Anderson downplays statements by Parker and Stone that complicate their supposedly conservative worldviews. The preceding statements, for instance, reveal that although Stone and Parker hate liberals more than conservatives, they nevertheless also hate conservatives. In fact, Parker and Stone have consistently expressed antipathy toward extremes on the left *and* the right throughout the show's history. When questioned about the term "South Park Republicans" in 2004, Parker maintained of himself and Stone, "[W]e're both just pretty middle-ground guys. We find just as many things to rip on the left as we do on the right. People on the far left and the far right are the same exact person to us" ("Interview"). Further still, Stone and Parker have routinely indicated an aversion to politics altogether. Less than a year after *South Park* premiered, Stone dismissed claims of the show's anti–PC agenda—a key premise for Anderson's antiliberal thesis—noting, "I don't give a shit about being PC or anti–PC. [. . .] We're not out to make statements" (Lim). He also confessed in 2001, "I don't think I'm registered to vote" (Brownfield) and declared in 2004, "there's no shame in not voting" (Wild 68). *South Park*, therefore, leans neither reliably right nor left and, instead, represents the attitudes of a "generation that's almost post-political" (Wild 68).

This chapter argues that the political worldview of *South Park* is consistent with that of Generation X, the birth cohort to which Parker and Stone belong. Rather than adherents of one political worldview or another, members of Generation X are characterized by irony, apathy, feelings of disenfranchisement, and deep cynicism toward official political institutions. *South Park* is therefore not simply antiliberal, nor anticonservative, but antipolitical—a sensibility that Anderson chooses to read only in terms that support his own political views. In addition, Gen Xers are typified by a generational worldview deeply influenced by popular culture, a dislike of 1960s radical youth culture, a leeriness of social formations such as the family, and a hesitation to assume responsibilities and roles associated with the "adult" world.[1] Through an analysis of key themes, characters, and episodes, this chapter demonstrates how all of these Gen X qualities inform the political themes of *South Park*, as well as the show's general sensibility.

"A Couple of Slackers"

South Park's creators embody key characteristics of Gen Xers. The birth years of Parker and Stone, 1969 and 1971, respectively, fall within those that bookend Generation X, the mid-1960s to the early 1980s. The children of professionals, the two grew up in mostly white, affluent Denver suburbs and were "from good families," notes Parker, and "had good upbringings" (qts. in Vincent). As Stone puts it, "Trey's mom is as close to June Cleaver as you can get" (qtd. in Span). They met in an introductory film production course at the University of Colorado at Boulder, where they bonded over their mutual dislike of class expectations. "We were basically the two guys who didn't want to make black-and-white lesbian art films," recalls Stone (qtd. in Kronke). They instead began to work with crude construction-paper animation and produced the film short, *The Spirit of Christmas* (1995), which introduced the main child characters and bawdy humor that would eventually become *South Park*. In these ways, Parker and Stone correspond with popular stereotypes of Gen Xers as white, middle-class youth raised in the conformity of affluent suburbia, who attend college and respect knowledge but who are nevertheless nonconventional and wary of educational institutions.

After college, the two explored nontraditional career paths and spent several years in low-wage employment as they searched for meaningful work—another common experience among Gen Xers that scholars link to trends of downward mobility that began in the 1970s (Hanson; Moore). Although Stone graduated with a mathematics degree (Parker was expelled in his senior year because he cut classes), he did not pursue a career related to this field. Instead, he and Parker went to Los Angeles, where they spent nearly two years working as landscapers and production assistants while they shopped their television and film projects (Span). In 1995 an executive for FOX studios saw *The Spirit of Christmas* and gave them $1,200 to remake it for a holiday video card for his industry friends (Goldman; Snead). The animated short became an underground bootleg phenomenon and eventually attracted the attention of Comedy Central. The cable channel struck a deal with Parker and Stone to develop a 30–minute cartoon series, with the two retaining the rights to executive produce, write, voice, animate, and score the show, power unheard of for youthful creators with no prior television experience (Goldman).

South Park was an immediate success and quickly attained the highest ratings in Comedy Central's history. Within its first few airings, the rating jumped from 1.3 to 1.6, with the 1997 Halloween episode pulling a 3.8—large numbers for cable television, although small for broadcast standards (Span). Along with continued high ratings, over the years the show has generated a wealth of associated merchandise and a devout fan base (Marin, Gegax, Rosenberg, Rhodes, Gill, and Angell). It has also been nominated for several prestigious awards and won an Emmy Award in 2005 and a Peabody Award in 2006 (*South Park*). In addition to the television series, Parker and Stone have written and directed several films, including the Academy Award–nominated *South Park: Bigger Longer & Uncut* (1999).

What explains such success for a show that has been described as "*Peanuts* on acid"? (Lim). A key reason is that the show's unique production techniques enable it to be remarkably topical. Because it is computer animated, an episode can be completed from start to finish in less than a week, and changes can be made as late as the night before it premiers. The extraordinary autonomy Parker and Stone enjoy in the creation of its content also means they do not need outside approval for their ideas (Justin). As a result, *South Park* is able to respond to current events virtually in real time. For example, with the 2006 controversy over the depiction of Mohammed in Danish cartoons still in the headlines, Parker and Stone produced "Cartoon Wars," parts 1 and 2, which showed a picture of the prophet that Comedy Central ultimately blacked out over fears it would incite further violence. This topicality is one reason some commentators view *South Park* as uncommonly reflective of the U.S. national consciousness. Nick Gillespie of *Reason* magazine suggests as much when he argues, "I suspect that *South Park* will prove every bit as long-lived in the American subconscious as Mark Twain's Hannibal, Missouri, or Laura Ingalls Wilder's prairie" (Walker and Gillespie). But this topicality also reflects the personal reactions of the show's creators to current events and thus provides insight into the worldviews of two prominent Gen Xers.

Indeed, according to Parker and Stone, *South Park* is produced from a particular generational viewpoint. In response to parents, schools, and public interest groups who argue that the cartoon's characteristic vulgarity negatively influences children, the two have routinely insisted that "it's not a children's show," as a then-29-year-old Parker put it in 1998, who emphasized his point by noting "the show is on at 10 o'clock at night" and that he and Stone "have refused all offers for merchandizing aimed at kids," including "our T–shirts," which are all "in adult sizes" (qtd. in Vincent). Rather, as a then-28-year-old Stone explained during that same year, "we're not making the show for kids; we're making the show for people our age" (qtd. in Aucoin). To describe this age, articles on Parker and Stone frequently evoke a Gen X identity. One 1997 *USA Today* article, for instance, called the two "slackers," a term that became synonymous with Generation X vis-à-vis director Richard Linklater's 1991 film *Slacker*, which documents the aimless lifestyles of underemployed and overeducated youth in Austin, Texas (Snead). The two also use this term for themselves, such as when Parker described the 1998 film *BASEketball*, in which he and Stone starred, as "the story of a couple of slackers. [. . .] Kind of like us" (qtd. in Rubin). And, at least in the late 1990s, the show's core audience was indeed comprised primarily of "people [their] age," and thus of fellow Gen Xers. As *Newsweek* noted in 1998, almost "60 percent of [the viewers] are 18 to 34" and characterized by "Generation X's [short] attention span" (Marin et al.).

That *South Park* is made by and for Gen Xers is demonstrated by one of its central sources of humor, breaking taboos of contemporary U.S. society. A primary approach of the show is "pushing [. . .] stereotypes," explains Parker, especially those that are controversial in contemporary America (qtd. in Kronke). The only black child who appears regularly is named "Token," for instance, and stereotypes of his race are referenced for comedic effect. Hence, in "Christian Hard Rock," when Token declines to play bass in Cartman's band because he has never played the instrument, Cartman counters: "Token, how many times do we have to go through this? You're black. You can play bass." Token angrily responds that he is tired of Cartman's stereotypes, but when Token picks up the instrument he can play like a professional. This willingness to exploit controversial stereotypes as a source of humor is one key reason conservative pundits such as Anderson laud *South Park* as anti–PC (76). But this willingness to break taboos around topics that are currently sensitive, such as racial stereotypes, also reveals Parker and Stone's generational perspective. For, although comedians from Shakespearian jesters to Richard Pryor have transgressed subjects proscribed by their respective societies as a means of comedy, not until the 1960s did influences such as the civil rights movement and feminism generate social norms pervasive enough to render stereotypes about race or gender (or similar identity traits) broadly taboo. Born in the late 1960s and early 1970s, for their entire lives Parker and Stone have understood these stereotypes as among the most potent taboos in American society and thus the most sacred of cows to satirize.

Popular Culture as Friend and Foe

South Park's Gen X sensibility is also revealed in the show's constant references to popular culture. As adolescents and preadolescents of the 1970s and

1980s, Gen Xers experienced changes and trends in mass media that affected television, films, and popular music both qualitatively and quantitatively. Unprecedented news coverage of the American War in Vietnam, socially relevant sitcoms like *All in the Family*, celebrity-centered "infotainment" programs such as *Entertainment Tonight*, and the explosion of cable were just some of the revolutions in television during these years. In film, "New Hollywood" offered innovative motion pictures that ranged from the radically left *Easy Rider* (1969) to the quirky *Harold and Maude* (1972) to the edgy *Taxi Driver* (1976) to the blockbusters *Jaws* (1975) and *Star Wars* (1977). Meanwhile, the proliferation of the video cassette recorder introduced an entire generation to a vast film library that they could now pause, rewind, and watch repeatedly in their living rooms. And in popular music, the "golden age" of FM radio in the 1970s gave way to the predominance of music videos in the 1980s. As a result of these changes and trends, Generation X developed a deeply symbiotic relationship with mass media that is suggested in the frequent, knowing, and often esoteric popular culture references that permeate its television, films, and music. In *South Park*, for instance, popular culture references abound and range from the commonplace (for example, *America's Funniest Home Videos*, Pokémon) to the more obscure (for example, the 1974 Rankin-Bass Christmas special, "T'was the Night before Christmas" and the fifth season of the 1980s sitcom *Night Court*).

Many of the popular culture references in *South Park* seem obscure because, like the Rankin-Bass and *Night Court* allusions, they refer to popular culture of the 1970s and 1980s. For example, the kids sing songs by musical acts such as Lou Rawls, Styx, Asia, and MC Hammer; their teacher Mr. Garrison refer to television shows such as *Barnaby Jones* and *The Love Boat*; and other icons from these decades (for example, skater Brian Boitano, Trapper Keepers, *Tic-Tac-Throw*) are prominently featured. These references play on Generation X knowledge and suggest that Parker and Stone indeed aim much of the show's content at people their own age who share aspects of their background. In this way, *South Park* is similar to other Gen X-produced popular culture, such as the films of Quentin Tarantino. In fact, just as Tarantino has employed actors such as John Travolta who were at the height of their popularity in the 1970s, the *South Park* character Chef was, until the 2006 season, voiced by musician Isaac Hayes, who rose to fame with his theme song for the 1971 blaxploitation film *Shaft*.

Informed by their symbiotic relationship with mass media, Gen X popular culture often takes an ambivalent approach to America's contemporary obsession with celebrity. While this obsession has a much longer history, in the past several decades it has taken new forms. The explosion of "infotainment" since the 1980s, in which famous stars comprise the news, has, on the one hand, helped reinforce an aura of glamour around celebrity. Yet, on the other, shows such as *Entertainment Tonight* also expose the trade secrets that make this glamour possible, as well as reveal the existence of turmoil in the personal lives of stars, both of which make celebrities seem "more human." And beginning in the 1990s, talk shows such as *The Jerry Springer Show* and reality television programs such as *Survivor* have helped create instant celebrities out of everyday people. Thus, films made by Gen Xers like *The Truman Show* (1998) and *Being John Malkovich* (1999) blur the lines between celebrity and everyday people, an approach that also informs *South Park*. Mr. Garrison, for instance, often lectures his class on entertainment industry topics in a straightforward manner normally reserved for such staid school subjects as biology and grammar. Additionally, much of the humor in *South Park*'s attacks on celebrities is based on their decidedly unglamorous personal quirks. Hence, in the two Starvin' Marvin episodes, the corpulence of *All in the Family* alum Sally Struthers is shown as discordant with her role as a famine relief spokesperson, and both Mel Gibson and Barbra Streisand are shown as egomaniacal and intolerant in "The Passion of the Jew" and "Mecha Streisand."

In keeping with their antipathy toward political extremes, Parker and Stone mock celebrities who use their fame and power to preach a hard-line sociopolitical worldview, whether from the left or the right. Thus, in "Butt Out," Rob Reiner, who is associated with the political left, is shown as an uncompromising and arrogant antismoking advocate, while in "The Passion of the Jew," Mel Gibson, who is associated with the political right, tells Stan and Kenny, who disliked his film *The Passion of the Christ* (2004), "You can't say my movie sucked, or else you're saying Christianity sucked!" Indeed, although Stone claims that he and Parker are "more right-wing than most people in Hollywood," he also explains, "to say that you're more right-wing than most people [in Hollywood] doesn't mean a whole lot because they're pretty left-wing," and he also adds, "I don't subscribe to either political ticket" (R. Owen).

Parker and Stone's weariness of politicized celebrity reveals a broader Gen X attitude toward the political roles and possibilities of popular culture, which, like politics in general, this generation views with disaffection and cynicism. Coming of age in a media-saturated environment characterized by unprecedented target marketing and product placement, Gen Xers are keenly aware of popular culture as a commodity, and thus that any political message it may communicate, whether overtly or covertly, is complicated and even compromised (Oake). As a result, they differ from their 1960s counterparts, who were more inclined to celebrate popular culture as a less corrupted source of political inspiration (Starr). Along with *South Park*, this generational difference was apparent at the 1999 Woodstock festival, a franchised version of the 1969 Woodstock festival that was sold to Gen Xers as an update of the original. But whereas the original "offered messages of love, hope, and communal possibilities," explained one *New York Daily News* article, against a backdrop of overpriced refreshments, ubiquitous credit card come-ons, and violent rioting, the 1999 simulacrum "specialized in defeat, anger, and isolation," with even the "one group sharing the lefty politics of the '60s," Rage against the Machine, delivering "its message with enough intolerance to impress the most accomplished fascist" (Farber).

South Park and Contemporary U.S. Political Ideologies

South Park suggests that one reason Gen Xers are weary of the politics of popular culture is that this generation considers this amalgamation of politics and popular culture a reason for the failure of 1960s' youth to effect broader social change. Thus, in "Die Hippie, Die" contemporary hippies bring a musical festival to the town of South Park to help raise consciousness about the collusion of corporations with the military. Yet, instead of addressing this issue, the hippies spend most of the time partying and talk only vaguely of a utopian society. The townspeople, who initially welcomed the newcomers, quickly find they are being overwhelmed by hippies and plot to drive them away. Similarly, Stan and Kyle, who at first sympathized with the hippies, eventually reject them as foolish. This episode therefore contends that the hippie counterculture's "politics of pot and rock" (Starr) creates only a hazy left-liberal politics that is ultimately ineffectual.

Such satirizing of the 1960s' left-liberal youth culture is frequent in South Park, and it speaks to a broader antipathy among Gen Xers toward the baby boom generation. The baby boomers were born during a period of high birthrates from the late 1940s to the early 1960s and comprise a massive generational cohort (around 75 million). As children, they were affected by fears of communism, tremendous affluence, suburban quiescence, racial segregation, rigid gender and sexual norms, and other characteristics of the post–World War II consensus culture (Hodgson). As they came of age in the 1960s, highly visible, predominately white and middle-class segments of the baby boomer generation began to rebel against what they saw as oppressive and repressive elements in this consensus culture. Hence, radical student groups such as Students for a Democratic Society joined with black civil rights workers to end southern racial segregation through voter registration drives, whereas the hippie counterculture hoped to effect change through radical cultural politics, such as countering status quo sexual mores with an ethos of free love. Unlike the baby boomers, the much smaller birth cohort of Generation X matured during a period of economic decline, high rates of unemployment and divorce, the onset of the AIDS epidemic, massive military expansion, and the dismantling of domestic programs designed to help youth and other vulnerable populations. For Gen Xers, the harsh environment of Reagan's America in which they matured suggested that left-liberal politics of 1960s youth had not only failed, but were possibly responsible for this harsh environment. Did the rising divorce rate of the 1980s, for instance, relate to the loosening of sexual mores and gender norms during the 1960s? Worse still, as the baby boomers aged, many seemed to embrace materialism and other values that they had condemned in their youth. Little wonder that one writer describes Parker and Stone as representative of a generation that is "as suspicious of hippie arrogance as they are amused by rampant youthful ignorance" (Wild 68).

This disdain for 1960s' youth culture is common in the popular culture generated by Generation X. At the beginning of *Reality Bites* (1994), perhaps the most emblematic Gen X Hollywood film, a main character muses in her valedictory address: "And they wonder why those of us in our twenties [. . .] aren't interested in the counterculture that they invented, as if we did not see them disembowel their revolution for a pair of running shoes." In *South Park*, hostility toward 1960s' youth culture, namely hippies, is expressed most vehemently by Cartman. His hatred of them is, in fact, a running gag. Cartman routinely derides other kids as "hippie" and has nightmares about hippies. In "Die Hippie, Die," he is portrayed as an exterminator of hippies who is the only one in town that instantly recognizes the threat these "parasites" pose. Cartman despises hippie traits (for example, hygiene customs, fashions) and values (for example, environmentalism, nonviolence). And like many Gen Xers, he abhors them as deeply hypocritical. Thus, in "Cartman's Silly Hate Crime 2000," when a lawyer accuses him of hating African Americans, Cartman responds, "No! I hate hippies! [. . .] I mean, the way they always talk about 'protectin' the earth' and then drive around in cars that get poor gas mileage and wear those stupid bracelets—I *hate* 'em! I wanna kick 'em in the nuts!"

Cartman's hostility toward hippies is representative not only of Gen Xers, however, but also of right-conservatives. Indeed, he verbalizes a broader backlash against the 1960s that has been championed by several right-conservative luminaries, ranging from George Wallace and Ronald Reagan to Rush Limbaugh and Bill O'Reilly. At the center of this backlash is a desire to restore a "traditional" American way of life that was supposedly disrupted in the 1960s by radical youth, African Americans, feminists, and other New Social movements when they challenged law-and-order policies, racial hierarchies, sexual mores, and gender norms. Not surprisingly, backlash politics appeal particularly to white males, who perceive these challenges as attacks on their social status. And because blatant racism, sexism, and homophobia are now considered vulgar in official culture (as Anderson might put it, because PC has prevailed), this backlash is often directed at the "big government" of the supposedly activist liberal state that facilitated the success of these challenges and continues to encourage them.

In the 1970s, the quintessential backlash stereotype was *All in the Family*'s Archie Bunker, whose belligerent racism, anti-Semitism, and open hostility toward feminists, homosexuals, and hippies was provocative, offensive, funny, and, for some, admirable. Parker and Stone looked to this character when they created Cartman, who they describe as a "misguided Archie Bunker" (qtd. in Bianculli). Like Bunker, Cartman is vigorously anti-Semitic and chauvinistic. He takes racial stereotypes at face value and, along with the other *South Park* kids, uses the term "gay" disparagingly. And, of course, he hates hippies. Yet, just as television producer Norman Lear, who created *All in the Family*, envisioned Bunker as a critique of such cultural narrow-mindedness (whether viewers actually interpreted him as such), Parker explains that *South Park* "is racist in the same way that Archie Bunker was racist [. . . it is] inhabited by stupid people, and stupid people say stupid things" (Rubin), and Stone calls Cartman "a racist bastard" (Lim). Thus, while the show lampoons policies that could be considered PC, its most anti–PC character is usually portrayed negatively.

Indeed, *South Park* strongly emphasizes tolerance of identity issues in episodes such as "Big Gay Al's Big Gay Boat Ride," "Conjoined Fetus Lady," "Chef Goes Nanners," "Ginger Kids," and "Cartman Sucks." In fact, because of its positive portrayals of homosexuality, the show was nominated for an award by the Gay and Lesbian Alliance Against Defamation (Lim). Similarly, episodes such as "Mr. Hankey, the Christmas Poo" and "Jewbilee" explore religious exclusion, whereas characters like the wheelchair bound, autistic Timmy are considered by the kids as just part of the group: "We think of Timmy and the boys think of Timmy as a full-fledged human being," notes Stone (*South Park*, season 4). *South Park* frequently suggests that discrimination against minority groups can lead to situations that create greater tolerance. Thus, in "Cripple Fight," when several dads complain to the Boy Scout council that their sons' troop leader is the openly homosexual character Big Gay Al, he is dismissed from the organization. But when his heterosexual replacement is revealed as a child molester, the dads realize that they have unfairly stereotyped Al because of his homosexuality. *South Park's* tolerance of identity issues reflects a similar tolerant attitude among Gen Xers who, along with the baby boomers, are generally more supportive of the idea of racial equality and more open-minded toward alternative lifestyles, such as homosexuality, than previous generations (Hill 122).

Yet, although *South Park* is tolerant of diversity, it is deeply suspicious of institutions that compel acceptance. Hence, in "Cripple Fight," after a court rules that the Boy Scouts must allow homosexuals, Big Gay Al explains that if he can freely express his sexuality, then the Boy Scouts can freely express their opposition to it, and that it is better to persuade, rather than force, the organization to change. In "The Death Camp of Tolerance," perhaps the show's strongest assault on institutionally-compelled acceptance, the kids complain of Mr. Garrison's homosexual behaviors during class (he hopes to provoke the school into firing him so that he can sue). The parents interpret these complaints as homophobia and send the kids to sensitivity training, which includes internment in a Nazi-like "tolerance camp" where they are forced to accept diversity. When the parents and the school attempt to give Mr. Garrison an award for coming out as gay, he chides that while tolerance is appropriate, forced acceptance is not. By mocking institutionally compelled acceptance, *South Park* derides contemporary liberalism's view that government action is both necessary and appropriate to promote equality.

But *South Park* is also disdainful of contemporary conservatism's view that government action is both necessary and appropriate to promote order based on a specific moral worldview. Thus, a persistent subtext in "Kenny Dies" is that banning stem-cell research on moral grounds shackles research that could cure disease, while in "Cartman Sucks" antihomosexual reeducation efforts by religious conservatives cause children to commit suicide. And in "Best Friends Forever," when Kenny enters a permanent vegetative state and is summoned by God to defend the universe from Satan's armies, a feeding tube keeps him both artificially alive and from his divine duty. When the tube is removed by court order, Satan's henchman vows to get the tube reinserted by doing "what we always do [to enact our plans]: Use the Republicans." Accordingly, the henchman is shown whispering into George W. Bush's ear directives such as, "It is God's will that he [Kenny] live," which the president then parrots at a White House news conference. Eventually Kenny is allowed to die and, in turn, save the universe. Such episodes deride the use of government to enforce a narrowly defined "right-to-life" moral agenda presented as representative of "God's will," a tactic predominately associated with right-conservatives. Yet episodes such as "My Future Self n' Me" and "Butt Out," both of which deal with the regulation of drugs, are equally contemptuous of similar moral agendas and tactics that Parker and Stone associate with left-liberals.

Instead, *South Park's* predominate ethos is that government should promote neither equality nor morality and, in this way, it presents a worldview more aligned with libertarianism. Indeed, in 2001 Parker indicated that he was registered with the Libertarian Party (Brownfield). Occasionally, however, *South Park* suggests that the government should advocate certain moral issues. In "Fun with Veal," for example, the kids get the U.S. Food and Drug Administration officially to change the word "veal" to "tortured baby cow," which represents "our stance," explains Parker, that "you can eat meat but don't eat babies" (*South Park*, season 6). Along with an abhorrence of paternalism and collectivism, libertarians—at least those aligned with the Libertarian Party—also believe in unfettered free market capitalism. Thus, when a Starbucks-like franchise threatens to take over a locally-owned coffee shop in "Gnomes," Kyle and Stan defend big corporations for delivering an array of consumer goods and for succeeding through good quality and management. Yet episodes such as "Chickenpox," "Chef Aid," "The Entity," and "Jared Has

Aides" send mixed messages about the fairness, efficacy, and honesty of the capitalist system. Similarly, in "Something Wall-Mart This Way Comes," when a Wal-Mart opens in the town of South Park and its low prices bankrupt local merchants and addict the townspeople to consumerism, the kids seek to shut it down. They learn from the company's president that the only way to stop a Wal-Mart is to destroy its heart, which turns out to be a mirror. Thus, although this episode proposes that Wal-Mart thrives because of consumer desire, there is also the sense that the unfettered free market capitalism the company represents creates social turmoil. In short, while *South Park* is predominately libertarian, some episodes cloud the purity of this worldview.

Even the Kids Are "Evil Little Bastards"

South Park's aversion toward an activist government relates to a broader theme of the show: Institutions of all types are generally corrupt, hypocritical, and inept. This includes institutions related to every level of government (global, national, state, and local) and to religions, businesses, and science. In fact, this view of institutions provides much of the show's humor. Running gags include a town policeman, Officer Barbrady, who is so dim-witted that he not only misses glaring crimes and clues but unwittingly assists the criminals; school lessons full of misinformation (for example, Columbus was the Indians' best friend); and a school cook, Chef, who answers the kids' questions with songs about his sexual prowess. This lampooning of institutions is frequently based on current events. Hence in 2002, with the Catholic priest/child molestation scandal in the news, Parker and Stone did "Red Hot Catholic Love," in which the local South Park priest attempts to persuade the Vatican to outlaw sex with boys, a campaign the Pope and prelates reject.

And, although Sullivan contends that South Park Republicans "believe we need a hard-ass foreign policy" (Anderson 99), episodes such as "Osama Bin Laden Has Farty Pants" are less definitive in their portrayal of U.S. militarism. Made shortly after the 9/11 terrorism attacks, this episode includes four virtuous Afghani children who look and act like the *South Park* boys and who are angry at the United States for indiscriminately bombing their country as well as for its general insensitivity toward the world. Thus, although the episode ends with a patriotic "America: love-it-or-leave" message, it also raises issues that complicate claims of U.S. benevolence. And when Wendy, a classmate of the *South Park* boys, informs a warmongering Cartman, "We're at war with terrorists, fat-ass, not with Afghanistan," she implicitly questions assertions that America acts militarily only in self-defense. Similarly, in "I'm a Little Bit Country," when the town of South Park divides into anti- and pro-war camps over the U.S. invasion of Iraq, Cartman travels back in time to learn of the Founding Fathers' opinion on the acceptability of antiwar protest and the wisdom of waging war. The episode concludes with Cartman explaining to the townspeople that antiwar and pro-war Americans need one another because the former "make the country look like it's made of sane, caring individuals," while the latter are necessary because if "our whole country was made up of nothing but soft pussy protesters, we'd get taken down in a second." "I'm a Little Bit Country" therefore suggests that those who oppose U.S. militarism are naïve, yet it also criticizes those who unconditionally support this militarism (and by extension military institutions in general) as irrational and brutal.

South Park's distrust of institutions relates closely to its Generation X sensibility. Although such distrust is not unique to this generation, research suggests that Gen Xers are less likely to register strong approval of official institutions, such as the presidency and Congress, than previous generations (D. Owen 94). Gen Xers matured during a period in which the legitimacy of official institutions was seriously undercut and, according to Diana Owen, they "have lived their entire lives in an environment in which damning messages about government and its leaders are the norm" (89). In the late 1960s and 1970s, traumas such as the War in Vietnam and the Watergate scandal evoked a sense of governmental and societal collapse that, in the 1980s and 1990s, was echoed by shocks such as the Iran-Contra scandal, the savings-and-loan debacle, televangelist scams, the AIDS epidemic, and the Rodney King beating. Gen Xers, as previously noted, also witnessed the baby boomers become the Establishment and infotainment remove the larger-than-life veneer from the entertainment industry. And during the years that Gen Xers came of age, school standards declined markedly at the same time that wealth disparities increased dramatically (Hanson 11, 58). Indeed, a declining standard of living might explain why a majority of Gen Xers oppose educational and job-related affirmative action despite their general support of racial equality (Hill 116), a conflicted stance mirrored in South Park's tolerance of diversity, yet dislike of institutionally compelled acceptance.

Generation X also experienced substantial changes in the dynamics of the family. Divorce rates rose from more than 300,000 to nearly 1.2 million between 1965 and 1985 (Hanson 11) and, for families that stayed intact, rising costs and other factors compelled both parents into the workforce, ballooning the number of latchkey kids. (We should note here that neither Stone's nor Parker's parents are divorced). Hence, Gen X-produced popular culture media, such as director Sam Mendes's American Beauty (1999), often present a jaded view of the family that debunks what right-conservatives tout as "traditional family values." In South Park, although an episode will occasionally include a theme that seems supportive of "traditional family values" (Anderson 85), much of the show's humor is based on mocking and transgressing these values. For example, the premarital sex and infidelity in "Cartman's Mom Is a Dirty Slut" are neither condemned nor condoned, whereas

"Two Guys Naked in a Hot Tub" portrays sexual experimentation between two fathers (in fact, all men) as normal. In addition, rather than nurturing or protective, parents in the show are generally deceitful, inept, shallow, mean, rash, childish, and basically unfit. They are also hazardous to their children's well-being. In "Cherokee Hair Tampons," for instance, Kyle's mom refuses to believe that holistic medicine is not curing her son's failed kidneys, even after Stan implores her to seek a doctor. And, unlike most sitcoms and other cartoons such as *The Simpsons*, in which central narrative tensions are frequently resolved by and in the family (Cantor), the *South Park* kids usually have to resolve issues on their own.

Indeed, the *South Park* kids look more to each other than their parents for guidance and, as such, function as a type of surrogate family—yet another common theme of Gen X-produced popular culture (for example, the films of director Paul Thomas Anderson) that suggests the impact changing family dynamics had on this generation. In fact, the idea that family is more about for whom you care than about whose blood you share is the central moral of "Ike's Wee Wee." But it is not only the *South Park* parents who are unreliable. As one observer notes of the show, Chef is "the only adult the kids can trust" (Schneider) and, in episodes such as "The Succubus," even he threatens to fail them. This character eventually does become a real threat to the children when he transforms into a predatory pedophile in the 2006 season. This cynical view of adults is, again, related to *South Park*'s Gen X sensibility. An estimated 40% of Gen Xers are children of divorce and many had to assume a greater role in their own upbringings (Hanson 11). They also came of age during an era that was less economically hospitable than that known by the baby boomers. As a result, Gen Xers show a greater hesitation to marry, enter careers, and assume other adult roles and responsibilities, leading some observers to term them the "postponed generation" (Littwin). *South Park*'s scathing view of adults reflects this hesitation to embrace adulthood, as does the prevalence of fart jokes and other puerile humor in the show, which suggests the desire to extend adolescence among both its Gen X creators and fans. "We still think like kids," explained a 34-year-old Parker to *Time* in 2006 (Poniewozik).

Possibly because Parker and Stone consider their approach to the world childlike, *South Park* offers a somewhat misty-eyed view of childhood. The kids in the show are usually the most commonsensical characters with the wisdom of uncorrupted youth. Yet Stone also notes that, whereas "most people" think of children as "innocent," the "essence of *South Park*" is that he and Parker "view kids as just evil little bastards" (*South Park*, season 3). Moreover, regardless of their youthful virtues, eventually the *South Park* kids will grow up presumably to become just as unpleasant as the show's adults, as episodes such as "Chickenlover" and "My Future Self n' Me" suggest, at least of Cartman.

In short, all of society in *South Park*—from institutions, to adults, to kids—is deeply corrupt. And in this way, it transgresses a—if not *the*—fundamental tenet of conservative thought, advocated from Edmund Burke to Ronald Reagan: Existing social and moral orders must be respected and changed only with great caution if at all. *South Park*, instead, suggests that existing social and moral orders are beyond contempt and redemption and should, therefore, not be maintained or "conserved." Hence, observers commonly describe the show as nihilistic or "anarchic," as Anderson puts it (xiv), for its contempt of all traditional institutions, a sensibility that can be interpreted, ultimately, as politically radical, revolutionary, and, indeed, liberal.

In response to claims that he and Parker are nihilistic, however, Stone explains: "We don't think mankind sucks. We just see the humor in everything" (Vincent). Indeed, to interpret *South Park* as completely awash in nihilism, we must overlook the potential positive effects of its equal-opportunity satire. Film critic Roger Ebert suggested this potential in his review of *South Park: Bigger Longer & Uncut* (1999)—a film in which "No target is too low, no attitude too mean or hurtful, no image too unthinkable"—when he described the laughter it engenders as sometimes "liberating, as good laughter can be, and sometimes it was simply disbelieving: How could they get away with this?" (*South Park*). Similarly, to interpret *South Park*, vis-à-vis its nihilism as ultimately liberal, we must ignore the numerous counterexamples of conservatism that saturate the show.

Despite occasional gestures toward one political outlook or another, however, the most consistent claim Parker and Stone make is that *South Park* straddles the political fence. When asked in a 2006 *Time* magazine interview whether Anderson's characterization of the show in *South Park Conservatives* as "antiliberal" was apt, Stone replied "I think that's a fair description of some of the show's politics. But you could easily write a book called *South Park Liberals*, because we've attacked a lot of funny stuff that conservative people and institutions do in America" (Poniewozik). Or, as Parker responded to one interviewer who noted that both the right and the left claim the show: "Absolutely" ("Interview"). Rather, Parker and Stone disdain the political extremity and certainty that pundits such as Anderson bring to their interpretation of the show. "What we are trying to do is represent the rest of America, basically those who believe that Bush is an idiot and that Michael Moore is an idiot, too," explains Stone. "We're kind of just in the middle going, 'I don't pretend to know shit'" (Wild 68). Tellingly, on the very front cover of Anderson's *South Park Conservatives* is a footnote that reads: "This book has not been prepared, approved, or licensed by any entity that created or produced the cable cartoon program *South Park*."

South Park must be seen as deeply politically ambivalent. This ambivalence makes the show an effective mirror for a politically polarized nation racked by culture wars because in it every political stripe can see its own ideologies reflected and thus seemingly justified. At the same time, however, because of its ambivalence, *South Park* offers no clear political worldview and therefore no political solutions. As Robert Ebert writes of the "vicious social satire" in *South Park: Bigger Longer & Uncut*, "All it lacks is a point to its message" (*South Park*). But it is Ebert's review of Parker and Stone's non–*South Park* project, the 2004 film *Team America: World Police*, which better identifies this political dead-endedness. Shot with marionettes, the film centers on a small group of ultrapatriotic U.S. special operatives who trot the globe hunting terrorists, but who instead mistakenly demolish the cultural landmarks of other countries, such as the Egyptian pyramids and the Eiffel Tower. An equal threat, however, comes from liberal Hollywood luminaries who attempt to thwart Team America's noble aims at every turn. The film thus satirizes the jingoism, incompetence, and ethnocentrism of U.S. foreign policy, as well as those who vocally oppose this foreign policy. "If I were asked to extract a political position from the movie, I'd be baffled," writes Ebert. "It is neither for nor against the War on Terrorism, just dedicated to ridiculing those who wage it and those who oppose it." It was this "nihilism" that most offended Ebert. "At a time when the world is in crisis and the country faces an important election, the response of Parker, Stone and company is to sneer at both sides—indeed at anyone who takes the current world situation seriously" ("*Team America*").

Such political ambivalence is central to Gen Xers, and it has resulted in their widespread disengagement from the political sphere. Nowhere is this disengagement more apparent than in the *South Park* episode "Douche and Turd," which aired only days before the 2004 presidential election. In it the children are asked to vote for either a giant douche or a turd sandwich to be their new school mascot. Given this choice, Stan refuses to vote, and only after a townsperson explains to him that "every election since the beginning of time has been between some douche and some turd" because they are "the only people who suck up enough to make it that far in politics," does he cast a ballot. Yet at end of the episode, he discovers that his vote did not matter. Parker and Stone point to this episode when asked who they voted for in the 2004 presidential election ("Pushing the Envelope). And, as the decline in political interest among youth in the United States since the 1960s indicates (Putnam), many of Parker and Stone's generation, regardless of their political leanings, share the view that regardless who is running, the choice is still essentially between a giant douche and a turd sandwich, so why bother voting for either one?

Notes

I would like to thank David Gray, Lary May, and Jeffrey Weinstock for their suggestions in improving this chapter.

1. This chapter uses the following sources to understand the parameters and attitudes of Generation X, as well as the broader social, political, and economic forces

that affect it: *After the Boom*, edited by Craig and Bennett, a collection of essays that draw their conclusions primarily from the American National Election Study surveys between 1972 and 1994, as well as several polls conducted on behalf of the Times Mirror/Pew Research Center for the People and the Press; Hanson, *The Cinema of Generation X*, which examines how films created by Generation X filmmakers both reflect and reveal a sensibility unique to this generation; and Moore, ". . . And Tomorrow Is Just Another Crazy Scam," which examines how the downward mobility confronted by Generation X influences its sense of nihilism, cynicism, and cultural exhaustion.

Works Cited

Anderson, Brian C. *South Park Republicans: The Revolt against Liberal Media Bias.* Washington, DC: Regency, 2005.

Aucoin, Don. "*South* Creators Do It for Laughs." *Boston Globe* 20 Jan. 1998: C8.

Bianculli, David. "'Bush' Creators to Test Limits." *Times Union* (Albany, NY) 22 Mar. 2001: D5.

Bozell, Brent L. "*South Park* Reconsidered, Sort Of." *L. Brent Bozell's Weekly Syndicated Entertainment Column* 11 Feb. 1998. <www.parentstv.org/PTC/publications/1bbcolumns/1998/col19980211.asp>.

Brownfield, Paul. "Fitting Square Pegs in an Oval Office." *Los Angeles Times* 4 Apr. 2001: F1.

Cantor, Paul. *Gilligan Unbound: Pop Culture in the Age of Globalization.* Lanham, MD: Rowman and Littlefield, 2003: 67–109.

Craig, Stephen C., and Stephen Earl Bennett. *After the Boom: The Politics of Generation X.* New York: Rowman and Littlefield, 1997.

Ebert, Roger. "*South Park: Bigger Longer & Uncut.*" 30 June 1999 <http://rogerebert.suntimes.com/apps/pbcs.d11/article?AID=/19990630/REVIEWS/906300301>.

———. "*Team America: World Police*, No Defense for Offensive 'Team America.'" 15 Oct. 2004 <http://rogerebert.suntimes.com/apps/pbcs.d11/article?AID=/20041014/REVIEWS/40921007>.

Farber, Jim. "Hurts So Good, Loud Bands, Mellow Fans and the Joy of Misery." *Daily News* (New York) 26 July 1999: 40.

Hanson, Peter. *The Cinema of Generation X: A Critical Study of Films and Directors.* Jefferson, NC: McFarland, 2002.

Hill, Kevin A. "Generations and Tolerance: Is Youth Really a Liberalizing Factor?" *After the Boom: The Politics of Generation X.* Ed. Stephen C. Craig and Stephen Earl Bennett. New York: Rowan and Littlefield, 1997.

Hodgson, Godfrey. *America in Our Time: From World War II to Nixon, What Happened and Why.* New York: Vintage, 1978: 67–98.

"Interview: Trey Parker and Matt Stone talk *Team America: World Police.*" *In Focus* 4 Oct. 2004 <www.movieweb.com/news/news.php?id=5406>.

Justin, Neal. "Cartman Celebrates a Decade of Decadence." *Minneapolis Star Tribune*, 1 Oct. 2006: F1, F11.

Kronke, David. "Luck with a Capital F: In *South Park*, Kids Fart Fire and Jesus Lives." *New Times Los Angeles* 31 July 1997: columns.

Lim, Dennis. "Television: Lowbrow and Proud of It." *Independent* (London) 29 Mar. 1998: 26.

Littwin, Susan. *The Postponed Generation: Why America's Grown-Up Kids Are Growing Up Later*. New York: Morrow, 1986.

Marin, Rick, T. Trent Gegax, Debra Rosenberg, Steve Rhodes, James Gill, and Elizabeth Angell. "The Rube Tube." *Newsweek* 23 Mar. 1998: 56.

Moore, Ryan. "'. . . And Tomorrow Is Just Another Crazy Scam': Postmodernity, Youth, and the Downward Mobility of the Middle Class." *Generations of Youth: Youth Cultures and History in Twentieth-Century America*. Ed. Joe Austin and Michael Nevin Willard. New York: New York University Press, 1998: 253–71.

Oake, Jonathon I. "*Reality Bites* and Generation X as Spectator." *The Velvet Light Trap*. Spring 2004, no. 53: 83–97.

Owen, Diana. "Mixed Signals: Generation X's Attitudes toward the Political System." *After the Boom: The Politics of Generation X*. Ed. Stephen C. Craig and Stephen Earl Bennett. New York: Rowan and Littlefield, 1997: 85–106.

Owen, Rob. "George W. as Ward Cleaver?" 19 July 2001 <www.post-gazette.com/tv/20010119owen1.asp>.

Poniewozik, James. "10 Questions for Matt Stone and Trey Parker." *Time* 13 Mar. 2006: 8.

"Pushing the Envelope." Interviewer: Jake Tapper, *Nightline*, ABC News, 9 Sept. 2006.

Putnam, Robert. *Bowling Alone: The Collapse and Revival of American Community*. New York: Simon and Schuster, 2000: 36.

Rubin, Sylvia. "TV's Foul-Mouthed Funnies: *South Park* Kids Say the %*&@—est Things." *San Francisco Chronicle* 26 Jan. 1998: D1.

Schneider, Michael. "Brash *South Park* Kids to Win Comedy Central Laughs." *Electronic Media* 21 July 1997: 8.

Snead, Elizabeth. "The Masters of the Chaotic *South Park* Universe." *USA Today* 27 Aug. 1997: 3D.

South Park. DVD Commentaries, Seasons 3, 4, 6. Creators. Trey Parker and Matt Stone. Comedy Central, 1999–2002.

Span, Paula. "On the Cussing Edge: 'South Park' Pushes the Taste Envelope." *The Washington Post* 14 Sept. 1997: G08.

Starr, Jerold. "Cultural Politics in the 1960s." *Cultural Politics: Radical Movements in Modern History*. Ed. Jerold Starr. New York: Praeger, 1985. 244–48.

Sullivan, Andrew. "South Park Republicanism." 10 Oct. 2003 <www.andrewsullivan.com/index.php?dish_inc=archives/2003_10_26_dish_archive.html#106727359457680686>.

Vincent, Mal. "Fame's a Bummer, Dude, but Pays Well." *Toronto Star* 31 July 1998: D10.

Walker, Jesse, and Nick Gillespie. "South Park Libertarians." *Reason*, Dec. 2006, http://www.reason.com/news/show/116787.html (accessed 5 Dec. 2006).

Wild, David. "Puppetmasters: *South Park* Bad Boys Take on Terror with Potty-Mouthed Puppets." *Rolling Stone* 28 Oct. 2004: 66–68.

CHAPTER 9

South Park Heretics

Confronting Orthodoxy through Theater of the Absurd

RANDALL FALLOWS

A t the end of "Bloody Mary," the final episode of the ninth season of *South Park*, Stan Marsh challenges his father for seeing himself as one who has to drink excessively or not at all. When Stan points out that a more reasonable solution might exist between these two extremes, his father replies "maybe I'm just the kind of person who needs to have it all or nothing." Stan counters his father's self-assessment by applying a lesson he learned from his karate teacher: "No, all or nothing is easy, but learning to drink just a little, that's a discipline." This snippet can be seen as *South Park* creators Trey Parker and Matt Stone's statement to the American people as a whole. The one thing that nearly all the episodes (including the movie) have in common is the notion that we have become a country that goes to absurd extremes, too lazy for the mental discipline to find a more reasonable path down the middle.

Though the show rarely offers realistic solutions to contemporary problems, it frequently reveals the ridiculous quality of the all-or-nothing thinking that not only characterizes Stan's father, but also has become increasingly common in American culture. By parodying the extreme orthodoxical views to which Americans often adhere, *South Park* encourages us to think beyond a mere repetition of ideological clichés and explore more creative ways of dealing with old problems. In essence, the show raises a distorted mirror to exaggerate the questionable qualities of American culture to help us see these qualities more clearly as we encounter them in the nonanimated world. This approach is neither as original as many of the show's fans might think, nor as pointless as some of its critics have accused it of being, but instead resonates with earlier satirical traditions.

Of course, many people whose opinions I respect disagree with my contention that *South Park* can function as social critique; they find the show too crude and too random to be anything more than a gross diversion. In answer to the first charge, I point out that crudity has always been a staple of satire. Trey Parker and Matt Stone were not the first to depict disgusting imagery and violence in a comedic fashion. Jonathan Swift, arguably the most important satirist in the English language, wrote "A Modest Proposal," which contains imagery that is just as revolting as anything Parker and Stone have given us. The central concept that the British could help the Irish out of poverty by buying and eating their babies reminds me of Cartman tricking his rival, Scott Tenorman, to eat his own parents. In fact, Swift even takes the gross imagery further by suggesting that "those who are more thrifty (as I confess the times require) may flay the carcass; the skin of which artificially dressed will make admirable gloves for ladies and summer boots for fine gentlemen" (1928). Without crude, disgusting imagery, many satires would lose the power to shock people out of their complacency.

Still Swift had a specific point to make about British insensitivity to the plight of the Irish. His humor may be crude at times, but he raised serious and consistent concerns about the government's responsibility to help those who cannot help themselves. Responding to the claim that *South Park* loses its edge by trying to be equally offensive to everyone, making it seem like a random hodgepodge of humor based on whatever is in the news at the moment each episode is released, is more difficult. Many of the show's fans probably see it as laughter for the sake of laughter, no more profound than the vast majority of shows that have always dominated television.

However, just because the show satirizes nearly everything does not mean that it loses its edge. The writers seldom rely on random humor, for each joke is consistent with the overall theme of the episode in which it appears. In "Cartoon Wars," the writers find a clever way to compare themselves to their counterparts on the FOX show, *Family Guy*, by having the kids watch the show as we watch them watch it. The snippet they see seems consistent with the overall nature of *Family Guy*; it presents a series of flashbacks in which Peter, the main character, finds himself caught up in seemingly random events from popular culture and politics. All the kids except Cartman seem to enjoy it. Later, when Kyle asks him why he does not like the show, given that it seems to be consistent with his humor, Cartman breaks character and responds as the writers of *South Park*, "I am nothing like *Family Guy*. When I make jokes, they are inherent to a story, deep situational and emotional jokes based on what is relevant and has a point, not just one random interchangeable joke after another." The *South Park* writers are not the only ones to see themselves in this way or their show would not have won a

Peabody Award for being a "notoriously rude, undeniably fearless lampoon of all that is self-important and hypocritical in American life, regardless of race, creed, color or celebrity status" (ABC News Web site, 6 Apr. 2006). For all these reasons, the show deserves to be taken seriously, although not lauded as something that just sprang out of nothing; it is an exemplarily incarnation of an older literary tradition, Theater of the Absurd.

Not surprisingly, this earlier tradition reached its apex during another period of extreme social duality, the early Cold War between the United States and the Soviet Union. Consider how closely President Bush's recent rhetoric regarding terrorists resembles that of the House Committee on Un-American Activities in a 1948 pamphlet explaining that the communist ideal was "that the world as we know it must be destroyed—religion, family, laws, rights, everything" (5). Of course, the Soviets had their own government propaganda machines that spewed out equally ridiculous statements about the intentions of the Western countries. Many playwrights of this period felt as the *South Park* writers evidently do now, that no system is without flaws and thus one should be careful not to follow any as absolute orthodoxy. Whether because of conscious intention or because they take similar rhetorical positions, *South Park*'s plots and purpose resemble many plays of this period.

In fact, as I wrote in "The Theology of *South Park*," the four main characters of the show strongly resonate with the four from the most famous play to come out of this tradition, Samuel Beckett's *Waiting for Godot*. Stan and Kyle, like Vladimir and Estragon, seem to be waiting for something or someone to make sense out of their world, but what they encounter instead is a selfish bully (Pozzo/Cartman) and an incomprehensible victim (Lucky/Kenny). Furthermore, the show, like the play, never comes to any easy moral resolution. As is the case with the end of each act of *Godot*, the lessons learned at the end of each episode of *South Park* are never remembered and the kids wind up in the same spot as they were the last time we saw them, confused and still waiting for someone to make sense out of their small community.

Of course, although the play has many comic moments, the tone of *Godot* is much more bleak than any single episode of *South Park*. The kids may have moments of depression, but imagining any of them lamenting their fate to the degree that Vladimir does is difficult, "Astride of a grave and a difficult birth. Down in the hole, lingeringly, the grave digger puts on the forceps. We have time to grow old. The air is full of our cries" (Beckett 193). Perhaps the reason the kids do not despair so deeply has to do with what Vladimir goes on to say, "habit is the great deadener" (193). The kids have simply gotten used to the fact that nothing makes sense and, although they would not know or be able to pronounce the word "existentialism," the concept permeates both their material and metaphysical universe. Not only are their parents and teachers deeply and obviously flawed, but so is the theological structure that surrounds them. While Jesus appears as a talk show host whose miraculous powers are based on tricks that cannot even rival those of magician David Blaine, God looks like a smaller version of Barney the dinosaur and is unavailable even to his own son. On the other end of the spectrum, Satan is more a figure to be pitied for all his failed homosexual relationships than an image that inspires fear or worship. With no role models and no clear-cut path to good or evil, the kids have to find their own meaning and most of the time they are unable to do so.

The townspeople as a whole, however, connect even more with the characters in the plays of Eugene Ionesco, who often shows large groups of people going to absurd extremes by following political and cultural trends. In *Rhinoceros*, the characters transform into the title animal and trample the weaker qualities of humanity. At first, Ionesco argued the play was about the rise of fascism, but later decided it also shows the consequences of following any political, religious, or cultural system too blindly. As he says in his introduction to this work, "*Rhinoceros* is certainly an anti-Nazi play, yet it is also and mainly an attack on collective hysteria and the epidemics that lurk beneath the surface of reason and ideas but are nonetheless serious collective diseases passed off as ideologies" ("Notes" 206). In short, when orthodoxy replaces critical thinking, people begin to accept the kind of absurd thought that leads to destructive actions.

One of the many times this happens in *South Park* is in the episode "Death," when Sheila Broflovski organizes the whole town to protest the airing of the *Terrance and Phillip Show*, a program the kids like but the parents find to be offensive because of its focus on flatulence jokes. Caught up in the ideology of their stance against such jokes occurring on television, they fail to see how much they engage in potty humor themselves in responding to how a flu that is going around has affected each of them with statements such as, "I have a case of the green apple splatters." In fact, the parents choose to leave their kids behind to go to New York City to protest in front of the Cartoon Central building to have the episode taken off the air. When the network president refuses to hear their demands, they catapult themselves against the building, reasoning that seeing their dead, splattered bodies on the news is better than hearing fart jokes.

Obviously, this reflects the absurd reasoning that many of the characters in *Rhinoceros* have for transforming, recognizing the thicker skin and greater power such creatures have but failing to see the obvious loss of humanity. In addition, the episode also contains the self-reflective quality inherent in most theater of the absurd plays. Just as the playwright makes reference to himself when Jean tells Beringer to go see an Ionesco play to obtain a greater degree of culture, so the *Terrance and Phillip* cartoon reflects the one in which it appears. While *South Park* is shown on Comedy Central, *Terrance and Phillip* appears on Cartoon Central. Furthermore, this episode contains more than its usual share of potty humor and, of course, reflects how *South Park* itself has been wrapped up in controversy since it first aired. This Brechtian strategy invites viewers to step outside the passive role of viewer and think about what they are seeing, hopefully making connections between the absurdity shown in the theater or on the television screen and the absurdity they have gotten used to in their own lives.

Furthermore, like Ionesco, the writers of *South Park* do not just reveal the more obvious violent consequences of people blindly following ideologies, such as the death of innocent victims (usually Kenny) or the constant destruction of the town; they also show the more internal costs. When they are not being violent, the *South Park* characters resemble those in another famous Ionesco play, *The Bald Soprano*, which reveals the members of an upperclass British family who are not so much outwardly destructive as they are inwardly innocuous, stupid, and soulless, following popular opinion and cultural trends without noticing the blatant absurdities and inherent contradictions their words and actions imply. For instance, Mrs. Smith, in one of her many moments of pointless blathering, points out the benefit of yogurt to her husband:

> Yogurt is excellent for the stomach, the kidneys, the appendicitis, and apotheosis. It was Doctor Mackenzie-King who told me that, he's the one who takes care of the children of our neighbors, the Johns. He's a good doctor. One can trust him. He never prescribes any medicine that he's not tried out on himself first. Before operating on Parker, he had his own liver operated on first, although he was not he least bit ill. (10)

Her speech has the air of someone trying to seem more clever than she really is, using a term such as "apotheosis" because it sounds intellectual but using it in a completely inappropriate manner and making herself an expert on medical procedures even when she has no idea how they actually take place.

Likewise, the citizens of South Park tend to follow trends over common sense. For example, in "Spontaneous Combustion" many of the characters in attempting not to appear flatulent to their new romantic partners end up exploding from all the gas they've built up inside them. When the rest of the town hears of this, they go to the opposite extreme, letting go of their gas to the point where they cause global warming with all the methane they inevitably add to the atmosphere. As usual, the kids come up with the reasonable solution in the middle: to fart only when absolutely necessary or when it's "really, really funny." And the town not only jumps on the current health bandwagon, but also embraces every celebrity trend. For instance, in "Stupid Spoiled Whore Video Playset," nearly everyone in the town gets excited when Paris Hilton pays them a visit. When Kyle asks why, what has she done that is so special, he gets the same answers: "She's rich," "she's a blatant whore." Obviously these qualities should not make her worthy of admiration, but only after Mr. Slave shows that she is not even very talented when looked at by these "standards" by beating her in a "whore-off" does the town lose interest in her. Typically, the townspeople soon forget the most important lesson and continue to embrace whatever trend comes their way even when backed by questionable scientific evidence or fatuous Hollywood personalities.

In this more than anything else, the town of South Park functions as synecdoche, a small part of the United States that reflects the essence of the whole. Thomas de Zengotita argues that Americans have become increasingly reliant on others to tell them how to think as their minds grow "clogged, anesthetized, numb" from a constant bombardment of partially fabricated information (33). Thinking for ourselves becomes too difficult and time-consuming, so we rely on our preexisting ideologies to make quick, efficient sense of events. This situation is compounded by the fact that many Americans consider one weak if one does not stick consistently to a single political position (recall, for instance, George Bush's effective characterization of candidate John Kerry during the 2004 election as a "flip-flopper"). In short, Americans in general arguably have become increasingly reliant on letting others stamp rigid ideological interpretations on every major issue or event. This was even true of the events of 9/11, which de Zengotita argues had less power to jolt Americans out of their complacency than they might have because "conditioned thus relentlessly to move from representation to representation, we got past the thing itself as well; or rather the thing itself was transformed into a sea of signs and upon it we were borne away from every shore, moving on, moving on" (40). The danger is that as we rely more on particular ideologies to navigate us through this "sea of signs," we might let them take us to places that are harmful to ourselves and others, to what Ionesco describes in the above quotation as "the collective hysteria and the epidemics that lurk beneath the surface of reason" (206).

Fortunately, Ionesco also offers us hope that one can avoid these dangerous consequences by learning to see the absurdities inherent in all ideologies: "Once we realize that History has lost its reason, that lying propaganda masks a contradiction between the facts and the ideologies that explain them, once we cast a lucid eye on the world as it is to-day, this is enough to stop us being taken in by irrational 'reasons' and so help us not to lose our heads" ("Notes" 206). Having lived in Romania and France during World War II, Ionesco witnessed the literal and figurative ways people "lost their heads" by adhering too closely to ideological systems, which were seen as beyond ridicule. Hopefully, with shows such as South Park carrying on the tradition that Ionesco, Beckett, and others developed, Americans will not only avoid falling into similar traps but also develop the mental discipline to notice and change the absurdities inherent in their own ideologies. I am not arguing that *South Park* alone can instigate a cultural renaissance in the United States, one based on reason as opposed to partisan loyalties, but perhaps it can help us to avoid those easy answers that have already led humanity down too many blind and dangerous alleys.

Works Cited

ABC News. <www.abcnews.go.com>. 6 Apr. 2007.

Beckett, Samuel. *Waiting For Godot*. New York: Grove, 1954.

de Zengotita, Thomas. "The Numbing of the American Mind: Culture as Anesthetic." *Harpers* Apr. 2002: 33–40.

Fallows, Randall. "The Theology of South Park." *Americana*. Jan. 2002. <http://www. americanpopularculture.com/archive/tv/theology_southpark.htm>.

Ionesco, Eugene. *Rhinoceros*. Trans. David Prouse. New York: Grove, 1960

——— . *The Bald Soprano*. In *Four Plays by Eugene Ionesco*. Trans. Donald M. Allen. New York: Grove, 1958.

——— . *Notes and Counternotes*. Trans Donald Watson. London: Calder, 1962.

Swift, Jonathan. "A Modest Proposal." 1729. *Harper Collins World Reader: The Modern World*. Ed. Mary Ann Caws. New York: Harper Collins, 1994.

United States. Cong. Committee on Un-American Activities. *100 Things You Should Know about Communism and Religion*, 80th Cong., 2nd Sess., 1948.

Prophetic Profanity

South Park on Religion or Thinking Theologically with Eric Cartman

MICHAEL W. DeLASHMUTT
and BRANNON HANCOCK

Introduction

Call us heretics, but we find *South Park* to be among the most theologically profound television available today. In the show's early seasons, creators Trey Parker and Matt Stone were not as quick to take aim at religion, but their confidence seems to have grown as the show has developed over its decadelong history. What began as the occasional self-deprecating Jewish humor has in more recent seasons evolved into more sophisticated analyses of religious traditions and of-the-moment responses to religiously themed current events.[1] Parker and Stone have covered everything from the clergy abuse scandal in the Catholic Church to Mel Gibson's *The Passion of the Christ* (2004) to everyone's favorite celebrity religion, Scientology.[2] However, while drawing fire from the Catholic Church and evangelical watchdogs such as Tim Wildmon's American Family Association, the show's commentary on religion has prompted little serious reflection by theological thinkers, especially those within academic or traditional faith communities; indeed, we suspect the former group regards the show as too low-brow and the latter as too debased to be treated with any seriousness. As scholars and religious practitioners, we wish to end this relative silence by exploring *South Park*'s often scathing critique of religion as a form of "secular prophecy"—secular in its origination if not always in its object or import—which, like the prophetic voice in the biblical tradition, employs profane speech and offensive imagery to issue a call to self-examination and a return to authenticity.

Popular Culture as (Secular) Prophecy

We agree with those suspicious of the recent advent of "religion-and-pop-culture" discourse that such endeavors should not be merely an excuse to baptize one's hobbies and side interests but rather must seek to provide an academically rigorous and mutually constructive critique of both religion/theology and popular culture. In *A Matrix of Meaning: Finding God in Pop Culture*, Craig Detweiler and Barry Taylor offer four compelling reasons why theologians and scholars of religion might wish to engage in the study of popular culture (19–23). First, they note that popular cultural forms provide a formative influence for the construction of identity, society, and value within contemporary Western society. Second, popular cultural forms are a means by which a culture's implicit ethical framework, its "strong evaluations" to use Craig Detweiler and Barry Taylor's language, are expressed. Films, television, music, literature, and art not only influence popular conceptions of value, beauty, and the good, but they also serve as the space in which such ideas are discussed. Third, literacy is no longer judged exclusively by way of one's familiarity with loci classicus of a particular discipline. Rather, to engage with the contemporary world, scholars of religion must be able to speak the lingua franca of the postmodern world, which for Detweiler and Taylor, are the forms of popular culture. Finally, the authors argue that popular culture must be pursued because, as Bruce Forbes has argued, "religion appears not only in churches, synagogues, mosques, and temples; it also appears in popular culture" (1), which is to say, religion is a frequent topic of popular cultural discourse, revealing an underlying conversation about the "sacred," which is deeply embedded in the forms of the secular.

In his *Understanding Theology and Popular Culture*, Gordon Lynch summarizes four ways in which scholars of religion and theologians have within recent scholarship pursued the task of relating theology and religious studies with popular culture (21). The first such approach is described as the study of religion in relation to everyday life (including the environment, resources, and practices thereof). This includes both the way in which expressions of religion are shaped by cultural forms, how religion is represented in popular culture, and how religion responds to popular culture.[3] Second, theology and religious studies can approach popular culture to understand its religious function. This approach seeks to understand how culture provides deep meaning to its participants by offering what could be identified as Ultimate Concern.[4] One could also seek to understand how popular cultural practices replace more well-established religious functions, such as the role of sport spectatorship as a substitute for religious community.[5] A third approach involves the study of the missiological engagement with popular culture, where either a system of controls is established to prevent a contamination of the sacred by secular forms of popular culture (conservative), or where popular culture forms are reread through a theological hermeneutic (liberal). Fourth, popular cultural forms can be understood as a source of theological reflection. Rather than rereading popular culture to force it to conform to a preexisting theological hermeneutic, this perspective encourages the cultural forms to speak on their own terms, whereby they are engaged dialogically from the perspective of theology and religious studies.[6]

This chapter concerns not only *South Park*'s depiction and critique of religion, but more significantly how *South Park*, wittingly or not, takes up the task of theologizing or "thinking religiously." Although popular culture can serve a religious function, in the case of *South Park*, this religious function is most likely well outside of the authors' intent and the general audience's awareness. In approaching *South Park* as a launching point for theological reflection, *South Park*'s secular prophetic message may very well speak in congress with other forms of sacred prophetic speech. In this sense, popular culture as an inroad to the biblical metaphor of prophetic speech both reflects the norms of the day and potentially offers a means of transforming those norms. This transformation is facilitated by the shock of the blasphemous and the scatological. *South Park*'s creators take shock humor to ridiculous extremes, and their use of animation rather than live-action heightens this effect. But *South Park*'s intent is not merely "shock-for-shock's-sake," like some kind of animated Howard Stern with children as central characters; nor is it a pornographic display of the grotesque merely for the sake of entertainment. Rather, we believe the show's antics are intended to rattle the viewer out of the intellectual stupor encouraged by passive television watching, often for the purpose of communicating a particular and fairly consistent message.

As the show's confrontational use of irreverent language and themes places the viewer outside the realm of appropriateness, the viewer is forced to engage in critical self-reflection. Indeed, we are motivated to regard *South Park* as a form of contemporary secular prophetic discourse precisely because it offers viewers both a call to critical reflection on one's complicit immersion in popular social and political life, as well as an admonition to change one's behavior and pursue a more authentic form of being-in-the-world. In our formulation, prophetic discourse, whether the divinely sanctioned speech-actions of the Hebrew Bible or the commentary of *South Park*, adheres to three key characteristics. First, prophecy seeks to jolt one out of the malaise of one's complicit habituation to a cultural ethos so as to convey a call to self-reflexivity or critical self-evaluation. Second, one is encouraged to seek some form of transformation or repentance. The Old Testament notion of "shuv," meaning to orient one's practices back toward the good and the New Testament term "metanoia," "to turn away from (sin)," are crucial for our notion of repentance. These biblical metaphors convey the practical or ethical dimension of a call to transformation, which is less a call for a moralistic turn away from sin than a turn toward righteous actions. Third, the prophetic voice is a calling to authentic life, or an authentic mode of being in the world, where one no longer pursues a passive (unreflective) capitulation to unjust social practices. Using the example of the prophet Ezekiel, we will elucidate the necessarily offensive element of the biblical prophetic voice, which is often accompanied by vulgar and scatological imagery, and defend *South Park*'s satire as a contemporary form of prophecy directed at a complacent American populace.

South Park and Religion

We share Mark Pinsky's sentiment that *South Park* is "one of the most religion-fixated shows on the small screen." Although an isolated and isolationist minority of the Christian demographic in the United States and abroad may remain practically unaware of the show and its send-up of religious institutions, by all indications the show is more than a blip on the radar of the religious and political right.[7] *South Park*'s creators embody a *via media*, situating themselves as though suspended between two poles—neither left nor right, conservative nor liberal, zealously religious nor cynically atheistic. In a 2004 interview with *In Focus* magazine, Parker describes their point of view:

> What we're sick of—and it's getting even worse—is: You either like Michael Moore or you wanna f***in' go overseas and shoot Iraqis. There can't be a middle ground. Basically, if you think Michael Moore's full of s***, then you are a super-Christian right-wing whatever. And we're both just pretty middle-ground guys. We find just as many things to rip on the left as we do on the right. People on the far left and the far right are the same exact person to us. (Russell)[8]

In sum, their ambiguous (which is not to say ambivalent) position in the center, their willingness to exist within the tensions inherent to the human condition, enables Parker and Stone to offer their profane critique in all directions. Although *South Park* may appear on the surface to be an unseemly bedfellow for Christian thought, its offensive, profane character places *South Park* in a long line of subversive and corrective pronouncements central to the prophetic within the Judeo-Christian tradition. A look at particular episodes will illustrate further *South Park*'s employment of over-the-top, scatological humor for what, in the end, serves as a prophetic call to contemporary culture to self-examination and, finally, change.

Popular culture can serve a religious function, even when this religious function is well outside the author's intent or the general audience's awareness, although this is not entirely the case with *South Park*. Certainly the show's creators deliberately and self-consciously criticize religion, but the implications and the potential religious value of their criticism might often extend beyond or even subvert their intention. For example, the episode "Red Sleigh Down" concludes with Santa Claus, having been rescued by Jesus from an Iraqi torture chamber, reminding the citizens of South Park that Christmas is about "a brave man named Jesus," who, quite literally, "gave his life to save me." While Parker and Stone are clearly making fun of born-again Christian catch-phrases and intend Santa's speech to be viewed more humorously than seriously, a profound truth slips through: While the boys of South Park are obsessing over presents, and the parents are preoccupied with their Christmas Eve tree-lighting ceremony, it takes Santa to remind them, and us, that Christmas is, in fact, about Jesus—a reminder all the more relevant as tensions over winter holiday semantics grow to unprecedented heights in U.S. society.

Audiences might attribute *South Park*'s religious episodes to the prevalence of such items in the media without realizing the profundity of either the show's commentary or its potential value to religious communities. Neither speculation about the authors' intention nor the audience's awareness should be considered a final litmus test for the significance of *South Park* as secular prophecy because the role of the prophet is simply to speak the truth, and it is often a truth even he fails fully to comprehend. In the end, the only responsibility of the prophet is to deliver the message, regardless of its reception.[9]

Cartman Rocks Christfest

"Christian Rock Hard" is, on several levels, an exemplary episode and a good place to begin a closer analysis. In a moment of (divine?) inspiration, Cartman quits his garage band, inexplicably named Moop, to form a Christian rock band. His now former bandmates Stan, Kyle, and Kenny are not amused, and they want nothing to do with it. "Think about it," Cartman explains. "It's the easiest, crappiest music in the world, right? If we just play songs about how much we love Jesus, all the Christians will buy our crap!" As is often the case with Cartman's half-cocked schemes, this leads to a wager with Kyle over which band can achieve a platinum album first: Moop, who are determined to maintain their artistic integrity, or Faith+1, Cartman's artificial contemporary Christian music venture. To his new bandmates, Butters and Token, Cartman elaborates on the genius of his plan: "All right, guys, this is gonna be so easy. All we have to do to make Christian songs is take regular old songs and add Jesus stuff to them. [*Some sheet music is shown. Cartman has already crossed out the original author's name*] See? All we have to do is cross out words like 'baby' and 'darling' and replace them with [*crosses out "baby" and writes*] 'Jesus.'" To be sure, in poking fun at the all-too-easily-mockable contemporary Christian music industry, the writers of *South Park* have done their homework. In calling attention to the pretension of band photos ("You can't look happy on the album cover! That's not cool!"), the likelihood of false motives ("You just start that way, Stan, then you cross over!"), and laughable lyrics that range from the trite ("Your love is my life") to the nonsensical ("I may be born again, but I wasn't born again yesterday") to the blasphemously homoerotic ("I just wanna feel you deep inside me, Jesus"), Parker and Stone pull back the curtain on what they identify as a damnably inauthentic expression of Christianity bred in the culture of late capitalism.

In fact, when Cartman responds to Stan's accusation that he cannot form a Christian band because he does not even know anything about Christianity by flatly stating, "I know enough to exploit it," he could be providing insight about Parker and Stone as well. Neither professes a religious faith, but the two

FIGURE 7
Cartman's Christian rock band, Faith + 1.

are such acute observers of Western culture that they are able to characterize, and caricaturize, the Religious Right and its often-laughable, often-lamentable extensions.[10] In so doing, they exploit what they do know from an outsider's perspective to accomplish their constant aim: exposing the dangers of every form of extremism and institutional dogmatism. Although his motivation is more about winning his bet with Kyle than fame or fortune, Cartman hopes to accomplish his aim, a platinum album, by taking the stage at "Christfest, the single largest gathering of Christians in the Midwest, each one of them a walking, praying wallet full of cash." Parker and Stone, like Cartman, seem to regard the Christian mainstream as a horde of mindless dupes, ready to slap down their money (or their ballot) for any product or cause touting itself as allegiant to Jesus or parading under the banner of "Christian," no matter how hollow or hypocritical. Their caricature, while hyperbolic, is not far off. The underlying danger they bring to the fore is the tendency of religion to numb practitioners into uncritical, thoughtless automatons. This also is captured exquisitely in the episode "Super Best Friends" by the Blainiacs, magician David Blaine's creepy cult of disciples, and also in "The Passion of the Jew" by the stand-off between South Park's Christian and Jewish communities brought to a head by Cartman's anti-Semitic "conversion" experience induced by his viewing of Mel Gibson's *The Passion of the Christ*. However, "religion"— of the self-promoting Pharisaical sort ripped to shreds by Jesus himself—is the object of *South Park*'s critique and not necessarily "faith."

In the final scene, the prophetic voice speaks. Throughout the episode, Cartman has been given ample opportunity to examine his motives and change his methods. His greed and selfishness are contrasted by the integrity of Kyle's band, which struggles to define its sound, goes on strike to protest illegal music downloading, and then realizes that the music should be more important than the money. The call to self-critique is ever present, but Cartman ignores it, to his own detriment. Cartman sells his million albums; indeed, the hordes of Christians, dependable as ever, rush out to "buy his crap." Unfortunately, his bet with Kyle was that Faith+1 would be the first to get a platinum album, and Cartman discovers only too late that the contemporary Christian music industry does not give platinum but rather myrrh albums. In front of record executives and countless fans, Cartman's anger gets the best of him, and his true self is revealed as he screams profanities, to the horror of the audience:

INDUSTRY EXEC: Oh, please don't take the Lord's name in vain.

CARTMAN: Who cares?! I can never win my bet because you stupid a**holes don't give out platinum albums!

INDUSTRY EXEC: But you spread the Word of the Lord. You've brought faith in Jesus.

CARTMAN: OH, F*** JESUS!!

BUTTERS: Eric, I'm pretty sure you shouldn't say the F-word about Jesus.

Still, he refuses to change his behavior, and stubbornly repeats his blasphemous phrase. Cartman's outburst alienates his fans, who run away screaming "My ears are bleeding!" In addition, he angers his bandmates because not only has he driven away their audience, but his ulterior motive to humiliate Kyle has led him also to spend all the money generated by their album sales on the absurdly elaborate but now ineffectual "myrrh-album" award ceremony. After hurling a racially charged insult at Token, who has been the object of such derision throughout the episode, Token decides he has had enough and beats up Cartman. His friends stand idly by, watching, then walk away, leaving him lying in a heap. Stan shrugs and says, "Hmm. Guess he got what he deserved." What Cartman "deserved"—not just the beating but the loss of his friends—is the direct result of his refusal to heed the prophetic voice, the call to self-reflexivity, transformation, and authenticity. This scene becomes a kind of intertextual twist on Jesus' parable of the Good Samaritan, who helps a stranger in need when others have passed him by. However, in this case the "victim" has brought the injury on himself and his friends exercise their just cause in abandoning him. Only Butters, the most kind-hearted of the South Park boys, lags behind. We wonder momentarily if he will be the Good Samaritan and reach out to Cartman. Instead, Butters farts in Cartman's face and, making the corresponding hand gesture, says "F*** you, Eric," and walks away.

Catholic in the Real World

Of course we could not, in the limits of this chapter, mention every religious reference in *South Park*, but to demonstrate further the operation of the show's prophetic voice, we turn to one final religiously themed episode. In "Red Hot Catholic Love," the parents of South Park are concerned about the widespread allegations of sexual misconduct within the Catholic Church. They grow distrustful of their priest, Father Maxi, who despite a few dalliances with a woman in the confessional chamber is usually portrayed as a loving pastor. The parents resolve to hire an outside counselor to talk to the boys in an attempt to ascertain whether their priest has molested them. While the parents wait outside, one father remarks, "What has Catholicism come to anyway? [. . .] If there was a God, why would he let our kids be molested in the first place?" They discuss their disillusionment with the Catholic Church and resolve to become atheists. Parker and Stone make light of their absurd decision:

CHRIS: [*angry, waving his fist in the air*] Yeah, let's kill God, yeah!

RANDY: Well uh, let's—let's just be atheists.

CHRIS: [. . .] Same thing.

As the parents oxymoronically become committed atheists, two additional subplots unfold. In one, Father Maxi undertakes a campaign to convince the Catholic Church that the solution to the problem of priestly sexual misconduct is for the church to loosen its policy on clerical celibacy. He takes his agenda all the way to the Vatican, where he is told sternly that "the Holy Document of Vatican Law cannot be changed." Parker and Stone clearly want to highlight the rigidity and, in their view, illogic underlying the religious establishment, yet, as the episode later shows, in a way that is distinct from the situation of the individual person of faith or local faith community.

The other subplot begins as a bet between Cartman and Kyle and turns out to be simply an ultravulgar device to serve the episode's prophetic denouement. A dinnertime scene at Stan's house highlights both the family's new, carefree atheist lifestyle and introduces Cartman's innovative process of eating, dubbed "intro-rectogestion."

RANDY: Oh boy, now that we're atheists we don't have to pray for our food.

SHARON: That's right, everyone just dig in. So, kids, anything happen with your whole Sunday off?

STAN: Uh, Cartman shoved his lunch up his ass and crapped out his mouth.

SHARON: Stanley!

STAN: What? He did.

RANDY: No, it doesn't work that way, son.

STAN: Yeah it does.

RANDY: No, it doesn't.

STAN: Yeah. It does.

The scene cuts to Stan's parents' bathroom. Stan's dad is kneeling before the toilet, attempting to defecate orally. After much effort, a turd comes out of his mouth and plops into the toilet. He is stunned and calls his wife to come witness this novel event. Now, we do not wish to dwell unnecessarily on this grotesque and quite literally unsavory image, but a later scene begins to clarify why Parker and Stone have elected to take this episode, the subject matter of which is otherwise fairly serious, in such a scatological direction. The parents of South Park have gathered at Stan's house for the first meeting of the South Park Atheists Club. They are seated in a circle in the living room around the coffee table underneath a banner bearing the name of the club. The purpose of their meeting is to discuss the difficulties of their new lives as atheists.

> RANDY: Well, Sharon and I are having a great time being atheists. I for one can't believe I used to live my life by what a very old and very fictional book used to say.
>
> LINDA STOTCH: Well it's true. I mean, what do a bunch of stories about people in robes slaughtering goats have to do with today's world?
>
> RICHARD: Atheism has definitely made our lives better.
>
> SHARON: [entering holding a tray of quesadillas and a wastebasket] I made some quesadillas, if anybody wants some. And if anybody needs to potty, there's a potty basket right here [indicates the wastebasket]. [. . .]
>
> MAN: You know, for Martha and I, we're worried we might have a hard time raising our son atheist. I mean—[taking a quesadilla from Sharon's tray] oh, thank you—I mean, it could end up being very difficult raising an atheist child in such a Christian society. [Unzipping his trousers.] I feel that everywhere my poor son goes he's being [straining to intro-rectogest the quesadilla] persecuted for his beliefs.
>
> RICHARD: That's true. If I'm gonna raise my son to be atheist, I don't want him saying "under God" every day at school. That could really damage him. "Under God" should be taken out of the—uh, 'scuse me [orally defecates into wastebasket]—"Under God" should be taken out of the Pledge of Allegiance.
>
> RANDY: That's right, I agree. And it should be taken off of money as well. The Religious Right in this country is trying to force our children to believe what they—[orally defecates into wastebasket]—and we can't let the Religious Right corrupt our kids. [A chorus of agreement from the others.]

As should now be apparent, the parents of South Park, having abandoned their formal religious principles, are only able to sit around and, quite literally, "talk shit." Adopting a clichéd liberal ideology that essentially substitutes one fundamentalism for another, the atheist parents, at least as much as their religious counterparts at Christfest, portray precisely the sort of phoniness that Parker and Stone rage against. The parents, failing to realize their own hypocrisy, become the same sort of impressionable suckers as the Christians who rush out to buy Cartman's schlocky contemporary Christian music album in "Christian Rock Hard."

All the while, Father Maxi grows increasingly annoyed with his lack of progress with the myopic Catholic leaders, who are more concerned with the testy Catholics from planet Gilgamec and gaining the approval of the Great Queen Spider (regarded as "the Highest Source") than they are about the very real and pressing problems they face in their contemporary situation. An enraged Father Maxi rips up the Holy Document of Vatican Law, which causes the Vatican to collapse and burn. Parker and Stone here reveal their ubiquitous anti-institutionalism once and for all. But this seemingly anti-Catholic, perhaps even blatantly antireligious move is followed and indeed transformed by the episode's closing scene. Again, the prophetic voice speaks clearly, this time in the form of a spokesperson of traditional religion.

[Vatican City. The clergy mill around in the ruins of the Vatican.]

ITALIAN CARDINAL: Gone! It's all gone!

BRITISH CARDINAL: Well, thanks a lot, Father Maxi. You've killed our religion.

FR. MAXI: No, I didn't! All that's dead are your stupid laws and rules! You've forgotten what being a Catholic is all about. This book. [Holds up the Bible.] You see, these are just stories. Stories that are meant to help people in the right direction. Love your neighbor. Be a good person. That's it! And when you start turning the stories into literal translations of hierarchies and power, well . . . Well, you end up with this [gestures toward the Queen Spider and the Gilgamecs]. People are losing faith because they don't see how what you've turned their religion into applies to them! They've lost touch with any idea of any kind of religion, and when they have no mythology to try and live their lives by, well, they just start spewing a bunch of crap out of their mouths!

[Cut to: Butter's house. The family is watching the news.]

RICHARD: [orally defecates into wastebasket] . . . What was that last bit?

[Cut to: Vatican City, via the news report on the television screen.]

FR. MAXI: Look, I'm proud to be a Catholic. But I'm a Catholic in the real world. In today's world! It's time for you all to do that, too. It is time . . . for change.

While the bureaucracy of the bishops and cardinals proves useless, this simple, local parish priest is able to see through the malaise and speak the truth, but this is possible only after he has accepted the truth about his religious institution, an epiphany incumbent on his willingness to heed the call to self-evaluation. Father Maxi desires repentance and the turn toward authentic religion, not only for his religious tradition, but also for his parishioners and even himself.

The families of South Park happily watch these events unfold on their television screens, beckoning their children in to share in their "victory"

("Stan, the Vatican is burning down"—"Score one for us atheists!"). But Father Maxi's speech sobers them, and, at least in the case of Stan's family, compels them toward self-critique:

> RANDY: He's right, Sharon. We don't have to believe every word of the Bible. They're just stories to help us to live by. We shouldn't toss away the lessons of the Bible just because some a**holes in Italy screwed it up.
>
> SHARON: [*relieved*] Oh Randy, I don't wanna put food up my butt anymore.
>
> RANDY: Gang, I think maybe we owe God an apology.
>
> STAN: [*disappointed*] Does this mean we have to go to church on Sundays again?
>
> RANDY: [*with saccharine sincerity*] No. It means we *get to*, son. It means . . . we get to [*Randy orally defecates as the credits begin to roll.*]

Parker and Stone apparently cannot resist the last-minute slam of institutional religion—that the family would find it at all appealing, much less necessary, to resume church attendance is perhaps impossible for them to comprehend. Still, the message rings clear: Authentic religion is not about institutions or hierarchies, but about stories and practices that guide the life of the individual and the faith community. Discarding the lessons of the Bible is throwing the baby out with the bathwater. The prophetic call is to the reform and, more important, the revitalization of religion—not its outright rejection. While some might take issue at the lowest-common-denominator vision of religion promoted by the episode ("Love your neighbor. Be a good person"), the emphasis is still on the particularity of one's religious beliefs, myths, and practices, albeit in a revised nonexclusivist, heterodox form. Furthermore, the episode leaves us with a two-way critique: While the parents are called to repent and return to a more authentic mode of religious faith and being, religion is itself challenged to repent of its tendency toward authoritarianism and to strive toward relevance, which to Parker and Stone, seems to be the trait of authentic religion, purged of its dogmatic insularity.

Prophets and Their Foul Mouths

Obviously, Parker and Stone are not the first to employ offensive and scatological speech in the service of moral admonition. Throughout the Old Testament, prophets are conscripted by Yahweh to scandalize conventional moralistic sensibilities to indict Israel's violation of their covenantal relationship with their God. Prophets and prophecy are weighty concepts that seem to have lost their resonance within a secular culture. Nonetheless the ideological critique that is facilitated by the profane humor of *South Park* is part of a long-standing tradition within the Judeo-Christian prophetic imagination.

Prophets were commonplace figures within the ancient Near Eastern cultures of the Levant. The societies from which the Hebrew scriptures emerged were familiar with the genre of prophetic critique. Broadly defined, "prophecy is human transmission of allegedly divine messages. [. . .] That is to say, prophets [. . .] do not employ methods based on systematic observations and their scholarly interpretations, but act as direct mouthpieces of gods whose messages they communicate" (Nissinen 1). This definition of prophecy pertains to both the function and the substance of the prophetic vocation. Although their words may be oriented toward various religious and social maladies of their day, ultimately the source of the critique is located in the Divine mind rather than human intentions.

Rather than relying on a substantive definition of the prophetic vocation, which would raise problems in our construal of *South Park* as "secular prophecy," we will prioritize the functional nature of prophetic speech acts, specifically those of Ezekiel, whose writings emerged from the postexilic period (from roughly the sixth century BCE). Although many earlier ancient Near Eastern prophets "provided mantic insights, worked miracles, proclaimed messages, visions and revelations at sanctuaries, royal courts and in public throughout the monarchies of Israel and Judah," the prophets of this later period in Israel's history aimed their proclamations to an exilic community and "preached against social injustice and oppression, warned of imminent catastrophes and occasionally sought to change the community's attitudes" (Carroll 7). Here we find a resonating echo of this sociopolitical prophetic critique, latently present within cultural forms such as *South Park*.

Although the Old Testament canon has a deep pool from which to draw many a scandalizing curio in which profanity and offensive language are used in service of the Divine Word—Isaiah's naked ramblings or Hosea's marriage to a woman of ill repute—we find Ezekiel's prophetic pronouncements to be the most "*South Park*–like" of all.[11] The prophet openly mocks Jerusalem's heritage as the fallen seat of divine favor (Ezk. 4–24), then recites graphic parables regarding the young Oholibah, who, like Jerusalem, flees fidelity and pursues harlotry.

The passages from Ezekiel's work which concern us (Ezk. 23:19–21) revolve around the covenantal violations of Judah and Jerusalem. According to the biblical narrative, the Kingdom of Israel had been divided into two autonomous kingdoms since 928 BCE. The Divided Kingdom consisted of the Southern Kingdom of Judah, with its capital city of Jerusalem, and the Northern Kingdom of Israel, with its capital city of Samaria. Ezekiel 24 casts the two kingdoms as two sisters who became the two wives of Yahweh. These wives are portrayed as being grossly unfaithful, lavishing their affection not on their "husband" but on the competing nations of Egypt and Assyria. Ezekiel's task is, therefore, to bring to the fore the gravity of their infidelity. As Ellen Davis notes: "Although there is no possibility that the judgment will be reversed, nonetheless it is necessary that Israel be brought to recognition of its own deserving. [. . .] Only this recognition, more humiliating than the destruction itself, can serve as the basis of a renewed relationship with Yahweh" (57).

Looking specifically at the text of Ezekiel 23, we note several instances of explicit vulgarity deliberately to offend the status quo. Ezekiel's use of profanity, in this case erotically charged, serves as a mocking offense against Israel's nationalist infidelities: "Yet she increased her whorings, remembering the days of her youth, when she played the whore in the land of Egypt and lusted after her paramours there, whose members were like those of donkeys, and whose emission was like that of stallions. Thus you longed for the lewdness of your youth, when the Egyptians fondled your bosom and caressed your young breasts" (Ezk. 23:19–21). Here, we see Jerusalem portrayed as a young, nubile whore, who lusts after the protection of a foreign power, rather than relying on divine protection as the source of her security. Like *South Park's* vulgarity, the sexual imagery of the prophet's judgment seeks to shock the audience into a form of ethical response. Given the scandalous career of this temporarily mute prophet, the ecstatic visions that launch his career (the chariot depicted by a wheel-within-a-wheel, the edible scroll of judgment), and the graphic language with which his judgments in chapters 16 and 23 are framed, Old Testament scholar Walter Brueggemann is justified in noting that "popular interpretations tend to dismiss Ezekiel as 'bizarre.' But Ezekiel may be exactly the right text for such a 'bizarre' time as ours" (51).

If this is the portrayal of the God in Ezekiel, whose justice has been maligned through stylized infidelities, it resonates with the portrayal of the hidden God who underpins the Catholicism "in the real-world" that is hinted at in the conclusion of "Red Hot Catholic Love." This is a God who is neither controlled by ecclesiastical heteronomy (the immutability of "the Holy Document of Vatican Law") nor replaced by graven idols (the Great Queen Spider) nor is it a God that is supplanted by atheistic autonomy (the parents' "South Park Atheists Club"). Like *South Park*, Ezekiel is an "imaginative practitioner" of renarration, who takes up the traditions of his nation and comments on them using the symbols and events of his day. Ezekiel "knows and affirms [a] tradition which is rooted in the oldest credo recitals, but he rereads the tradition in light of his own incongruous situation" (Brueggemann 59). One must wonder if, likewise, the secular prophetic of *South Park* only works so well as a profane societal critique because its authors are so in tune with the incongruity of their own experiences within late capitalist U.S. culture. Like Ezekiel, Parker and Stone levy their critique at that culture of which they are a part, and employ effectively cutting shock humor because they possess both an intimate familiarity with the history of their nation and the structures of religious and political taboo within their day and age. The "lewd and shocking" rereading of history in Ezekiel conveys a remarkably "radical rereading" of his tradition. It offers his audience a subversive history that forces them to "discover things about memory," which had been "suppressed" by the dominant ideology of the day (Brueggemann 60). Likewise, *South Park* forces its viewers to confront a radically renarrated vision of typical American values. Through their imaginative and offensive re-presentation the excesses of our culture can be judged.

Contemporary television, according to Dominic Strinati, is a postmodern medium whose "regular daily and night-time flows of images and information bring together bits and pieces from elsewhere, and create its sequences of programmes on the basis of compilations and surface simulations" (213). The claims that televised media stake on their viewers are both universal and individualistic, contributing to what Strinati notes as an increasingly "fragmented" experience of the world (220).

A degree of resonance is found between the sociocultural fragmentation Strinati's analysis of postmodern entertainment culture describes and the exilic community to which Ezekiel preached. Like our contemporary televisual society, the exilic community felt the foundations of the corporate identity erode. For ancient Israel, universality (socioreligious homogeneity) and particularity (fragmented isolationism) coalesced in the experience of exile as foreign armies destroyed their loci of cultural identity (land and temple). Ezekiel's message to this fragmented people is one of both judgment (to explicate their situation) and hope (to point to a future return to the Promised Land). We believe that South Park, like Ezekiel, speaks to a fractured and "exiled" people today, who suffer a loss of ground and common experience through the fracturing consequences of postmodern entertainment culture.

Conclusion

This chapter has been guided by a concern for finding the emergence of deeper meaning within popular culture and noting how this deeper meaning can serve an ultimately redemptive purpose. Artifacts such as film and television are a means by which social, political, and religious concerns are articulated, serving as a forum wherein conceptions of value, beauty, and the good can be discussed. Theologians and theological practitioners, rather than shying away from the medium out of a concern for piety or purity, should instead approach the "positive potential of Jesus' teaching: 'If your eyes are good, your whole body will be full of light' (Matt. 6:22). We are called to develop good eyes, not blind eyes" (Detweiler and Taylor 202). Only when we approach media with a "good eye" can we be liberated from the apathy of passive television watching and begin to engage with the message of the media.

For scholars of religion, the ability to dialogue with culture is measured not only by way of one's familiarity with the loci classicus of a particular discipline, but it is also marked by one's ability to speak the lingua franca of the postmodern world—popular culture. This chapter has demonstrated how popular cultural forms can be understood as a source of theological reflection. Rather than rereading popular culture to force it to conform to a preexisting theological hermeneutic, here *South Park* speaks on its own terms. Although neither *South Park* nor its community of viewers constitute a religion, we have sought to employ *South Park* as a form of secular prophecy that resonates with other forms of authentic religious critiques. The balance between authenticity and fakery, or the sacred and the secular, is one that teases out the liminality of expressions of religion within popular cultural forms.

Nonetheless, using popular culture as an object for theological reflection is not without its detractors. In particular, one may call into question the merit of a popular prophetic voice such as that of *South Park*'s, arguing that its transformative message may ultimately fall on deaf ears and never effect the change for which it was intended. Yet again, like prophetic discourse discussed earlier, reception is secondary to delivery. Prophecy is a performative exercise that seeks to confront injustice with the just ideal regardless of the effect. Indeed, Ezekiel's own career was prefaced on the fact that his prophetic voice would not effect a change, but merely offer an interpretation of Israel's exilic situation: "But the house of Israel will not listen to you, for they are not willing to listen to me; because all the house of Israel have a hard forehead and a stubborn heart" (Ezk. 3:7).

So, which is more offensive or more profane: Ezekiel's confrontational attack on the sacred city of his exiled people's mythology or *South Park*'s willingness to challenge excessive ecclesial heteronomy and uncritical atheistic autonomy? How does *South Park*'s depiction of contemporary religious life—the mob mentality of Christfest or the atheist parents' crapping out of their mouths—compare to Ezekiel's painful jabs at the sacred socioreligious ideology? Although on the surface Parker and Stone appear very far removed from the prophetic role, perhaps Ezekiel and *South Park* do originate from a common authorial wellspring where crassness and critique meet together to overturn faulty, even dangerous, assumptions about the nature of nationality and true religion. In a Jerusalem where one's neighbors could be sold for the price of one's own freedom, and in an America where the poor are oppressed for the sake of cheap sneakers and carbonated beverages, perhaps we should turn our attention to the prophecy of *South Park* as a self-reflexive call for repentance and a turn toward a life of authenticity.

Notes

The information contained herein was presented at an earlier stage to the Religion and Popular Culture Group of the American Academy of Religion on November 19,

2005. The work, at that time titled "Parody and Prophecy: A Serious Look at *South Park*," was included as part of a panel on "Religion and the Politics of Parody." We are grateful to panel chair Gary Laderman, our fellow panelists, and those in attendance who provided helpful feedback. Students at the University of Aberdeen and the Centre for Literature, Theology and the Arts at Glasgow University were also subjected to our *South Park* treatment, and we appreciate their patience and constructive criticism as well.

1. For example, consider "All about the Mormons?" and "Bloody Mary." Although full treatment of the relationship between *South Park*'s unique animated style and the efficacy of its prophetic voice would require an additional chapter, the show's rudimentary computer animation, which facilitates an amazingly concise production time, allows the creators to respond to current events with stunning immediacy. *South Park*'s treatment of the cultural furor surrounding the life and death of permanently vegetative patient Terri Schiavo—"Best Friends Forever," wherein Kenny, in like condition, is the object of similar disputes among the South Park community and is eventually taken off life support—is an excellent example. This Emmy Award–winning episode aired on 30 Mar. 2005, 12 days after the removal of Terri Schiavo's feeding tube (18 Mar. 2005) and within 24 hours of her death (31 Mar. 2005).

2. *South Park*'s satirizing of Scientology ("Trapped in the Closet") has made recent news for contributing to the resignation of Scientologist Isaac Hayes, the voice of Chef, from the show. In a comment to the Associated Press, Stone noted the irony of Mr. Hayes's reaction: "He has no problem—and he's cashed plenty of checks—with our show making fun of Christians" (Associated Press).

3. See Romanowski for more on religion as shaped by cultural forms, especially 90, and Pinsky, as a prime example of this pursuit with regard to animated television.

4. "Ultimate Concern" is a term the twentieth-century German-American protestant theologian Paul Tillich used. In *The Protestant Era*, Tillich defines religion as "the state of being grasped by something unconditional, holy, absolute," which he refers to as being grasped by ultimate concern (58).

5. See Hoffman, as well as Detweiler and Taylor, especially 243–69.

6. This approach is encouraged, although not always practiced, by Detweiler and Taylor.

7. We take this cue from Andrew Sullivan's phrase "South Park Republican," later morphed into "South Park Conservatives" in the title of a book by Brian C. Anderson. These monikers, and the right-wingers who have coined them, appropriate the libertarianism expressed in *South Park* to characterize a "new wave" within the younger generation of American political conservatives. See Sullivan. As an additional note, the authors wish to acknowledge that they are aware of their tendency to conflate, in a way that might be judged problematic, the political conservatism with religious fundamentalism and political liberalism with an antireligious or atheist ideology. We believe such a conflation is often evident in *South Park* and would defend this correlation on these grounds, while admitting that things are, of course, not that simple: Indeed, we have met religious liberals, theistic libertarians, nonreligious conservatives, and so forth.

8. Or Matt Stone's pithier quip: "I hate conservatives, but I really f***ing hate liberals" (Anderson). To be sure, both Stone and Parker often skirt questions about their political affiliation, but they are most often identified with libertarianism; Parker is in fact a registered Libertarian and Stone has claimed he is unsure if he is even registered to vote (Brownfield).

9. Often the prophetic voice falls on deaf ears. Even more often, the prophet is disregarded as a raving lunatic and ignored or cast out—indeed, as Jesus himself noted, the prophet becomes a pariah when his words hit too close to home: "And they took offense at him. But Jesus said to them, 'Only in his hometown and in his own house is a prophet without honor'" (Matt.13:57).

10. Stone describes himself as an "agnostic Jew" (Pinsky) and claims he remained unaware of the fact of his family's Jewish heritage until well into his teenage years. In at least one venue, Parker has claimed to believe in God, whereas Stone denied any such belief (Thompson).

11. In a similar way that *South Park* is, in its very form, a parody of animated television, Ezekiel himself is a parody of a prophet. A vocation, such as that of the prophet, was historically tied to the proclamation of a verbal message, whether in the form of words of judgment, words of hope, or words of salvation. Being called to an orally fixated vocation, Ezekiel is scandalized when in his first encounter with his God he is instructed to internalize his message: "He said to me, O mortal, eat what is offered to you; eat this scroll" (Ezk. 3:1). He is then struck dumb as a result, "I will make your tongue cling to the roof of your mouth, so that you shall be speechless and unable to reprove them; for they are a rebellious house" (Ezk. 3:25).

Works Cited

Anderson, Brian C. "We're Not Losing the Culture Wars Anymore." *City Journal* 13.4 (Autumn 2003). 13 June 2006. <http://www.city-journal.org/html/ 13_4_were_ not_losing.html>.

Associated Press. "Scientologist Isaac Hayes Quits 'South Park.'" (21 Mar. 2006). 13 June 2006. <http://www.msnbc.msn.com/id/11812699/>.

Brownfield, Paul. "Fitting Square Pegs in an Oval Office." *Los Angeles Times* 4 Apr. 2001: F1.

Brueggemann, Walter. *Hopeful Imagination: Prophetic Voices in Exile*. London: SCM, 1986.

Carroll, Robert P. *When Prophecy Failed: Reactions and Responses to Failure in the Old Testament Prophetic Traditions*. London: SCM Press, 1978.

Davis, Ellen F. *Swallowing the Scroll: Textuality and the Dynamics of Discourse in Ezekiel's Prophecy*. Sheffield: Almond Press, 1989.

Detweiler, Craig, and Barry Taylor. *A Matrix of Meanings: Finding God in Pop Culture*. Grand Rapids, MI: Baker Academic, 2003.

Forbes, Bruce David, and Jeffrey H. Mahan, eds. *Religion and Popular Culture in America*. Berkeley: University of California Press, 2000.

Hoffman, Shirl J., ed. *Sport and Religion*. Champaign, IL: Human Kinetics Books, 1992.

Lynch, Gordon. *Understanding Theology and Popular Culture*. London: Blackwell, 2005.

Nissinen, Martti. *Prophets and Prophecy in the Ancient Near East*. Atlanta, GA: Society of Biblical Literature, 2003.

Pinsky, Mark I. "Jesus Lives in South Park." *Beliefnet* (15 Aug. 2005). 13 June 2006. <http://www.beliefnet.com/story/174/story_17498_1.html>.

Romanowski, William D. *Eyes Wide Open: Looking for God in Popular Culture*. Grand Rapids, MI: Brazos, 2001.

Russell, M. E. "Puppetry of the Meanest: An Interview with Trey Parker and Matt Stone." *In Focus* IV.10 (Oct. 2004). 13 June 2006. <http://www.infocusmag.com/04october/puppetryuncut.htm>.

Strinati, Dominic. *An Introduction to Theories of Popular Culture*. London: Routledge, 2004.

Sullivan, Andrew. "South Park Republicanism." 12 Oct. 2003. <www.andrewsullivan.com/index.php?dish_inc=archives/2003_10_26_dish_archive.html#106727 359457680686>.

Thompson, Stephen. "Is There a God?" *The Onion AV Club* (9 Oct. 2002). 15 June 2006. <http://www.avclub.com/content/node/24569>

Tillich, Paul. *The Protestant Era*. Trans. James Luther Adams. Chicago: University of Chicago Press, 1957.

PART FOUR

Specific Critiques

CHAPTER 11

"You Know, I Learned Something Today . . ."

Cultural Pedagogy and the Limits of Formal Education in *South Park*

JAMES RENNIE

Despite being stuck in the fourth grade for the past several years, Kyle, Stan, Cartman, and Kenny have learned a lot at South Park Elementary School. They have made and lost millions of dollars, saved their town from countless apocalyptic threats, and explored the (often graphic) intricacies of human sexuality. Yet how many of these lessons have actually been learned in the classroom? Mr. Garrison rarely succeeds in teaching the boys much of anything. Ms. Choksondik fared just as poorly in her brief tenure. In fact, classroom practices and curricular goals are almost totally unsuccessful in the world of *South Park*. Try as the system might, it just cannot seem to teach the kids much of anything.

With its narrative reliance on the schoolhouse, Trey Parker and Matt Stone's *South Park* routinely undermines the pedagogical influence and function of formal education. From Chef's paternal advice to the life-changing results of Internet searches, the most important lessons come from the least likely of sources. Consequently, *South Park* presents an important critique of contemporary public education and its role in youth culture and development. In recognizing the importance of the school yard, the Internet, and the bus stop, South Park not only plays with the conventions of situational comedies, but it also unapologetically diminishes the supreme importance of schooling in childhood education. Kyle, Stan, Cartman, Kenny, and their classmates learn about the world at large the same way that young people in the real world do—they watch television, they listen to the adults around them, and they discuss matters among themselves with a degree of sophistication parents and teachers rarely recognize. Although public schooling undoubtedly plays an important role in this process of exploration, *South Park* reminds Western society that most contemporary definitions of "education" exclude the bulk of real childhood learning.

This chapter explores *South Park*'s contribution to contemporary discussions of education, youth development, and public schooling. As a social construction, "childhood" has been used to attack and defend an unlimited number of causes, projects, and programs. By repositioning the role of public schooling, *South Park* uses the artificiality of "childhood" as a satiric weapon to undermine the ideological stability of the same list of causes, projects, and programs. Young people learn to read the world around them with or without the direct tutelage of adults; when adults exaggerate the pedagogical significance of the classroom, they fail to give young people sufficient space to develop on their own.

South Park, the School Yard, and the Politics of Cynicism

Although *South Park* has often been compared to shows such as *The Simpsons* (*South Park* itself drew attention to the difficulty of working in such a large shadow—see Weinstock's chapter in this collection), casting a slightly wider net when looking for predecessors and distant cousins is helpful. Arguably the show has more in common with the narrative structures and devices employed in Charles Schulz's *Peanuts* than with *The Simpsons*; young children are at the center of each episode instead of the classic family unit found in traditional sitcoms (of which *The Simpsons* has undoubtedly become an example). Parents, teachers, and celebrities become the peripheral characters in most episodes, allowing Parker and Stone to use the younger children to drive the stories. Many episodes feature adult characters learning lessons from events, but the children usually instigate the action or deliver critical information that informs the adults' lessons ("Something Wall-Mart This Way Comes," "The Death Camp of Tolerance," "Rainforest Schmainforest," and so forth).

Placing children at the center of contentious social debates has had numerous unusual consequences, including an astonishing array of ideological criticism from every conceivable direction. As Becker discusses herein, in *South Park Conservatives*, for example, Brian C. Anderson argues that Stan, Kyle, Kenny, and Cartman represent a fundamental political shift across the American landscape, citing as proof that "Parker and Stone have made their show not only the most obscenity-laced but also the most hostile to liberalism in television history" (88). Anderson goes on to argue that younger audiences embrace the show's antiliberalism, and that, "Together with the FOX-ification of cable news, this new attitude among the young, reflected in the hippest cable comedy, promises a more conservative future" (100).

South Park's politics, however, are somewhat more complex than Anderson's own hopeful model. As Robert Bolton, professor of communications at the University of North Carolina, notes, "I don't think that South Park has a particular political agenda, and I think it shares this kind of very profound political ambivalence with an awful lot of popular culture in America [. . .]. What it does do is open up as a source of humor an awful lot of things that could either be read as being left or right" (qtd. in Slade 98). To the casual viewer, Parker and Stone may indeed serve a specific political agenda, whether it is anticorporate ("Chef's Salty Chocolate Balls"), pro-corporate ("Gnomes"), antiwar ("I'm a Little Bit Country"), or pro-war ("I'm a Little Bit Country"). Regarded as a whole, however, South Park episodes demonstrate little political consistency. Critics and pundits who search for deeper meanings and partisan leanings ignore the role the audience plays in interpreting South Park's deeper cultural significance. As Christina Slade observes, "Interestingly, the diametrically opposed views of the critics share a fundamental assumption: that the moral impact of the program is the responsibility of the program producers and writers. Even those who understand the vagaries of audiences tend to treat the audience as monolithic when discussing shows such as South Park" (98).

Rather than seeking common political themes, considering the ideological assumptions South Park makes, particularly as they relate to cultural notions of childhood and learning, is helpful. What is often perceived of as cynicism, antiliberalism, antipolitical, or simply antisocial behavior may actually conceal South Park's deeper cultural relevance.

Childhood Revisited: South Park and Moral Panic

One of the most striking aspects of South Park's originality is the incredibly young age of its main characters. Setting the show in the third (now fourth) grade at South Park Elementary allows Parker and Stone to challenge fundamental notions of childhood and its construction. Whereas live-action television programs use teenagers to address issues of violence, sexuality, and power (see Degrassi High, Dawson's Creek, The O.C., or Beverly Hills 90210, for example), animation—particularly of the crude, highly abstracted variety South Park uses—frees writers from certain moral and legal restrictions. (Can anyone imagine Dakota Fanning and Haley Joel Osment calling each other uncle-fuckers or pleasuring Ben Affleck in a convertible? Is simply imagining these scenarios grounds for arrest?) Much of South Park's comedy stems from

basic mismatches between "adult" themes and the experiences of "children."
To understand why many of these mismatches seem so shocking to many
viewers, exploring Western culture's relatively recent obsession with the
sanctity and purity of childhood is necessary.

South Park's most effective critique of contemporary culture stems from
its unique construction of childhood, which presents itself in stark contrast
to dominant social models of youth and development. Whereas the children
of *South Park* have been exposed to countless episodes of grotesque violence,
explicit sexuality, and untold criminal horrors, the vast majority of children
in Western societies continue to be sheltered—as much as possible—from
such experiences. As a culture, we have transformed the realm of childhood
into a sacred sanctuary, where any significant intrusion is apt to generate
fierce moral panic. However, as Joe Kincheloe and Shirley Steinberg write,
"Changing economic realities coupled with children's access to information
about the adult world have drastically changed childhood. The traditional
childhood genie is out of the bottle and is unable to return" (3). Furthermore,
although childhood is once again undergoing intense transformation, many
critics and observers are warning of dire consequences. "Recent writing about
childhood in both the popular and scholarly presses speaks of 'childhood lost,'
'children growing up too fast,' and 'child terror in the isolation of the fragmented home and community'" (3).

So where does this precious model of childhood, which television, the
Internet, and all other "corrupt" media forces are now attacking, come from
in the first place? Were children ever truly as innocent as moral crusaders
would like them to be now? To understand fully the absurdity of our current
situation, we must compare contemporary attitudes toward young people
with historical precedents. Simply stated, we have not always felt the need to
protect young people from the crude realities of adult life. In fact, our current
attitudes toward children and childhood are more recent than many would
care to appreciate. Stephen Kline writes:

> During the nineteenth century a powerful idea came to prevail as the
> dominant view of child development: that children are innocent beings
> in need of formation and learning, to be protected from the harsher real-
> ities of industrial society. Historically, this was a radical idea [. . .]. Chil-
> dren were being excluded more and more from the crucial arenas of life
> and the inherent conflicts and struggles that had shaped so much of the
> rest of history. (48)

For thousands of years, children were essentially small adults who would
one day grow into fully functional members of a community; children young
enough to be Kyle and Stan's peers contributed to the work and well-being of
their communities in whatever ways possible. During a period of labor

reforms in the Industrial Revolution, young people began to be excluded from the world of work, and they were eventually excluded from participating in many other vital aspects of community life.

As Western society entered the twentieth century, the rapid expansion of public schooling, coupled with the existing authority of the household, provided nearly constant supervision of young people's development. Protecting children from physical labor had become the full-time job of teachers, nannies, mothers, and fathers. By the 1920s, raising children was a full-fledged science through which experts (mostly men) could instruct parents (mostly mothers) in the subtle art of sheltering children from adult life. As Lynn Spigel observes, at the core of this science was "the idea that children were pliable, innocent creatures who needed to be guided by adults. The adult's responsibility was to generate moral values in the young by guarding the gates to knowledge"; by strictly adhering to "scientifically" established stages of development, "parents could ensure that children would carry the torch of progress for future generations. A mistake in this regard, the experts warned, could prove fatal—not only for the individual child, but for the moral character of the entire nation" (113–14).

Throughout the history of television programming, most sitcoms have adhered to this cultural belief that good parenting translates into good citizenry and that good parenting involves protecting children from the dangers of "adult" ideas and activities. Whether Bill Cosby is keeping the Huxtable girls from dating too soon, Marge Simpson is chastising Bart for using foul language in the house, or June Cleaver is reminding the Beaver to stay out of any and all trouble, sitcom parents reinforce acceptable childhood behaviors to maintain the clear boundaries between childhood and adult life. Western culture, as reflected in many of television's families, entrusts parents and teachers with the sacred role of gatekeeping, ensuring that young people remain at a safe distance from mature matters until just the right time. Treating children as immature bodies, incapable of any real decision-making, provides television sitcoms with a very basic—and culturally recognizable—narrative device; children will always learn a valuable lesson from their mistakes because parents and teachers show them the errors they have made. *South Park* clearly revels in mocking this infantilizing function of adult society; as Chef advises:

> CHEF: It's very simple, children. The right time to start having sex is seventeen.
>
> KYLE: Seventeen?
>
> CHEF: Seventeen.
>
> SHEILA BROFLOVSKI: So you mean seventeen as long as you're in love?
>
> CHEF: Nope. Just seventeen.

GERALD BROFLOVSKI: But, what if you're not ready at seventeen?

CHEF: Seventeen. You're ready. ("Proper Condom Use")

Rather than pretend that adults must dole out all knowledge at controlled intervals, *South Park* embraces a rather sophisticated model of childhood learning and development. As an example, consider *South Park*'s position on sexuality and sex education. Although public schools often shoulder much of the burden of teaching young people the basics of human sexuality, South Park Elementary is woefully inadequate in this field, demonstrated painfully by Mr. Mackey's admission that he cannot remember where he put "that damned thing" the last time he had sex ("Proper Condom Use"). In their role as educators, most teachers strive to be honest with their students; in their role as gatekeepers, however, teachers must also protect young students from certain categories of knowledge that society deems to be too sophisticated or obscene. The subject of human sexuality is particularly murky terrain; adults must continually reevaluate the needs of cultural discretion in relation to the demands of sheer pragmatism. If students are engaging in sexual behavior at younger ages, then proper education must slowly work its way down to lower age groups. In a study of how British children process sexual content from media sources, David Buckingham and Sara Bragg note that whereas schools "obviously provided significant opportunities for sexual learning—and not just through the explicit instruction provided in sex education lessons," on another level, "schools operate to 'police' sexuality, preventing it from manifesting itself in certain ways" (45).

South Park illustrates this educational function quite explicitly, ensuring that the fourth grade girls' first exposure to sexuality comes in the form of graphic images of diseased genitals ("Proper Condom Use"). Between the extreme pedagogies of fear-mongering and blatant ignorance, the students at South Park Elementary come to understand the broader implications of sexuality only when they gossip with one another. Buckingham and Bragg describe a similar solution, arguing for a Foucauldian construction of sexuality, insofar as "what seem to be our most intimate personal experiences and relationships are in fact intensively socially organised and managed" (14). Rather than accessing sexual knowledge through the culturally authorized filters of parents and teachers, the children of *South Park*, like most children in the real world, learn about sex from a variety of sources, including school yard gossip and numerous media sources (consider Stan's eye-opening Internet search for information on the clitoris in *South Park: Bigger Longer & Uncut* [1999]). One of the greatest moral panics fueled by the *South Park* model of childhood is that young people may be able access "adult" information on their own, circumventing the information gatekeepers put in place to protect their "fragile little minds."

Modern media outlets therefore play an integral part in *South Park's* repositioned model of childhood development. The media's role in childhood learning is also among the most contentious issues parents, teachers, and media scholars debate because the benefits of additional learning are greatly overshadowed by fears of unbridled, unsupervised access. The resulting calls for media regulation and censorship are a last, desperate attempt to protect the gatekeeping roles parents and teachers have played in childhood development for the past century. Summarizing the perceived scope of this threat to childhood, David Marr observes, "One of the great achievements of the censorship advocates [. . .] has been to establish in the public imagination the image of the extraordinarily vulnerable and extraordinarily ingenious child who wanders about the house, barely parented, sleepless at 3 A.M., looking for mischief and finding it on television [. . .] or on the Internet" (qtd. in Slade 122). If children are indeed navigating media outlets without traditional forms of supervision, what exactly are they finding? Just as important, which traditional social role is most at risk in this new arrangement: the children or the gatekeepers?

Cultural Pedagogy, Moral Development, and the Media

Although *South Park* relies heavily on the schoolhouse for narrative development, the school clearly lacks any significant educational authority in the lives of South Park's children. Sex ed is best learned on the playground, Chef can answer most of the student's more personal questions at lunchtime, and an extraordinary number of Mr. Garrison's lesson plans are based on cancelled television programs. As adults who would traditionally aid in the children's educational and moral development, the teaching staff at South Park Elementary serves to undermine outdated modes of understanding childhood growth. In the early days of the modern childhood model, Kline notes, "It was at school, after all, that children would derive their first sense of their position in the broader social matrix of jobs, civic duty, social responsibility and moral choices" (50). Although Stan, Kyle, Cartman, and Kenny have undoubtedly come to grasp their place in the world, South Park Elementary can hardly take much credit for their advances.

South Park's model of childhood learning deliberately ridicules public schooling's inability to contribute meaningfully to major aspects of development; instead, it advances the argument that schools alone cannot take credit for the personal development of young people. This model can be seen as one that advocates the notion of "cultural pedagogy," "which refers to the idea that education takes place in a variety of social sites including but not limited to schooling. Pedagogical sites are those places where power is organized and deployed, including libraries, TV, movies, newspapers, magazines, toys, advertisements, video games, books, sports, and so on" (Kincheloe and Steinberg 3–4). Contemporary models of cultural pedagogy naturally include a significant focus on media outlets, which play a substantial role in modern childhood development, regardless of whether concerned adults like it.

Media analyses in the study of cultural pedagogy are rarely conclusive, however, as they have tended to focus on individual instances of media production and consumption. To ascertain the pedagogical effectiveness of particular programs and resources, for example, considering content alone is not sufficient. In their study of how teenagers respond to British television, Buckingham and Bragg discuss the pedagogical function of television drama, distinguishing between "overt" and "covert" pedagogy: "By overt pedagogy, we are referring to clearly defined moral or health-related 'lessons' that viewers perceive the programmes to be putting across. Covert pedagogy refers to more general attitudes or beliefs about relationships which viewers infer from their viewing, whether or not they see these as intended on the part of the producers" (161). Although the distinction between overt and covert pedagogical functions is certainly essential to understanding media impacts, considering the ways in which specific programs and resources fit into broader cultural categories is equally important. In the case of television comedy, for example, shows such as *South Park* can be read as both belonging to a specific genre (the sitcom) and transgressing established boundaries of the genre. As Buckingham and Bragg note, although "Comedies may also promote more overt moral lessons—for example in the homilies about trust or sharing with which more traditional U.S. sitcoms tend to conclude," nevertheless, "the defining characteristic of comedy is precisely that it is not to be taken seriously. If comedy teaches, it must surely seek to do so with a very light touch" (168–69). Programs such as *South Park* complicate what seem to be straightforward interpretations of media content, as they manipulate established frameworks for both comedic and critical purposes. If the children of *South Park* could watch a show such as *South Park* (Terrance and Phillip often play this very role on the show), how would they respond? Can parents and teachers assume that children in the real world are as media-savvy as Stan, Kyle, Cartman, and Kenny, or is much of *South Park*'s cultural satire lost on younger audiences?

Returning to the issue of sexuality and sex education, the cultural pedagogy model of childhood learning need not be so terrifying for parents and teachers. Although young people may access controversial materials through media outlets, a degree of education undoubtedly takes place that cannot be duplicated in the classroom. In their discussion of the benefits of learning about sex from the media, Buckingham and Bragg note, "In general, the media were seen to possess several advantages over other potential sources of information. They addressed topics directly that many children found embarrassing to discuss with their parents or teachers, or that parents might feel they were not 'ready' for. [. . .] The media also seemed to offer the benefit of anonymity, particularly if they were consumed privately" (60). Young people may not wish to discuss particular topics with parents and teachers, but they also recognize the limited authority that their peers have when discussing other topics. Television and Internet sources can provide additional information with which children can begin to formulate concrete knowledge and personal beliefs. In this way, learning about "mature" matters can be seen "as a form of *bricolage*, a matter of 'piecing it together' from a range of potential sources," as well as "a collective process, conducted among the peer group" (61).

We should note, of course, that cultural pedagogy does not guarantee any degree of accuracy, nor does it present a superior, coherent framework of learning. Mr. Mackey may not have answers to all of the children's questions on *South Park*, but at least he is consistent, as opposed to Stan's Internet search for basic sexual knowledge that resulted in the boys discovering Cartman's mother performing in a German *Scheisse* fetish video. Learning about sexuality from media sources may provide some benefits for young people, but it cannot adequately replace all traditional venues of learning. As Buckingham and Bragg note of their study, "the easy availability of such information does not mean that learning about sex has somehow become scientific and rational. On the contrary, it is still surrounded by shame, embarrassment and ambivalence, in which romantic aspirations co-exist with a knowledge of sordid realities" (238).

What cultural pedagogy, as displayed on *South Park*, provides young people with is a model of learning and development that uses young peoples' own curiosity with the world as a point of departure. While public schooling continues to use common frameworks of knowledge as the building blocks of curricula (mathematics, literacy, history, and so forth), media sources and schoolyard gossip help children develop critical skills in making personal, social, and moral decisions. Recognizing the importance of cultural pedagogy, however, does not mean abandoning well-established educational practices. As Kincheloe and Steinberg write, we need not "embrace anarchy but instead understand and learn even to appreciate the desire, the libidinal impulse that begins to bubble in childhood and reaches full expression in adolescence. [. . .] A critical pedagogy of childhood is aware and unafraid of childhood desire, often connecting it to children's efforts to understand the world and themselves" (27). Although collective discussion of sexuality and its complexities ultimately provided the most sound understanding at South Park Elementary, the children would not have had the fundamental knowledge of anatomy and biology needed to instigate their exploration without some form of curricular planning.

In its examination of cultural pedagogy and the limits of traditional schooling, *South Park* therefore brings attention to an aspect of development that is often overlooked in educational research. Emphasis on curricular goals and cognitive abilities has tended to overshadow the importance of moral development in young people's education; while moral development never fully disappeared from public debate, as Lawrence Rosenkoetter notes, "For decades, the study of moral development was at the very least dormant" (463). The lessons learned on *South Park*, whether related to human sexuality, genetic engineering, or even racial prejudice, often contain a moral element that traditional forms of schooling simply cannot contain. The children are thrust headfirst into complex and controversial situations in which they rely on their relatively inexperienced moral reasoning to navigate some sort of solution. In this way, *South Park* refutes any social construction of childhood that places young people and adults in two distinct categories of ethical maturity. All human beings, regardless of their age, are forced to make difficult decisions throughout their lives; while age and experience can sometimes simplify these matters, they do not guarantee a more satisfactory outcome. As Henry Jenkins writes of children, morality, and identity:

> Children, no less than adults, are active participants in [the] process of defining their identities, though they join those interactions from positions of unequal power. When children struggle to reclaim dignity in the face of a schoolyard taunt or confront inequalities in their parents' incomes, they are engaged with politics just as surely as adults are when they fight back against homophobia or join a labor union. Our grown-up fantasies of childhood as a simple space crumble when we recognize the complexity of the forces shaping our children's lives and defining who they will be, how they will behave, and how they will understand their place in the world. (4)

In this way, *South Park* presents its young protagonists as fundamentally moral beings in a supposedly adult world. Without any substantial assistance from the structures and content of public education, Stan, Kyle, Cartman, and Kenny develop sophisticated foundations for addressing moral crises, employing the same types of ethical mechanisms (both personal and social) commonly attributed to the adult world. Whereas the adults of *South Park* are often swayed by the type of mob mentality and peer pressure often attributed to childhood ("Butt Out," "Something Wall-Mart This Way Comes," "I'm a Little Bit Country"), the younger characters often attempt to work through dilemmas rationally and thoughtfully. Rosenkoetter, drawing on the work of Lawrence Kohlberg, argues that this type of reasoning is characteristic of "a moral person," which he defines as "an individual who has developed advanced cognitive structures by which to differentiate between good and evil" (464). Although the controversies and dilemmas presented on *South Park* tend not to favor simplistic resolutions (thus discouraging pedantic partisan use of the show for political advantage), Parker and Stone do demonstrate how individuals can develop rational, mature, and even ethical positions on such issues, using young children to illustrate how basic this process can be when approached properly.

None of this should lead parents and teachers to believe that cultural pedagogy, relying on a heavy diet of media content, can guarantee that children will grow into fully matured moral citizens. In the case of television programs, moral lessons can be especially difficult to untangle and interpret, even among adult audiences. As Rosenkoetter notes, "Although research is clearly limited, there is no evidence to date that heavy television usage leads to more advanced moral reasoning. It may be that the moral dilemmas most often presented on television are deficient in that the major characters spend so little time sharing their reflections and ethical considerations" (465). In this regard, *South Park* is particularly interesting because it often condenses potentially moral lessons into short, satirical epilogues with Stan or Kyle addressing the audience (both within the story and within the framework of a traditional, homily-laden sitcom) and explaining how they "learned something today." Whereas most television comedies present the resolution of a child's conflict as the site of a moral lesson (for example, "Listen to your parents/teachers, because they know best"), *South Park* mocks this act of summarizing a lesson learned, focusing the audience's attention on the process of moral reasoning: The particular outcome of a child's ethical struggle may be of far less value than the ethical struggle itself.

Although recognizing the pedagogical significance of these satirical moments may be difficult, the recurrence of this "I learned something today" critique tends to support *South Park*'s adherence to a model of childhood development grounded in cultural pedagogy. As with the show's ability to escape narrow political definition, an articulation of its philosophy of education relies on reading the show as a collection of episodes, rather than analyzing specific characters or stories. *South Park*'s critique of traditional childhood education and its subsequent advocacy of moral development based in part on cultural pedagogy is therefore consistent with a model of learning known among researchers as Cultivation Theory. Whereas many studies and their explanatory models tend to focus on singular programs and episodes, Cultivation Theory stems from "the realization that television represents a coherent (although not invariant) system of messages that cumulatively present the viewer with a stable worldview, including the moral sphere" (Rosenkoetter 470). *South Park*'s worldview may be far from stable in many respects (Kenny's numerous deaths and rebirths, the town's numerous apocalypses, and Stan's father's seemingly endless back story come to mind) but the overarching model of moral development has remained exceptionally consistent throughout the show's history. Accordingly, if a coherent cultural lesson is to be learned from *South Park*, it is to be found in the most enduring, coherent aspects of the program. Stan and Kyle's tongue-in-cheek claims to have "learned something" are about as stable a theme as can be found in the *South Park* universe.

Conclusion: The Pedagogical Value of *South Park*

While most parents want to prevent their children from watching programs such as *South Park*, we must recognize *South Park*'s critique of childhood learning as an exceptionally valuable addition to teaching and learning in a media landscape. More important, however, we must remember that childhood itself is a cultural fiction, insomuch as it shapes our beliefs and educational principles concerning young people. Preventing children from accessing shows such as *South Park* may protect them from ideas and images that may be difficult for them properly to understand, but parents and teachers know that children will eventually access these materials on their own; supervising and contextualizing such media use may be far more helpful to a child's development than simply censoring their media diet in an effort to "protect" them. "Too often," writes Jenkins, "our culture imagines childhood as a utopian space, separate from adult cares and worries, free from sexuality, outside social divisions, closer to nature and the primitive world, more fluid in its identity and its access to the realms of imagination, beyond historical change, more just, pure, and innocent, and in the end, waiting to be corrupted or protected by adults. Such a conception of the child dips freely in the politics of nostalgia" (3–4). In an age of media saturation and limitless information access, critical media literacy is essential; highly reflexive shows such as *South Park* may offer children and adults alike a surprisingly effective model for navigating and understanding what they see.

Although many *South Park* episodes are undoubtedly indecent by almost any cultural standard, discarding the show as mere juvenile potty humor would be a mistake. As Slade notes, the overwhelming preponderance of adult themes on *South Park* "is a trick for garnering attention and can serve to persuade children to focus on issues of some importance" (97). What *South Park* offers audiences (of all ages) is a refreshingly honest interpretation of moral crises in Western society; rather than establishing and presenting firm ideological stances on a particular issue, the show demonstrates the urgent need for both individual and collective reflection. As Buckingham and Bragg conclude from their study of British children and television, although media sources can be valuable resources for confronting complex moral issues, they:

> are likely to be much more effective in this respect if they are used as a means of generating discussion, rather than as a surrogate form of propaganda. The value of the media in this respect is precisely that they appear

to offer a forum for debate, both in schools and in homes; and there is certainly room for both teachers and parents to be given more advice about how this debate can be encouraged and promoted. (251)

What is critical in this analysis is that educational media texts need not display the conventional characteristics of "educational programming" for children; innocuous role models and direct moralizing cannot provide children with adequate space for personal and moral growth. Teachers and parents need to look for media content that allows young learners to generate their own opinions and beliefs about the world in which they live—a world no less frightening, fast-paced, and incredible than the one that we adults inhabit.

The world of *South Park* is often obscene, violent, and absurd. Kyle, Stan, Cartman, and Kenny navigate moral crises that few children will ever directly confront in their own development. Nevertheless, children in the real world might be better prepared for dealing with obstacles and issues if they were encouraged to begin thinking about the "adult world" at an earlier age. The strength of the media texts Buckingham and Bragg studied was that they "constitute their audiences in ethical terms—that is, they invite them to engage actively with the dilemmas and issues they portray and to take responsibility for their responses and views"; as the researchers observed, "young people repeatedly expressed particular preferences for more open storylines that appeared to allow them to 'make up their own minds'" (244). Television can be incredibly effective at encouraging young people to think critically about the complexity of moral issues, but only when it recognizes the ethical maturity of its audience. *South Park's* greatest strength is that it refuses to treat young people like children.

Works Cited

Anderson, Brian C. *South Park Conservatives: The Revolt against Liberal Media Bias*. Washington, DC: Regnery, 2005.

Buckingham, David, and Sara Bragg. *Young People, Sex and the Media: The Facts of Life?* New York: Palgrave MacMillan, 2004.

Jenkins, Henry. Introduction. *The Children's Culture Reader*. Ed. Henry Jenkins. New York: New York University Press, 1998. 1–37.

Kincheloe, Joe L., and Shirley R. Steinberg. Introduction. *Kinderculture: The Corporate Construction of Childhood*. Ed. Joe L. Kincheloe and Shirley R. Steinberg. Boulder, CO: Westview, 1997.

Kline, Stephen. *Out of the Garden: Toys, TV and Children's Culture in the Age of Marketing*. Toronto: Garamond, 1993.

Rosenkoetter, Lawrence I. "Television and Morality." *Handbook of Children and Media.* Ed. Dorothy G. Singer and Jerome L. Singer. Thousand Oaks, CA: Sage, 2001. 463–73.

Slade, Christina. *The Real Thing: Doing Philosophy with Media.* New York: Peter Lang, 2002.

Spigel, Lynn. "Seducing the Innocent: Childhood and Television in Postwar America." *The Children's Culture Reader.* Ed. Henry Jenkins. New York: New York University Press, 1998. 110–30.

"Omigod, It's Russell Crowe!"

South Park's Assault on Celebrity

DAMION STURM

When Cartman wakes to find Ben Affleck lying nude beside him and evidence of lovemaking on his hand (which has mysteriously taken on the persona of Jennifer Lopez), not only are Affleck and Lopez being mocked, but the entire economy of celebrity in the U.S. media as well. This chapter explores representations of celebrity on the animated series *South Park*. Rather than "celebrating" celebrity, however, *South Park* undoes or dismantles celebrity in relation to elements of production, circulation, and consumption in American culture. In particular, *South Park* exposes and mocks the manufacturing of celebrity, distorts celebrity representations and public images, and undermines the authenticity or merit conventionally invested in most celebrities. To demonstrate these aspects, the status of celebrity is first discussed, providing an academic insight into the cult of celebrity, as well as its cultural currency and use within popular media forms. My focus then turns to *South Park*, examining the role of television satire and animation in critiquing celebrity, as well as how *South Park*'s distinctive style of representational politics contributes to this dismantling process through a comparative consideration of celebrity representation in another well-known animated series, *The Simpsons*. Finally, I discuss five well-known celebrities—Mel Gibson, Winona Ryder, Paris Hilton, Jennifer Lopez, and Russell Crowe—demonstrating how *South Park*'s humiliating, vulgar, and scathing representations dismantle their status in relation to celebrity production, circulation, and consumption.

First, our attention turns to the cult of celebrity. Academics have tried to make sense of celebrity culture, exploring and understanding the term through a range of lenses. Conceived of as multifaceted, academics have considered celebrity as a social function (Evans and Wilson), as a sign or star text (Dyer), as contributing to cultural identity (Marshall; Rojek; Turner), or as a process of manufacture with the celebrity as a commodity (Cashmore; Gamson; McDonald; Rein, Kotler, and Stoller; Schickel). However, a unified approach and clear definition of celebrity has proved elusive in academia. Rojek's four categories for celebrity are a useful starting point, suggesting that celebrity status is either *ascribed*, predetermined through lineage; *achieved*, the recognition of an individual for his accomplishment in the public sphere (which is more useful when considering notions of stardom); or *attributed*, those who gain attention but may lack specific talent (perhaps best understood as packaged celebrity). Rojek also conceives of the *celetoid*, a subset of attributed celebrity, for the ordinary and everyday celebrity, whose fame is fleeting, made famous one day and forgotten the next (the latest lottery winner, the next *Big Brother* contestant).

Based on the academic literature, three factors are necessary for assigning celebrity status: the mass mediation and continual exposure of these individuals, well-knownness and a public interest in and recognition of these individuals, and an interest in their private lives that often circulates outside any connection to work, performance, or merit (particularly in relation to scandal and intrigue). Turner's discussion of celebrity succinctly ties these key components together. Turner says:

> We can map the precise moment a public figure becomes a celebrity. It occurs at the point at which media interest in their activities is transferred from reporting on their public role (such as their specific achievement in politics or sport) to investigating the details of their private lives. Paradoxically, it is most often the high profile achieved by their public activities that provides the alibi for this process of "celebritisation." Conversely, the celebrity's general claim on public attention can easily outstrip the public awareness of their [sic] original achievements. (8)

What the body of research on celebrity reveals is the complex and volatile mix of self-promotion, cultural currency and exchange, media exposure, and sustained public interest that is fundamental to the contemporary culture of celebrity.

The celebrity literature also appears to have a gendered dynamic, and some authors reveal not only an overwhelming interest in the private lives of female celebrities but also, more important, an explicit (and often sexualized) focus on their appearance. Within film, Geraghty suggests that actresses tend to operate as spectacles both inside and outside the cinema. Geraghty's concept reinforces Mulvey's well-documented idea of women as objects and passive supports of the male imaginary in cinema, while also accounting for the large, subsidiary circulation actresses have across a range of noncinematic media forms. Similar findings are also applicable to sport, with Harris and Clayton, and Wensing and Bruce suggesting that an emphasis on the beauty of female stars outweighs coverage of their actual athletic performance. Whereas various male celebrities may also be objectified, females operate disproportionately as spectacles across diverse media forms, such as the cinema, television, sport, and music videos. The Internet is also a prominent site for an increasingly provocative array of representations, with Turner noting the invasiveness of nude celebrity Web sites that post images without their subjects' consent. Thus, while the three interconnected themes of mass mediation, well-knownness, and an interest in private lives categorize contemporary celebrity, the celebritization of "famous" females is often also based on the perceived desirability, circulation, and exchange of their appearance.

Returning to populist accounts and representations of celebrity, the mass exposure and circulation of celebrities tend both to celebrate and elevate these individuals within popular culture. This is discernible in most mainstream media accounts that emphasize the unique talents, glamour, or beauty of celebrities. This is especially salient in tabloid-style, celebrity-focused television shows such as *The Insider* or *Entertainment Tonight* and in the abundance of women's and fashion magazines that seek to reveal and expose celebrities' glamour, beauty, private lives, and even scandalous behavior. Furthermore, most Hollywood films act as a showcase for emphasizing the talent, beauty, or "extra-ordinary" (Dyer; Ellis) qualities of film stars, whereas television facilitates broader access to famous individuals through its domestic reception and conventions of familiarity and repetition. These versions of popular culture all share in embellishing celebrities and their perceived qualities through glowing or flattering representations, constant and continual mediated exposure, and they ultimately confer a status above the general populace, which is admirable, desirable, and yet unattainable for most.[1]

In marked contrast to these processes of celebrification, the animated series *South Park* not only offers a challenge to this privileged reproduction of celebrity, but also dismantles the basis of their production, circulation, and consumption. Through elements of parody, irony, and satire, *South Park* provides both a comical and insightful critique of celebrity by mocking their manufacture and flattering representations, as well as questioning why celebrity continues to be celebrated, what underlines this public infatuation, and precisely who is being celebrated.[2] Such an approach to celebrity, of course, is not unique to *South Park*, and television satire has a long tradition of such assaults. Indeed, many forms of satire have appeared on television that have challenged, critiqued, or provided social commentary on contemporary culture, politics, and celebrity through comedy (*Saturday Night Live*,

The Late Show, or from Britain, *Spitting Image*, *The New Statesman*, and *Filthy Rich and Catflap*). However, while *South Park* shares the focus of televisual satire on recent and well-known events and individuals from popular culture, it is also able to use this material in far broader ways than other conventional or "real" satirical television shows. Through the medium of animation, the creators are less bound by or accountable to the "real" than are nonanimated, live-action, skit-based shows such as *Saturday Night Live*. Thus, celebrities can be depicted in a bizarre array of unflattering and demeaning situations, as the absurd scenario of Jennifer Lopez as a "living" hand puppet or Mel Gibson's despicable antics and behavior demonstrate. The often vulgar, objectionable, and offensive celebrity representations extend beyond the fixed conventions tenable in "real" satire, allowing *South Park's* excessive animated depictions not only to ridicule particular celebrities, but also to raise questions about the process of celebrification itself.

The role and significance of *South Park's* animation warrants further consideration. Various academics have noted usefully how animation contributes to the effectiveness, cultural currency, and longevity of another well-known animated series, *The Simpsons*. For Dobson, although the medium of animation works against a "true 'verisimilitude,'" the use of "cultural references and even the 'real life' issues dealt with in the series [. . .] create a strong sense of being 'about the real'" (89). Mullen notes "animation eliminates any need to meet expectations of verisimilitude" (82), yet observes viewers approach these cartoons with "suspended disbelief, and in the process absorb significant social commentary" (82). This notion is reinforced by Alberti, who suggests the show is able "to treat serious and even controversial issues under the cover of being 'just a cartoon'" (xiii). These findings have broader significance for both *South Park* and animated comedy in general. Like *The Simpsons*, *South Park* also relies heavily on media culture, intertextuality, and satirizing contemporary issues under the rubric of being "just a cartoon." Both shows also permit a wider audience by catering to children and adults through their use of animation.

Animation appears to have three important functions within *South Park's* assault on celebrity. The first of these is that, by not being bound by the real, the creators can exaggerate their depictions of celebrities. Thus, *South Park* can push the perceived flaws or exploits of celebrities to excess to achieve a satirical comment on, parody of, and fundamental dismantling of the elements of an individual celebrity's manufacture, circulation, consumption, or a combination thereof. As Slade comments on the animated representation of *South Park*, "television humour in cartoons is essentially iconic, not representational. The aim is to develop the aspects of characters that could not be emphasized were the characters real actors" (109). Celebrities become an easy target for ridicule because their images and exploits saturate media coverage and popular culture. This "raw material" can be manipulated and pushed to excess through animation, facilitating the overemphasis on, for example, Paris Hilton's "real" sexual exploits that, through a satirical and iconic depiction, transform her into a "stupid whore" or "total slut." A similar process is also at play with the utterly absurd scenario of Jennifer Lopez being replaced by a hand puppet. Obviously ridiculous, this premise becomes the basis for *South Park*'s scathing critique of Lopez's perceived manufactured image and lack of authentic talent. These animated representations clearly go beyond the "real" and predominantly celebratory celebrity images continuously reproduced and circulated in popular culture. Rather, these iconic depictions emphasize absurd, perverse, and devalued reconstructions to dismantle the production, circulation, and consumption of the celebrity image.

Continuing with this theme of dismantling celebrity, the second function of an animated representation is to reduce the opportunity for recelebrification. As noted, various forms of scandal and intrigue may allow for the recelebrification of well-known individuals. This is countered in the animated *South Park* depictions; although the mocking of celebrities in the series is primarily derived from actual well-known events, the celebrity is mocked and ridiculed to such an extent that nonironic recelebrification is nearly impossible. The depictions are unfavorable and undesired by the celebrity because they take up, extend, and exaggerate the already publicized scandalous elements of the celebrity's persona. Despite the fact that Cashmore argues that any publicity is good publicity, *South Park* humiliates and ridicules celebrities to such an extent that no opportunity is left for recelebrification. *South Park*'s closed narrative (*South Park* as episodic), fictional dynamic (a story presented as fictional but loosely derived from "real" and often publicly known events), and extremity of representation does not cater to the process of recelebrification. Rather, the celebrity image is dismantled through an often vulgar, humiliating, or degrading representation, and the celebrity generally has no opportunity to participate in, rebuke, react to, or recover from the events portrayed due to the show being an animated and fictional depiction. As an animated program, *South Park* works differently from other media forms in which nonconsensual, unflattering "real" images can subsequently be redressed through more flattering images, and bad publicity can be reformed or redeemed through good behavior: Fundamentally, *South Park* is perceived to be "just a cartoon" (Alberti, xiii). Additionally, *South Park*'s use and manipulation of "real" and well-known events ensures that the notoriety of individual celebrities remains in the public consciousness, but now circulates in an even more perverse, vulgar, and undesirable form.[3]

To demonstrate the offensive representations employed by *South Park*, let us briefly consider some depictions of well-known celebrities. Leonardo DiCaprio appears on *South Park* thanking Cartman (who dreamed he was a Vietnamese prostitute) and waving goodbye after paying for sex with him ("Cow Days"). In the episode, "Starvin' Marvin," a very overweight Sally

Struthers raises awareness of the plight of the starving people in Africa, all the while secretly hoarding and eating a large private stash of food. She subsequently reappears in the series resembling the obese *Star Wars* character Jabba the Hut ("Starvin' Marvin in Space"). *South Park* is particularly scathing of Barbra Streisand, depicting her as an evil mechanical robot attempting to destroy the earth ("Mecha Streisand"), using her face to frame the episode "Spooky Fish" (thus being presented in "Scary Vision"), and her name becomes a key obscene word that kills Saddam Hussein (*South Park: Bigger Longer & Uncut* [1999]). The *Queer Eye for the Straight Guy* cast is represented as being evil "crab people" in disguise who both pretend to be gay and use their celebrity status as a means to conquer the world ("South Park Is Gay"); and the series presents Christopher Reeve as having a lust for consuming dead fetuses as he promotes the validity of stem-cell research ("Krazy Kripples"). Finally, some celebrities are reduced to insignificant entities in the show, such as representing Patrick Duffy as the leg of a monster called Scuzzle-Butt ("Volcano"), making the head of David Hasselhoff Mr. Garrison's head after a nose job ("Tom's Rhinoplasty"), and limiting Brooke Shields's dialogue in the movie to the one line, "I farted once on the set of *Blue Lagoon*," which results in her being slapped in the face for the remark (*South Park: Bigger Longer & Uncut*).

Clearly many of these representations of celebrities are scathing, combining elements of parody, ridicule, and even absurdity. *South Park* is not unique within animation in this respect; other shows, such as *The Simpsons*, also challenge and mock celebrity through parody. However, *South Park*'s distinctive treatment of celebrity can be illustrated through a comparative consideration of the representational politics employed by both shows. Visually, celebrities are usually represented in one of two forms. The first is unique to *South Park* in which a photographic image of the celebrity's face and head is placed on a cartoon body. Examples in the series include David Hasselhoff on Mr. Garrison's body ("Tom's Rhinoplasty"), Saddam Hussein ("Terrance & Phillip in 'Not Without My Anus,'" "Do the Handicapped Go to Hell?" and *South Park: Bigger Longer & Uncut*), or Tony Danza in the woods ("Rainforest, Schmainforest"). The more common version appears in most animated shows in which caricatures represent celebrities. The types of celebrities depicted on *South Park* are also common to *The Simpsons*, both of which primarily draw on celebrities from the entertainment industry (film, television, and music), although political figures such as George Bush, Bill Clinton, Adolf Hitler, Osama Bin Laden and, most notably, Saddam Hussein have also appeared on both programs.[4]

Although celebrity permeates both of these shows, a major distinction is that *South Park* seldom invites celebrities to be involved in the parody of themselves. Indeed, each episode begins with the following disclaimer, "All characters and events in this show—even those based on real people—are entirely fictional. All celebrity voices are impersonated . . . poorly. The following program contains coarse language and due to its content should not be viewed by anyone."[5] Clearly, the disclaimer is humorous and may assist the show with legal and censorship matters, but it also positions *South Park* as an outsider discourse. Not inviting celebrity involvement allows the show free rein to ridicule the production, circulation, and consumption of celebrities without their permission or the constraints of their presence. This is particularly notable when considering the visual representation of a photographic head on a cartoon body. The audience will recognize the celebrity, yet the disclaimer dismisses the association as fictional, allowing the creators to manipulate and place well-known figures in a range of humiliating, bizarre, and degrading positions and situations.

South Park occasionally uses celebrity voice-overs, but generally these celebrities portray a character; for example, Jennifer Aniston voices Mrs. Stevens ("Rainforest, Schmainforest"), and Natasha Henstridge voices the children's substitute teacher, Ms. Ellen ("Tom's Rhinoplasty"). Furthermore, George Clooney and Jay Leno are reduced to nonspeaking voice-overs as animals (Clooney as Sparky the dog in "Big Gay Al's Big Gay Boat Ride" and Leno as Kitty the cat in "Cartman's Mom is a Dirty Slut").[6] What is significant in this use of celebrities is that *South Park* is not using their involvement either to draw on the celebrities as themselves or inviting them to mock themselves. This is commonly how *The Simpsons* draws on celebrities, inviting their celebrity guests to participate in a parody of themselves. In opposition to this, *South Park* seems to operate as an outsider discourse that facilitates a less restrictive assault on the cult of celebrity.

Additionally, by reducing a film star such as George Clooney to the infrequent gruffs and barks of a dog, *South Park* belittles or subverts the perceived status these celebrities offer as a guest star voice-over. That is, with George Clooney as a guest star, one would expect him to fulfill a more substantial role; Clooney as a nonspeaking dog ostensibly dismantles his star power.[7] Although appearing to work in a contradictory way, this use of celebrity voice-overs including those by Clooney, Leno, Aniston, and Henstridge actually works in a celebratory manner and endears them to the *South Park* audience. Although these guest stars are not fictionally parodied as celebrity characters, their willingness to be involved provides the ironic duplicity or doubleness (Hutcheon) of both recognizing their own celebrity status while simultaneously subverting this status by poking fun at their own self-importance as celebrities (especially by accepting nonspeaking roles). Rather than being the butt of a joke or able to control the means and extent of their ridicule through self-parody such as in *The Simpsons*, *South Park* guests parody their own celebrification through the association and (often limited) involvement with this controversial show.

Celebrities have been invited on a few occasions to play themselves. In various episodes, the series has included Jonathan Katz as Dr. Katz ("Summer

Sucks"); Jay Leno ("City on Edge"); and musicians or groups such as Robert Smith ("Mecha Streisand"), Korn ("Korn's Groovy Pirate Ghost Mystery"), Ozzy Osbourne, Primus, Elton John, and others performing as themselves ("Chef Aid"). This treatment is rare and, of all the entertainers represented on *South Park*, musicians are most likely to escape overt ridicule as they are invited to perform and are represented solely through their performance. This does not apply to all musicians, however; Céline Dion ("Terrance & Phillip in 'Not Without My Anus'"), Barbra Streisand ("Mecha Streisand" and "Spooky Fish"), Jennifer Lopez ("Fat Butt and Pancake Head"), and Michael Jackson ("The Jeffersons") all are recipients of scathing attacks on their celebrity status.

Although some musicians may get off lightly, thematically *South Park* is consistent in its representation of celebrities. Celebrities are generally ridiculed, mocked, and depicted unfavorably through a representational style that generally is more overtly offensive than *The Simpsons*. Slade has commented on this stylistic differentiation, noting, "*South Park* takes *The Simpsons* even further," suggesting "*South Park* is even more vulgar and shocking" (104), whereas Savage finds *South Park* generally has a darker tone, concluding, "*South Park* definitely pushes the envelope farther than *The Simpsons*, especially regarding racial, ethnic, and sexual humor" (220). On *South Park*, fame is belittled, representations are unflattering, personae lack depth, achievements are without merit, and the processes of celebrity manufacture and commodification are exposed. Therefore, I agree with Slade and Savage that, through *South Park*'s more scathing treatment of celebrities and the manner in which it debases them through humiliation, vulgarity, and absurdity, *South Park* moves beyond *The Simpsons* in its critique of celebrity status. Although both shows challenge celebrity through parody and the satirical conventions of televisual comedy, *South Park*'s harsher representational politics move beyond the "safe" or "fun" mocking of celebrity apparent in *The Simpsons* to dismantle the elements of celebrity production, circulation, and consumption in contemporary culture.

To demonstrate further this mocking and ridicule of celebrity, I focus on five particular cases where high-profile celebrities are dismantled. The distorted and unflattering representations of Mel Gibson, Russell Crowe, Winona Ryder, Paris Hilton, and Jennifer Lopez belittle their fame and subvert dominant representations of their celebrity. Instead of lionizing these celebrities, *South Park* mocks their celebrity status through vulgarity (Ryder), humiliation (Hilton), absurdity (Lopez), and unflattering portrayals of psychotic behavior (Gibson), and violent tendencies (Crowe). I will first examine the representations provided for the two male celebrities, Mel Gibson and Russell Crowe, before considering how *South Park* dismantles their celebrity status through these violent depictions. The three female celebrities (Winona Ryder, Paris Hilton, and Jennifer Lopez) will then be discussed, suggesting that, collectively, their celebrity status is dismantled by representations that devalue the merit and basis of their fame, and particularly for Ryder and Hilton, emphasize their sexuality as spectacle.

The representation of Mel Gibson provides a useful celebrity case study because a direct comparison can be made between the representational style and politics of celebrity in *The Simpsons* and *South Park*. On *The Simpsons*, the episode "Beyond Blunderdome" revolves around Gibson's new film, with Homer becoming a coproducer after initially giving it a poor review; ultimately Homer turns the film into a violent action picture that fails. The presentation of Mel Gibson is favorable with his caricature represented as charismatic and handsome. Gibson guest stars by performing his own voice-over and therefore has been invited to participate in the process of mocking himself. Although a level of parody pokes fun at Gibson and the violent content of his films, essentially *The Simpsons*'s representation is safe, weak in its criticism, avoids attacking Gibson directly, and brushes over an overt critique of the culture of celebrity. Rather than chastising Gibson, the representation seems to celebrate his status, suggesting that the people of Springfield are enamored with Mel, while Gibson's character finds "it's hell being Mel" as everyone is always nice to him.

If this pandering to celebrities on *The Simpsons* makes "it hell to be Mel," I suspect the scathing and brutal depiction of Gibson on *South Park* makes it positively awful to be Mel. The *South Park* episode, "The Passion of the Jew," also revolves around the notion of audience reception to Gibson's films. In this episode Kyle finds Gibson's film *The Passion of Christ* disturbing with its horrific violence and unfavorable depiction of Jews (a theme Cartman embraces in his Nazi-like rally and fandom for Gibson), whereas Stan labels it a "snuff-film" and sets out with Kenny to confront Gibson and get their money back. Rather than a parody that celebrates his status, *South Park*'s representation distorts Gibson's profile, placing a photographic image of his head on the caricature body, while implying he is a deranged religious zealot, a sadist, and utterly despicable. Gibson's behavior is presented as psychotic, as he argues with the boys over the merits and accuracy of his film ("You can't NOT like *The Passion*. I just followed the Bible. Christ died for you"), as well as the value of his work ("You CAN'T say my movie sucked, or else you're saying Christianity SUCKS!"), all the while maiming and torturing himself to win their approval.

Furthermore, Gibson is presented as a crazy, egotistical, and power-hungry figure who literally defecates on people and buildings, and who is utterly obsessed with his religious, sadistic, and cinematic convictions with which he expects total adherence. Clearly, this representation is operating outside the safe realms of *The Simpsons*'s depiction; rather, *South Park* assaults Gibson's celebrity status as an actor, filmmaker, and moral crusader through a scathing and brutal assault on Gibson that portrays him as a deranged and psychotic figure. Not surprisingly, Gibson is not involved in this process or redeemed at the end of the episode (in the final scene Kyle labels him a "big wacko douche" before Gibson defecates on Cartman), and I suspect Gibson himself would not endorse such an uncharismatic and unflattering portrayal.

Russell Crowe also does not escape the gaze and ridicule of *South Park*. Although an acclaimed film star, Crowe's celebrity status arguably has gained a good deal of currency from his notorious drunken escapades and fist fights with various people. *South Park* exposes and ridicules this aggressive behavior. In the episode, "The Terrance & Phillip Movie Trailer," the boys are anxiously waiting to view the trailer for this film that will appear during an advertising break on Crowe's (fictional) television show, *Russell Crowe: Fighting 'Round the World*. The boys become increasingly annoyed at having to sit through Crowe's show and watch his behavior and exploits while they wait for the short trailer. The *South Park* representation metaphorically pulls no punches, with Crowe's show being a half hour of violence and a series of fight scenes. As the preview to Crowe's television show suggests, "He loves to act but he loves one thing more! Fighting 'round the world!" In the program, a temperamental Crowe takes exception to nearly everyone he encounters on his show. When Crowe is recognized by fans at different locations ("Ain't that that *Gladiator* guy?" or "Omigod, it's Russell Crowe!"), Crowe patronizes them (a sarcastic "Omigod, it's Russell Crowe" response), abuses them ("Why don't you mind your own business, ya scrotum"), and proceeds to beat them up, rather than oblige them with autographs and pictures.

Crowe also finds adapting to different cultures difficult, and he is shown "fighting 'round the world" in China and India, as well as in Brooklyn (he even beats up the show's editor for cutting the Brooklyn scenes: "My fighting is poetry. You don't edit Russell Crowe's poetry, ya testicle"). His one friend on the show, a tugboat named Tugger, gets tired of his antics and shoots himself when Crowe begins to sing a song from his new album. Crowe surmises that to get his old friend Tugger back on his side he needs a cause; thus, Crowe decides to "fight cancer," dragging a sick old man laden with an IV–drip out of bed and beating him up to cure the disease ("take that, cancer"). Through such an aggressive representation, *South Park* portrays Crowe as a temperamental thug who always resorts to violence. With his gruffness and a propensity toward thuggery, Crowe's acting is unacknowledged and his singing/songwriting is lampooned; primarily, he is depicted as a bully, thug, and brawler in *South Park*'s representation.

South Park's depiction of these two actors works to dismantle the circulation and consumption of their celebrity status. Overall, their production as celebrities is not interrogated in any depth, although one aspect of Crowe's representation hints at his own image manufacturing. Crowe pronounces, "most great actors take up causes and I'm the greatest of them all!" with *South Park* implying that celebrities often adopt causes to sustain their fame; thus,

Crowe's decision to "fight cancer" may be motivated more by the acquisition of good publicity, rather than a genuine concern for Tugger's well-being. Nevertheless, Crowe's violent tendencies undermine such an endeavor, while the violent behavior of both male celebrities is the chief dismantling tool the *South Park* creators use. In particular, the violence associated with the circulation and consumption of Gibson and Crowe as celebrities is deplored. Both actors have been reliant on violent filmic roles to establish and sustain their fame, but *South Park* subverts this success to suggest that violence is the sole basis for their fame. Representing violence as intrinsic to their off-screen persona ridicules the depthlessness of their public image. With Gibson, *South Park* plays on insanity and an inability for Gibson to distinguish between his films and reality as he lives out his *Mad Max* (1979) and *Braveheart* (1995) roles, coupled with incessant requests for people to torture him. For Crowe, *South Park* can draw on an already publicly known history of violence to imply his fists and a proclivity for fighting underscore his fame. Therefore, rather than acknowledging any acting ability, talent, or warranted filmic success, *South Park* dismantles the celebrity status of Mel Gibson and Russell Crowe by exposing the depthlessness of their public images through the overemphasis on, and embellishment of, their violent claims to fame.

Winona Ryder also cannot be impressed with her depiction on *South Park*. Ryder's caricature makes a guest appearance at the USO show to entertain U.S. troops in *South Park: Bigger Longer & Uncut*. While she is introduced as "the pint-sized pixie and darling of the Indie movie scene," her "talent" lies in her ping-pong ball trick. After a banal consideration of the war with Canada ("I mean war, man. Wow, war. You know? Wow"), Ryder lies back on the stage and proceeds to shoot ping-pong balls out to the crowd. This scene, framed from behind Ryder, plays on vulgarity, showing her legs spread wide as the balls shoot out into the stunned crowd. For viewers, these appear to emanate from her vagina, connoting a sex act and effecting the sexualization of Ryder via this apparently lewd act. The scene is altered by cutting to a frontal shot, showing Ryder with a bat hitting the remaining balls and a big smile on her face as she exclaims, "There. I didn't miss one." However, parody has already served to dismantle Ryder's celebrity status. Through this vulgar representation, her acting and social commentary are devalued; instead, the movie implies Ryder's real talent is to be a sexualized object who performs lewd acts (for example, lying on her back and shooting out ping-pong balls).

Paris Hilton's celebrity status is also mocked as being reliant on overt sexualization. In the episode "Stupid Spoiled Whore Video Playset," Hilton arrives in South Park primarily to promote her new store ("Stupid Spoiled Whore") and sell her wares. Wendy asks what she does and gets the simple response, "she is a stupid, rich whore," who all the girls of South Park wish to emulate (two teenage girls in Hilton's store assert that "all the girls in South Park are going to be total sluts from now on"). Procuring Hilton's "Stupid

FIGURE 8
Paris Hilton with Mr. Slave.

Spoiled Whore Video Playset," or her new perfume, "Skanque," the girls mimic Hilton by dressing like "sluts" and wanting to become "little whores," while Wendy struggles to fit in and seeks advice on how to become a whore. Throughout the episode Hilton is given an unflattering, overtly sexual portrayal articulated through the terms "whore" and "slut" and her skimpy attire.

Paris Hilton is also represented as a highly sexualized object through engaging in perverse acts. Hilton continually coughs up balls of cum from her "partying" the night before, in addition to passing out on Butter's bed as he proceeds to poke her with his finger. The sexualization of Hilton is complete in the "whore-off" scene she has with Mr. Slave. Paris wishes to prove she is the bigger whore and fits a whole pineapple into her vagina (in a scene with connections to Winona Ryder's ping-pong ball trick). Ultimately, Mr. Slave wins, engulfing her "where the sun don't shine" and in the process turns Hilton into a "real" sexual object (the symbolism of Hilton as a walking dildo is apparent). Through such a scathing representation, *South Park* is attacking the circulation and commodification of Hilton's overt sexualization as a celebrity, while also questioning the basis and merit of her fame.

While humiliation underscores Paris Hilton's representation, Jennifer Lopez's celebrity status is dismantled through sheer absurdity. In the episode

FIGURE 9
The other Jennifer Lopez.

"Fat Butt and Pancake Head," Cartman uses his own hand as a puppet, which, with a little makeup and a Latino accent, he calls Jennifer Lopez. Cartman's motive is purely to put one over on Kyle, with the intention of making Kyle believe his puppet is real so he can taunt him for being fooled. However, the J-Lo hand puppet seemingly begins to take on a life of its own. When the hand puppet is offered a recording contract and is set to replace J-Lo, the real Lopez comes to South Park to confront the hand puppet, screaming profanities and beating her up as she tries to save her career. Clearly, the events are absurd but, through this absurdity, *South Park* challenges the manufactured basis of the real Jennifer Lopez's celebrity.

In particular, it is the pop music stardom of J-Lo that is ridiculed. The hand puppet is instantly successful, making a disposable brand of music that is easy to produce and sell. Indeed, Cartman, having written three of the required ten songs in a short space of time while lying on his bed, reflectively says, "your style of music is so simple, it doesn't even require any thought." With most of the lyrics revolving around tacos and burritos, ("forget about all your wishes, I'll give you taco-flavored kisses"), *South Park* is dismissive of Lopez's talent, while also taking a swipe at her ethnicity. Furthermore, the self-important, egotistical, and divalike behavior that Lopez is purported to indulge in is incorporated into the program as coinciding with the hand-puppet's success is a contemptuous or "bitchy" attitude, illustrated through the constant rebuking of others.

Lopez's very public love life is also mocked, with *South Park* again using absurdity to represent her fiancé at that time, Ben Affleck. Affleck accompanies Lopez to remove her competitor, but becomes infatuated with the hand puppet. In a series of absurd scenes, Affleck romances the hand puppet with flowers, tongue kisses it, and, most disturbingly, Cartman awakes to discover a nude Ben Affleck in his bed and evidence of lovemaking still on his hand. Clearly these depictions insult Affleck directly ("I've been meaning to write a song or a poem," Affleck tells the hand puppet, "but I have no talent"), but they also ridicule the media-hype that surrounds their relationship. Through the construction of an absurd series of events that (fictionally) threatens Jennifer Lopez's career, *South Park* attacks Lopez's manufactured and commodified fame, belittles her perceived talent and musical success, and ridicules her very public lifestyle.

South Park's treatment of these three female celebrities dismantles the production, circulation, and consumption of their celebrity status. The production of celebrity is evident in the absurd scenario of Lopez being replaced by a hand puppet and reveals two manufactured aspects of her celebrity. The first is the manufactured quality of Lopez's work, which is criticized for its simplistic production and lack of artistry (Cartman's ease at writing her songs), and points out the ephemeral and fleeting impact of her music as a recycled, repetitive, and disposable brand of music (in this instance revolving exclusively around tacos and burritos). Second, the ease at which a hand puppet cannot only resemble but take over the career of a "real" celebrity suggests that Lopez (like her music) is also a simplistic and manufactured version of celebrity that is both ephemeral and easily replicated, while ultimately undermining Lopez's actual talent. This devaluing of Lopez's "authenticity" is central to *South Park*'s assault on the consumption of all three female celebrities.

The manufacture of Ryder's and Hilton's celebrity is less overt, although *South Park* calls attention to the basis for their prominence by emphasizing the centrality of their sexualized representation. By depicting Ryder and Hilton in particular as sexual objects, these representations reinforce the celebrity research that suggests females have a significant subsidiary circulation as spectacle often disassociated from their performance or specific talent(s).[8] In many ways, *South Park* reiterates Mulvey's finding of active men and passive women in the cinema by portraying this gendered dynamic through macho (violent) men and women as sexy props. However, *South Park* also distorts the notion of desirability through extreme, exaggerated, and excessive representations of Ryder and Hilton that transmogrify their sexualization into a disturbing and abhorrent spectacle.

Primarily, however, *South Park* dismantles these female celebrities by mocking and devaluing the basis for their consumption. Like the male celebrities, Ryder, Hilton, and Lopez are not recognized as possessing any specific talent or redeeming features, and *South Park* dismantles their authenticity by asserting that they are reliant on overt sexualization (Hilton and Ryder) or manufacture (Lopez) to be famous. Ultimately, *South Park* dismantles the celebrity status of these three females by exposing the depthlessness of their fame, implying that they circulate as manufactured or sexualized commodities lacking in authentic talent or merit.

As my case studies indicate, *South Park* offers a challenge or disruption to most popular media accounts of celebrity. Rather than celebrating or elevating these famous individuals, *South Park* belittles or mocks their talent, manufacture, circulation, and commodification. Such an approach is common to challenges to popular culture, politics, and celebrity employed in other versions of televisual satire. However, as an animated show, *South Park* can construct, manipulate, and exaggerate celebrity representations, extending their severity beyond other "real" television comedy conventions. Whereas other animated shows, such as *The Simpsons*, also lampoon celebrity, *South Park* goes beyond a "safe" and "fun" challenge to (and parody of) celebrity, fundamentally dismantling their production, circulation, and consumption. Thus, on *South Park*, various high-profile celebrities are derided, degraded, and devalued through a range of unflattering, distorted, and offensive representations. *South Park*'s two-dimensional style of cartooning emphasizes the depthlessness of contemporary celebrity and ridicules the promise of a rich, warm, and deep personality behind the public face. The notion of authentic talent and merit is also discarded. *South Park*'s satirical challenge to celebrity becomes dismantling at the moment when the shallowness of celebrity is revealed, positioning celebrities as empty receptacles only given meaning through reproduction, circulation, consumption, and public desire.

Notes

1. Even the "exposure" of scandalous behavior within popular culture is arguably favorable (depending on the circumstances obviously) in the sense that it allows the celebrity to continue to garner attention, be well-known, and circulate in the popular consciousness (Cashmore), as well as offers the chance for redemption (and hence further mediated exposure). Therefore, the drunken exploits of Tara Reid, sex acts of Pamela Anderson (both of which are also applicable to Paris Hilton), or Russell Crowe's bar fights allow their celebrification (media exposure, well-knownness, an interest in their private lives), to flourish, in addition to providing the opportunity for redemption. Cynically, even nonconsensual nude images of celebrities are often favorable as, like images of celebrities without makeup, with cellulite, and so forth, these also perpetuate celebrification (celebrities can be glamorous again with makeup). In

particular, nude images emphasize the "extraordinary" beauty and desirability of the individual celebrity, which in turn facilitates more exposure and perhaps greater levels of public consciousness and desire.

2. Interestingly, while scathing of celebrity, *South Park* is also reliant on the cult of celebrity as a staple source of material. Many episodes draw on celebrity at some point, either visually representing these individuals or making reference to them (primarily as the butt of a joke).

3. We may also find implications for the "fictional" component of these depictions when viewed at a later date or due to subsequent events, such as Mel Gibson's drunken anti-Semitic tirade in 2006.

4. *The Simpsons* uses political figures more frequently than *South Park*, although generally the *South Park* versions are depicted in a harsher manner. For example, Saddam Hussein is represented both as a tyrannical dictator ("Terrance & Phillip in 'Not Without My Anus'") and as the power hungry, sex-crazed, gay lover of Satan in the *South Park* movie (*South Park: Bigger Longer & Uncut* [1999]).

5. The film *South Park: Bigger Longer & Uncut* also uses a similar disclaimer during the end credits, stating "Conan O'Brien, Brooke Shields, President Clinton, the Baldwin Brothers and Winona Ryder did not authorize the use of their names or contribute any performance to this motion picture."

6. Clooney is however the voice of Dr. Gouache in the *South Park* movie.

7. Similarly, Natasha Henstridge is not advertised by name, but rather is presented as "the chick from *Species*," downplaying her status and emphasizing her appearance for those familiar with her highly sexualized role in the *Species* films. This is supported by the fireside chat the *South Park* creators Trey Parker and Matt Stone provide on *South Park*: Volume Four, in which they excitedly tell the audience who the guest star is and discuss how they love to freeze-frame her "acting" in *Species* (1995) on their videotape player and then play with themselves.

8. Jennifer Lopez's appearance and sexualization is less explicit than that of Ryder and Hilton, although the title of this episode plays on her appearance, as Lopez's rear end is often talked about as desirable in both men's and women's magazines. The term "fat butt" demeans, rather than expresses, this desirability (she is also referred to in the episode as "the slut with the large ass"), while "pancake head" seems to be an unflattering reference to Affleck's appearance.

Works Cited

Alberti, John. "Introduction." *Leaving Springfield:* The Simpsons *and the Possibility of Oppositional Culture*. Ed. John Alberti. Detroit: Wayne State University Press, 2004. xi–xxxii.

Cashmore, Ellis. *Celebrity/Culture*. New York: Routledge, 2006.

Dobson, Nichola. "Nitpicking *The Simpsons*: Critique and Continuity in Constructed Realities." *Animation Journal* 11 (2003): 84–93.

Dyer, Richard. *Stars*. London: BFI, 1979.

Ellis, John. *Visible Fictions. Cinema: Television: Video*. London: Routledge, 1992.

Evans, Andrew, and Glenn D. Wilson. *Fame: The Psychology of Stardom*. London: Vision, 1999.

Gamson, Joshua. "The Assembly Line of Greatness: Celebrity in Twentieth-Century America." *Popular Culture: Production and Consumption*. Ed. C. Lee Harrington and Denise D. Bielby. Malden, MA: Blackwell, 2001. 259–82.

Geraghty, Christine. "Re-examining Stardom: Questions of Texts, Bodies and Performance." *Reinventing Film Studies*. Ed. Christine Gledhill and Linda Williams. London: Arnold, 2000. 183–201.

Harris, John, and Ben Clayton. "Femininity, Masculinity, Physicality and the English Tabloid Press. The Case of Anna Kournikova." *International Review for the Sociology of Sport* 37 (2002): 397–413.

Hutcheon, Linda. *The Politics of Postmodernism*. London: Routledge, 1989.

Marshall, P. David. *Celebrity and Power: Fame in Contemporary Culture*. Minneapolis: University of Minneapolis, 1997.

McDonald, Paul. *The Star System: Hollywood's Production of Popular Identities*. London: Wallflower, 2000.

Mullen, Megan. "*The Simpsons* and Hanna-Barbera's Animation Legacy." *Leaving Springfield. The Simpsons and the Possibility of Oppositional Culture*. Ed. John Alberti. Detroit: Wayne State University Press, 2004. 63–84.

Mulvey, Laura. "Visual Pleasure and Narrative Cinema." *Screen* 16 (1975): 6–18.

Rein, Irving, Philip Kotler, and Martin Stoller. *High Visibility: The Making and Marketing of Professionals into Celebrities*. Chicago: NTC Business Books, 1997.

Rojek, Chris. *Celebrity*. London: Reaktion, 2001.

Savage, William J. "'So Television's Responsible!': Oppositionality and the Interpretive Logic of Satire and Censorship in *The Simpsons* and *South Park*." *Leaving Springfield: The Simpsons and the Possibility of Oppositional Culture*. Ed. John Alberti. Detroit: Wayne State University Press, 2004. 197–224.

Schickel, Richard. *Common Fame: The Culture of Celebrity*. London: Pavilion, 1985.

Slade, Christina. *The Real Thing: Doing Philosophy with the Media*. New York: Lang, 2002.

Turner, Graeme. *Understanding Celebrity*. London: Sage, 2004.

Wensing, Emma, and Toni Bruce. "Bending the Rules: Media Representations of Gender during an International Sporting Event." *International Review for the Sociology of Sport* 38 (2003): 387–96.

List of Episodes Cited

"Best Friends Forever." Production number 904. Original airdate: 30 Mar. 2005. Writer: Trey Parker.

"Big Gay Al's Big Gay Boat Ride." Production number 104. Original airdate: 3 Sept. 1997. Writers: Trey Parker and Matt Stone.

"Biggest Douche in the Universe, The." Production number 615. Original airdate: 27 Nov. 2002. Writer: Trey Parker.

"Bloody Mary." Production number 914. Original airdate: 7 Dec. 2005. Writer: Trey Parker.

"Butt Out." Production number 713. Original airdate: 3 Dec. 2003. Writer: Trey Parker.

"Cartman Gets an Anal Probe." Production number 101. Original airdate: 13 Aug. 1997. Writers: Trey Parker and Matt Stone.

"Cartman's Mom Is a Dirty Slut." Production number 113. Original airdate: 25 Feb. 1998. Writers: Trey Parker and David Goodman.

"Cartman's Mom Is Still a Dirty Slut." Production number 202. Original airdate: 22 Apr. 1998. Writers: Trey Parker and David Goodman.

"Cartman's Silly Hate Crime 2000." Production number 401. Original airdate: 12 Apr. 2000. Writer: Trey Parker.

"Cartman Sucks." Production number 1102. Original airdate: 14 Mar. 2007. Writer: Trey Parker.

"Cartoon Wars (1)." Production number 1003. Original airdate: 5 Apr. 2006. Writer: Trey Parker.

"Cartoon Wars (2)." Production number 1004. Original airdate: 12 Apr. 2006. Writer: Trey Parker.

"Cat Orgy." Production number 307. Original airdate: 14 July 1999. Writer: Trey Parker.

"Chef Aid." Production number 214. Original airdate: 7 Oct. 1998. Writers: Trey Parker and Matt Stone.

"Chef Goes Nanners." Production number 408. Original airdate: 5 July 2000. Writer: Trey Parker.

"Chef's Salty Chocolate Balls." Production number 209. Original airdate: 19 Aug. 1998. Writers: Trey Parker, Matt Stone, and Nancy Pimental.

"Cherokee Hair Tampons." Production number 407. Original airdate: 28 June 2000. Writer: Trey Parker.

"Chickenlover." Production number 203. Original airdate: 27 May 1998. Writers: Trey Parker, Matt Stone, and David Goodman.

"Chickenpox." Production number 210. Original airdate: 26 Aug. 1998. Writers: Trey Parker, Matt Stone, and Trisha Nixon.

"Child Abduction is Not Funny." Production number 611. Original airdate: 24 July 2002. Writer: Trey Parker.

"Chinpokomon." Production number 310. Original airdate: 3 Nov. 1999. Writer: Trey Parker.

"Christian Rock Hard." Production number 709. Original airdate: 29 Oct. 2003. Writer: Trey Parker.

"City on the Edge of Forever (Flashbacks)." Production number 207. Original airdate: 17 June 1998. Writers: Trey Parker, Matt Stone, and Nancy Pimental.

"Conjoined Fetus Lady." Production number 205. Original airdate: 3 June 1998. Writers: Trey Parker, Matt Stone, and David Goodman.

"Cow Days." Production number 213. Original airdate: 20 Sept. 1998. Writers: Trey Parker and David Goodman.

"Cripple Fight." Production number 503. Original airdate: 27 June 2001. Writer: Trey Parker.

"Death." Production number 106. Original airdate: 17 Sept. 1997. Writers: Trey Parker and Matt Stone.

"Death Camp of Tolerance, The." Production number 614. Original airdate: 20 Nov. 2002. Writer: Trey Parker.

"Die Hippie, Die." Production number 902. Original airdate: 16 Mar. 2005. Writer: Trey Parker.

"Do the Handicapped Go to Hell?" Production number 410. Original airdate: 19 July 2000. Writer: Trey Parker.

"Douche and Turd." Production number 808. Original airdate: 27 Oct. 2004. Writer: Trey Parker.

"Entity, The." Production number 511. Original airdate: 21 Nov. 2001. Writer: Trey Parker.

"Fat Butt and Pancake Head." Production number 705. Original airdate: 16 Apr. 2003. Writer: Trey Parker.

"Fat Camp." Production number 415. Original airdate: 6 Dec. 2000. Writer: Trey Parker.

"Follow that Egg." Production number 910. Original airdate: 2 Nov. 2005. Writer: Trey Parker.

"4th Grade." Production number 412. Original airdate: 8 Nov. 2000. Writer: Trey Parker.

"Freak Strike." Production number 601. Original airdate: 20 Mar. 2002. Writer: Trey Parker.

"Fun with Veal." Production number 605. Original airdate: 27 Mar. 2002. Writer: Trey Parker.

"Ginger Kids." Production number 911. Original airdate: 9 Nov. 2005. Writer: Trey Parker.

"Gnomes." Production number 217. Original airdate: 16 Dec. 1998. Writers: Trey Parker, Matt Stone, and Pam Brady.

"Goobacks." Production number 806. Original airdate: 28 Apr. 2004. Writer: Trey Parker.

"Good Times with Weapons." Production number 801. Original airdate: 17 Mar. 2004. Writer: Trey Parker.

"Here Comes the Neighborhood." Production number 512. Original airdate: 28 Nov. 2001. Writer: Trey Parker.

"Hooked on Monkey Phonics." Production number 313. Original airdate: 10 Nov. 1999. Writer: Trey Parker.

"Ike's Wee Wee." Production number 204. Original airdate: 20 May 1998. Writer: Trey Parker.

"I'm a Little Bit Country." Production number 701. Original airdate: 9 Apr. 2003. Writer: Trey Parker.

"It Hits the Fan." Production number 502. Original airdate: 20 June 2001. Writer: Trey Parker.

"It's Christmas in Canada." Production number 715. Original airdate: 17 Dec. 2003. Writer: Trey Parker.

"Jared Has Aides." Production number 602. Original airdate: 6 Mar. 2002. Writer: Trey Parker.

"Jeffersons, The." Production number 807. Original airdate: 21 Apr. 2004. Writer: Trey Parker.

"Jewbilee." Production number 309. Original airdate: 28 July 1999. Writer: Trey Parker.

"Kenny Dies." Production number 513. Original airdate: 5 Dec. 2001. Writer: Trey Parker.

"Korn's Groovy Pirate Ghost Mystery." Production number 312. Original airdate: 27 Oct. 1999. Writer: Trey Parker.

"Krazy Kripples." Production number 702. Original airdate: 26 Mar. 2003. Writer: Trey Parker.

"Mecha Streisand." Production number 112. Original airdate: 18 Feb. 1998. Writers: Trey Parker, Matt Stone, and Philip Stark.

"Mexican Staring Frog of Southern Sri Lanka, The." Production number 206. Original airdate: 10 June 1998. Writers: Trey Parker and Matt Stone.

"Mr. Garrison's Fancy New Vagina." Production number 901. Original airdate: 9 Mar. 2005. Writer: Trey Parker.

"Mr. Hankey, the Christmas Poo." Production number 110. Original airdate: 17 Dec. 1997. Writer: Trey Parker.

"Mr. Hankey's Christmas Classics." Production number 315. Original airdate: 1 Dec. 1999. Writer: Trey Parker.

"My Future Self n' Me." Production number 616. Original airdate: 4 Dec. 2002. Writer: Trey Parker.

"Osama Bin Laden has Farty Pants." Production number 509. Original airdate: 7 Nov. 2001. Writer: Trey Parker.

"Passion of the Jew, The." Production number 804. Original airdate: 31 Mar. 2004. Writers: Daisy Gardner and Trey Parker.

"Probably." Production number 411. Original airdate: 26 July 2000. Writer: Trey Parker.

"Proper Condom Use." Production number 507. Original airdate: 1 Aug. 2001. Writer: Trey Parker.

"Quest for Ratings." Production number 811. Original airdate: 17 Nov. 2004. Writer: Trey Parker.

"Rainforest Schmainforest." Production number 301. Original airdate: 7 Apr. 1999. Writers: Trey Parker and Matt Stone.

"Red Hot Catholic Love." Production number 608. Original airdate: 3 July 2002. Writers: Daisy Gardner and Trey Parker.

"Red Sleigh Down." Production number 617. Original airdate: 11 Dec. 2002. Writer: Trey Parker.

"Return of the Fellowship of the Ring to the Two Towers, The." Production number 613. Original airdate: 13 Nov. 2002. Writer: Trey Parker.

"Simpsons Already Did It." Production number 607. Original airdate: 26 June 2002. Writer: Trey Parker.

"Something Wall-Mart This Way Comes." Production number 809. Original airdate: 3 Nov. 2004. Writer: Trey Parker.

"Something You Can Do with Your Finger." Production number 409. Original airdate: 12 July 2000. Writer: Trey Parker.

"South Park Is Gay!" Production number 708. Original airdate: 22 Oct. 2003. Writer: Trey Parker.

"Spontaneous Combustion." Production number 302. Original airdate: 14 Apr. 1999. Writers: Trey Parker, Matt Stone, and David Goodman.

"Spooky Fish." Production number 215. Original airdate: 28 Oct. 1998. Writer: Trey Parker.

"Starvin' Marvin." Production number 109. Original airdate: 19 Nov. 1997. Writer: Trey Parker.

"Starvin' Marvin in Space." Production number 311. Original airdate: 17 Nov. 1999. Writers: Trey Parker, Matt Stone, and Kyle McCulloch.

"Stupid Spoiled Whore Video Playset." Production number 812. Original airdate: 1 Dec. 2004. Writer: Trey Parker.

"Succubus, The." Production number 303. Original airdate: 21 Apr. 1999. Writer: Trey Parker.

"Summer Sucks." Production number 208. Original airdate: 24 June 1998. Writers: Trey Parker and Nancy Pimental.

"Super Best Friends, The." Production number 504. Original airdate: 4 July 2001. Writer: Trey Parker.

"Terrance & Phillip in 'Not Without My Anus.'" Production number 201. Original airdate: 1 Apr. 1998. Writers: Trisha Nixon and Trey Parker.

"Terrance and Phillip Movie Trailer, The." Production number 604. Original airdate: 3 Apr. 2002. Writer: Trey Parker.

"Timmy! 2000." Production number 404. Original airdate: 19 Apr. 2000. Writer: Trey Parker.

"Tom's Rhinoplasty." Production number 111. Original airdate: 11 Feb. 1998. Writer: Trey Parker.

"Trapper Keeper." Production number 413. Original airdate: 15 Nov. 2000. Writer: Trey Parker.

"Two Guys Naked in a Hot Tub." Production number 308. Original airdate: 21 July 1999. Writers: Trey Parker, Matt Stone, and David Goodman.

"Very Crappy Christmas, A." Production number 417. Original airdate: 20 Dec. 2000. Writer: Trey Parker.

"Volcano." Production number 103. Original airdate: 20 Aug. 1997. Writers: Trey Parker and Matt Stone.

"Weight Gain 4000." Production number 102. Original airdate: 27 Aug. 1997. Writers: Trey Parker and Matt Stone.

"Wing." Production number 903. Original airdate: 23 Mar. 2005. Writer: Trey Parker.

"You Got F*cked in the Ass." Production number 805. Original airdate: 7 Apr. 2004. Writer: Trey Parker.

Complete Episode Guide, Seasons 1-11

Each episode below is listed chronologically by title, production number, original airdate in the United States on Comedy Central, and writers. Detailed information on each episode can be obtained the online titles and airdates guide at <http://epguides. com/SouthPark/>.

Season 1 (1997-1998)

"Cartman Gets an Anal Probe." Production number 101. Original airdate: 13 Aug. 1997. Writers: Trey Parker and Matt Stone.

"Weight Gain 4000." Production number 102. Original airdate: 27 Aug. 1997. Writers: Trey Parker and Matt Stone.

"Volcano." Production number 103. Original airdate: 20 Aug. 1997. Writers: Trey Parker and Matt Stone.

"Big Gay Al's Big Gay Boatride." Production number 104. Original airdate: 3 Sept. 1997. Writers: Trey Parker and Matt Stone.

"An Elephant Makes Love to a Pig," Production number 105. Original airdate: 10 Sept. 1997. Writers: Trey Parker, Matt Stone, and Dan Sterling.

"Death." Production number 106. Original airdate: 17 Sept. 1997. Writers: Trey Parker and Matt Stone.

"Pinkeye." Production number 107. Original airdate: 29 Oct. 1997. Writers: Trey Parker, Matt Stone, and Philip Stark.

"Damien." Production number 108. Original airdate: 4 Feb. 1998. Writers: Trey Parker and Matt Stone.

"Starvin' Marvin." Production number 109. Original airdate: 19 Nov. 1997. Writer: Trey Parker.

"Mr. Hankey, the Christmas Poo." Production number 110. Original airdate: 17 Dec. 1997. Writer: Trey Parker.

"Tom's Rhinoplasty." Production number 111. Original airdate: 11 Feb. 1998. Writer: Trey Parker.

"Mecha Streisand." Production number 112. Original airdate: 18 Feb. 1998. Writers: Trey Parker, Matt Stone, and Philip Stark.

"Cartman's Mom Is a Dirty Slut." Production number 113. Original airdate: 25 Feb. 1998. Writers: Trey Parker and David Goodman.

Season 2 (1998–1999)

"Terrance & Phillip in 'Not Without My Anus.'" Production number 201. Original airdate: 1 Apr. 1998. Writers: Trisha Nixon and Trey Parker.

"Cartman's Mom Is Still a Dirty Slut." Production number 202. Original airdate: 22 Apr. 1998. Writers: Trey Parker and David Goodman.

"Chickenlover." Production number 203. Original airdate: 27 May 1998. Writers: Trey Parker, Matt Stone, and David Goodman.

"Ike's Wee Wee." Production number 204. Original airdate: 20 May 1998. Writer: Trey Parker.

"Conjoined Fetus Lady." Production number 205. Original airdate: 3 June 1998. Writers: Trey Parker, Matt Stone, and David Goodman.

"The Mexican Staring Frog of Southern Sri Lanka." Production number 206. Original airdate: 10 June 1998. Writers: Trey Parker and Matt Stone.

"City on the Edge of Forever (Flashbacks)." Production number 207. Original airdate: 17 June 1998. Writers: Trey Parker and Nancy Pimental.

"Summer Sucks." Production number 208. Original airdate: 24 June 1998. Writers: Trey Parker and Nancy Pimental.

"Chef's Salty Chocolate Balls." Production number 209. Original airdate: 19 Aug. 1998. Writers: Trey Parker, Matt Stone, and Nancy Pimental.

"Chickenpox." Production number 210. Original airdate: 26 Aug. 1998. Writers: Trey Parker, Matt Stone, and Trisha Nixon.

"Roger Ebert Should Lay Off the Fatty Foods." Production number 211. Original airdate: 2 Sept. 1998. Writers: Trey Parker and David Goodman.

"Clubhouses." Production number 212. Original airdate: 23 Sept. 1998. Writers: Trey Parker and Nancy Pimental.

"Cow Days." Production number 213. Original airdate: 20 Sept. 1998. Writers: Trey Parker and David Goodman.

"Chef Aid." Production number 214. Original airdate: 7 Oct. 1998. Writers: Trey Parker and Matt Stone.

"Spooky Fish." Production number 215. Original airdate: 28 Oct. 1998. Writer: Trey Parker.

"Merry Christmas, Charlie Manson!" Production number 216. Original airdate: 9 Dec. 1998. Writers: Trey Parker and Nancy Pimental.

"Gnomes." Production number 217. Original airdate: 16 Dec. 1998. Writers: Trey Parker, Matt Stone, and Pam Brady.

"Prehistoric Ice Man." Production number 218. Original airdate: 20 Jan. 1999. Writers: Trey Parker and Nancy Pimental.

Season 3 (1999–2000)

"Rainforest Schmainforest." Production number 301. Original airdate: 7 Apr. 1999. Writers: Trey Parker and Matt Stone.

"Spontaneous Combustion." Production number 302. Original airdate: 14 Apr. 1999. Writers: Trey Parker, Matt Stone, and David Goodman.

"The Succubus." Production number 303. Original airdate: 21 Apr. 1999. Writer: Trey Parker.

"Tweek vs. Craig." Production number 304. Original airdate: 23 June 1999. Writer: Trey Parker.

"Jackovasaurus." Production number 305. Original airdate: 16 June 1999. Writers: Trey Parker, Matt Stone, and David Goodman.

"Sexual Harassment Panda." Production number 306. Original airdate: 7 July 1999. Writer: Trey Parker.

"Cat Orgy." Production number 307. Original airdate: 14 July 1999. Writer: Trey Parker.

"Two Guys Naked in a Hot Tub." Production number 308. Original airdate: 21 July 1999. Writers: Trey Parker, Matt Stone, and David Goodman.

"Jewbilee." Production number 309. Original airdate: 28 July 1999. Writer: Trey Parker.

"Chinpokomon." Production number 310. Original airdate: 3 Nov. 1999. Writer: Trey Parker.

"Starvin' Marvin in Space." Production number 311. Original airdate: 17 Nov. 1999. Writers: Trey Parker, Matt Stone, and Kyle McCulloch.

"Korn's Groovy Pirate Ghost Mystery." Production number 312. Original airdate: 27 Oct. 1999. Writer: Trey Parker.

"Hooked on Monkey Phonics." Production number 313. Original airdate: 10 Nov. 1999. Writer: Trey Parker.

"The Red Badge of Gayness." Production number 314. Original airdate: 11-24-1999. Writer: Trey Parker.

"Mr. Hankey's Christmas Classics." Production number 315. Original airdate: 1 Dec. 1999. Writer: Trey Parker.

"Are You There, God? It's Me, Jesus." Production number 316. Original airdate: 29 Dec. 1999. Writer: Trey Parker.

"Worldwide Recorder Concert." Production number 317. Original airdate: 12 Jan. 2000. Writer: Trey Parker.

Season 4 (2001)

"Cartman's Silly Hate Crime 2000." Production number 401. Original airdate: 12 Apr. 2000. Writer: Trey Parker.

"The Tooth Fairy's Tats 2000." Production number 402. Original airdate: 5 Apr. 2000. Writers: Trey Parker, Matt Stone and Nancy Pimental.

"Quintuplets 2000." Production number 403. Original airdate: 26 Apr. 2000. Writer: Trey Parker.

"Timmy! 2000." Production number 404. Original airdate: 19 Apr. 2000. Writer: Trey Parker.

"Pip." Production number 405. Original airdate: 29 Nov. 2000. Writer: Trey Parker.

"Cartman Joins NAMBLA." Production number 406. Original airdate: 21 June 2000. Writer: Trey Parker.

"Cherokee Hair Tampons." Production number 407. Original airdate: 28 June 2000. Writer: Trey Parker.

"Chef Goes Nanners." Production number 408. Original airdate: 5 July 2000. Writer: Trey Parker.

"Something You Can Do with Your Finger." Production number 409. Original airdate: 12 July 2000. Writer: Trey Parker.

"Do the Handicapped Go to Hell?" Production number 410. Original airdate: 19 July 2000. Writer: Trey Parker.

"Probably." Production number 411. Original airdate: 26 July 2000. Writer: Trey Parker.

"4th Grade." Production number 412. Original airdate: 8 Nov. 2000. Writer: Trey Parker.

"Trapper Keeper." Production number 413. Original airdate: 15 Nov. 2000. Writer: Trey Parker.

"Helen Keller! The Musical." Production number 414. Original airdate: 22 Nov. 2000. Writer: Trey Parker.

"Fat Camp." Production number 415. Original airdate: 6 Dec. 2000. Writer: Trey Parker.

"The Wacky Molestation Adventure." Production number 416. Original airdate: 13 Dec. 2000. Writer: Trey Parker.

"A Very Crappy Christmas." Production number 417. Original airdate: 20 Dec. 2000. Writer: Trey Parker.

Season 5 (2001)

"Scott Tenorman Must Die." Production number 501. Original airdate: 11 July 2001. Writer: Trey Parker.

"It Hits the Fan." Production number 502. Original airdate: 20 June 2001. Writer: Trey Parker.

"Cripple Fight." Production number 503. Original airdate: 27 June 2001. Writer: Trey Parker.

"Super Best Friends, The." Production number 504. Original airdate: 4 July 2001. Writer: Trey Parker.

"Terrance and Phillip: Behind the Blow." Production number 505. Original airdate: 18 July 2001. Writer: Trey Parker.

"Cartmanland." Production number 506. Original airdate: 25 July 2001. Writer: Trey Parker.

"Proper Condom Use." Production number 507. Original airdate: 1 Aug. 2001. Writer: Trey Parker.

"Towelie." Production number 508. Original airdate: 8 Aug. 2001. Writer: Trey Parker.

"Osama Bin Laden Has Farty Pants." Production number 509. Original airdate: 7 Nov. 2001. Writer: Trey Parker.

"How to Eat with Your Butt." Production number 510. Original airdate: 14 Nov. 2001. Writer: Trey Parker.

"The Entity." Production number 511. Original airdate: 21 Nov. 2001. Writer: Trey Parker.

"Here Comes the Neighborhood." Production number 512. Original airdate: 28 Nov. 2001. Writer: Trey Parker.

"Kenny Dies." Production number 513. Original airdate: 5 Dec. 2001. Writer: Trey Parker.

"Butter's Very Own Episode." Production number 514. Original airdate: 12 Dec. 2001. Writer: Trey Parker.

Season 6 (2002)

"Freak Strike." Production number 601. Original airdate: 20 Mar. 2002. Writer: Trey Parker.

"Jared Has Aides." Production number 602. Original airdate: 6 Mar. 2002. Writer: Trey Parker.

"Asspen." Production number 603. Original airdate: 13 Mar. 2002. Writer: Trey Parker.

"The New Terrance and Phillip Movie Trailer." Production number 604. Original airdate: 3 Apr. 2002. Writer: Trey Parker.

"Fun with Veal." Production number 605. Original airdate: 27 Mar. 2002. Writer: Trey Parker.

"Professor Chaos." Production number 606. Original airdate: 10 Apr. 2002. Writer: Trey Parker.

"Simpsons Already Did It." Production number 607. Original airdate: 26 June 2002. Writer: Trey Parker.

"Red Hot Catholic Love." Production number 608. Original airdate: 3 July 2002. Writers: Daisy Gardner and Trey Parker.

"Free Hat." Production number 609. Original airdate: 10 July 2002. Writer: Trey Parker.

"Bebe's Boobs Destroy Society." Production number 610. Original airdate: 17 July 2002. Writer: Trey Parker.

"Child Abduction Is Not Funny." Production number 611. Original airdate: 24 July 2002. Writer: Trey Parker.

"A Ladder to Heaven." Production number 612. Original airdate: 6 Nov. 2002. Writer: Trey Parker.

"The Return of the Fellowship of the Ring to the Two Towers." Production number 613. Original airdate: 13 Nov. 2002. Writer: Trey Parker.

"The Death Camp of Tolerance." Production number 614. Original airdate: 20 Nov. 2002. Writer: Trey Parker.

"The Biggest Douche in the Universe." Production number 615. Original airdate: 27 Nov. 2002. Writer: Trey Parker.

"My Future Self N' Me." Production number 616. Original airdate: 4 Dec. 2002. Writer: Trey Parker.

"Red Sleigh Down." Production number 617. Original airdate: 11 Dec. 2002. Writer: Trey Parker.

Season 7 (2003)

"I'm a Little Bit Country." Production number 701. Original airdate: 9 Apr. 2003. Writer: Trey Parker.

"Krazy Kripples." Production number 702. Original airdate: 26 Mar. 2003. Writer: Trey Parker.

"Toilet Paper." Production number 703. Original airdate: 2 Apr. 2003. Writer: Trey Parker.

"Cancelled." Production number 704. Original airdate: 19 Mar. 2003. Writer: Trey Parker.

"Fat Butt and Pancake Head." Production number 705. Original airdate: 16 Apr. 2003. Writer: Trey Parker.

"Lil' Crime Stoppers." Production number 706. Original airdate: 23 Apr. 2003. Writer: Trey Parker.

"Red Man's Greed." Production number 707. Original airdate: 30 Apr. 2003. Writer: Trey Parker.

"South Park Is Gay!" Production number 708. Original airdate: 22 Oct. 2003. Writer: Trey Parker.

"Christian Rock Hard." Production number 709. Original airdate: 29 Oct. 2003. Writer: Trey Parker.

"Grey Dawn." Production number 710. Original airdate: 5 Nov. 2003. Writer: Trey Parker.

"Casa Bonita." Production number 711. Original airdate: 12 Nov. 2003. Writer: Trey Parker.

"All about Mormons?" Production number 712. Original airdate: 19 Nov. 2003. Writer: Trey Parker.

"Butt Out." Production number 713. Original airdate: 3 Dec. 2003. Writer: Trey Parker.

"Raisins." Production number 714. Original airdate: 10 Dec. 2003. Writer: Trey Parker.

"It's Christmas in Canada." Production number 715. Original airdate: 17 Dec. 2003. Writer: Trey Parker.

Season 8 (2004)

"Good Times with Weapons." Production number 801. Original airdate: 17 Mar. 2004. Writer: Trey Parker.

"AWESOM-O." Production number 802. Original airdate: 14 Apr. 2004. Writer: Trey Parker.

"Up the Down Steroid." Production number 803. Original airdate: 24 Mar. 2004. Writer: Trey Parker.

"The Passion of the Jew." Production number 804. Original airdate: 31 Mar. 2004. Writers: Daisy Gardner and Trey Parker.

"You Got F*cked in the Ass." Production number 805. Original airdate: 7 Apr. 2004. Writer: Trey Parker.

"Goobacks." Production number 806. Original airdate: 28 Apr. 2004. Writer: Trey Parker.

"The Jeffersons." Production number 807. Original airdate: 21 Apr. 2004. Writer: Trey Parker.

"Douche and Turd." Production number 808. Original airdate: 27 Oct. 2004. Writer: Trey Parker.

"Something Wall-Mart This Way Comes." Production number 809. Original airdate: 3 Nov. 2004. Writer: Trey Parker.

"Preschool." Production number 810. Original airdate: 10 Nov. 2004. Writer: Trey Parker.

"Quest for Ratings." Production number 811. Original airdate: 17 Nov. 2004. Writer: Trey Parker.

"Stupid Spoiled Whore Video Playset." Production number 812. Original airdate: 1 Dec. 2004. Writer: Trey Parker.

"Cartman's Incredible Gift." Production number 813. Original Airdate: 8 Dec. 2004. Writer: Trey Parker.

"Woodland Critter Christmas." Production number 814. Original airdate: 15 Dec. 2004. Writer: Trey Parker.

Season 9 (2005)

"Mr. Garrison's Fancy New Vagina." Production number 901. Original airdate: 9 Mar. 2005. Writer: Trey Parker.

"Die Hippie, Die." Production number 902. Original airdate: 16 Mar. 2005. Writer: Trey Parker.

"Wing." Production number 903. Original airdate: 23 Mar. 2005. Writer: Trey Parker.

"Best Friends Forever." Production number 904. Original airdate: 30 Mar. 2005. Writer: Trey Parker.

"The Losing Edge." Production number 905. Original airdate: 6 Apr. 2005. Writer: Trey Parker.

"The Death of Eric Cartman." Production number 906. Original airdate: 13 Apr. 2005. Writer: Trey Parker.

"Erection Day." Production number 907. Original airdate: 20 Apr. 2005. Writer: Trey Parker.

"Two Days before the Day after Tomorrow." Production number 908. Original airdate: 19 Oct. 2005. Writer: Trey Parker.

"Marjorine." Production number 909. Original airdate: 26 Oct. 2005. Writer: Trey Parker.

"Follow that Egg." Production number 910. Original airdate: 2 Nov. 2005. Writer: Trey Parker.

"Ginger Kids." Production number 911. Original airdate: 9 Nov. 2005. Writer: Trey Parker.

"Trapped in the Closet." Production number 912. Original airdate: 16 Nov. 2005. Writer: Trey Parker.

"Free Willzyx." Production number 913. Original airdate: 30 Nov. 2005. Writer: Trey Parker.

"Bloody Mary." Production number 914. Original airdate: 7 Dec. 2005. Writer: Trey Parker.

Season 10 (2006)

"The Return of Chef!" Production number 1001. Original airdate: 22 Mar. 2006. Writer: Trey Parker.

"Smug Alert!" Production number 1002. Original airdate: 29 Mar. 2006. Writer: Trey Parker.

"Cartoon Wars (1)." Production number 1003. Original airdate: 5 Apr. 2006. Writer: Trey Parker.

"Cartoon Wars (2)." Production number 1004. Original airdate: 12 Apr. 2006. Writer: Trey Parker.

"A Million Little Fibers." Production number 1005. Original airdate: 19 Apr. 2006. Writer: Trey Parker.

"ManBearPig." Production number 1006. Original airdate: 26 Apr. 2006. Writer: Trey Parker.

"Tsst." Production number 1007. Original airdate: 3 May 2006. Writer: Trey Parker.

"Make Love, Not Warcraft." Production number 1008. Original airdate: 4 Oct. 2006. Writer: Trey Parker.

"Mystery of the Urinal Deuce." Production number 1009. Original airdate: 11 Oct. 2006. Writer: Trey Parker.

"Miss Teacher Bangs a Boy." Production 1010. Original airdate: 18 Oct. 2006. Writer: Trey Parker.

"Hell on Earth 2006." Production 1011. Original airdate: 25 Oct. 2006. Writer: Trey Parker.

"Go God Go (1)." Production 1012. Original airdate: 1 Nov. 2006. Writer: Trey Parker.

"Go God Go XII." Production 1013. Original airdate: 8 Nov. 2006. Writer: Trey Parker.

"Stanley's Cup." Production 1014. Original airdate: 15 Nov. 2006. Writer: Trey Parker.

Season 11 (2007)

"With Apologies to Jesse Jackson." Production 1101. Original airdate: 7 Mar. 2007. Writer: Trey Parker.

"Cartman Sucks." Production 1102. Original airdate: 14 Mar. 2007. Writer: Trey Parker.

"Lice Capades." Production 1103. Original airdate: 21 Mar. 2007. Writer: Trey Parker.

"The Snuke." Production 1104. Original airdate: 28 Mar. 2007. Writer: Trey Parker.

"Fantastic Easter Special." Production 1105. Original airdate: 4 Apr. 2007. Writer: Trey Parker.

"D-Yikes!" Production 1106. Original airdate: 11 Apr. 2007. Writer: Trey Parker.

"Night of the Living Homeless." Production 1107. Original airdate: 18 Apr. 2007. Writer: Trey Parker.

Contributors

MATT BECKER is a Ph.D. candidate in the American Studies Department at the University of Minnesota, Twin Cities. He is currently finishing a dissertation on the goth subculture and has published in *The Velvet Light Trap*. His chapter in this volume comes from research for his next project on American youth and comedic popular culture since the 1980s.

JASON BOYD received his Ph.D. in English literature from the University of Toronto in November 2005. He is an instructor at the University of Toronto, and project manager and coeditor of the Patrons and Performances Web site <http://link.library.utoronto.ca/reed/>. He is currently working on a book tentatively titled *Oscar Wilde's Fabulous Lives: Biography, Tragedy and Exegesis in Wilde Studies*.

LINDSAY COLEMAN is a Ph.D. candidate in the cinema studies program at the University of Melbourne, Australia. His publications include interviews with film directors Ian Mune and Paul McGuigan, and with cinematographer Roger Deakins in the online magazine, *The Big Picture*.

MICHAEL W. DELASHMUTT is a lecturer in theology and the study of the Christian Church at the University of Exeter where he is helping to establish the Centre for the Learning Church. His research interests include the study of theology and everyday life and the ongoing relationship between theology, culture, technology, and the sciences. His publications can be found in the *Scottish Journal of Theology*, *Zygon: The Journal of Science and Religion*, and *Crucible*.

RANDALL FALLOWS is a lecturer in the Writing Programs Department at the University of California at Los Angeles. His work has appeared in the

243

Journal of Popular Film and Television, American Drama, Rhetoric Review, Americana, and the *Journal of Popular Culture.* He is currently working on a textbook on how to write analyses.

STEPHEN GROENING is a Ph.D. candidate in the Comparative Studies in Discourse and Society program at the University of Minnesota, Twin Cities. His work has been published in *Cultural Critique* and *Scope.* He is currently finishing his dissertation, "Connected Isolation: Mobile Screens and Globalized Media Culture."

ALISON HALSALL is an adjunct professor at York University, Toronto, Canada. Her dissertation, *Rendering Siddall: H.D.'s Version of the Pre-Raphaelite "cult of youthful beauty,"* focuses on the visual and literary interconnections between the Victorian and modernist periods. Currently, she is teaching courses on visual cultures, film adaptation, and children's literature. She has published articles on various topics, including vampires, the Pre-Raphaelites, and Harry Potter.

BRANNON HANCOCK studied English and music at Trevecca Nazarene University (Nashville, Tennessee) before moving to Scotland to pursue interdisciplinary research in theology, contemporary culture, and hermeneutics. He is currently a doctoral student of the University of Glasgow's Centre for the Study of Literature, Theology and the Arts, and is a recipient of the Overseas Research Students award. His published work has appeared in *Literature and Theology* and the *Journal of Religion and Film.*

BRIAN L. OTT is an associate professor of media studies in the Department of Speech Communication at Colorado State University. He received his Ph.D. from Pennsylvania State University in 1997. His previous scholarship has appeared in *Critical Studies in Media Communication, Communication and Critical/Cultural Studies, Cultural Studies<=>Critical Methodologies, Journal of Popular Culture, Rhetoric and Public Affairs,* and *Western Journal of Communication.* His first book, *The Small Screen: How Television Equips Us to Live in the Information Age,* is forthcoming from Blackwell.

MARC R. PLAMONDON received his Ph.D. in English literature from the University of Toronto where he wrote his doctoral dissertation on the interrelation of music and poetry, focusing on Robert Browning and Alfred Tennyson. He has published a study of the importance of music to two of Robert Browning's dramatic monologues in Victorian poetry. He is currently a sessional instructor with the English Department at the University of Toronto and a database programmer with the Department of Information Technology

Services of the University of Toronto Libraries. Two articles on computer applications to the study of English poetry are forthcoming. He recently became associate editor of *Representative Poetry Online*.

JAMES RENNIE is finishing work toward his master's degree in Communication at Simon Fraser University, where his current research deals with technology and pedagogical practice in public schools. His background is in film and media studies, and he plans to pursue doctoral studies to combine the strengths of critical cultural studies with the practical applications of education research.

ROBERT SAMUELS is president of the University of California, American Federation of Teachers faculty union and a lecturer in the Writing Programs at the University of California at Los Angeles. He is the author of *Between Philosophy and Psychoanalysis*, *Hitchcock's Bi-Textuality*, *Writing Prejudices*, and *Integrating Hypertextual Subject: Computers, Composition, and Academic Labor*. He is currently writing a critical students' guide to the university.

DAMION STURM is a Ph.D. candidate with the Departments of Screen and Media and Sport and Leisure Studies at the University of Waikato, Hamilton, New Zealand. His thesis analyzing Formula One motor racing cuts across both media and sport disciplines, exploring theories of stardom and celebrity, the point-of-view shot, fandom, the spectacle and representation from a postmodern cultural studies perspective. His other research interests include experimenting with ethnographic writing forms, video games, and subversive media representation.

JEFFREY ANDREW WEINSTOCK is associate professor of American literature and culture at Central Michigan University. He is the author of *The Rocky Horror Picture Show* (part of Wallflower Press's "Cultographies" series) and has edited collections on American ghosts, *The Blair Witch Project*, and Charlotte Perkins Gilman. His work has appeared in journals including *American Literature*, *Studies in American Fiction*, and *Arizona Quarterly*, and he has forthcoming books or edited collections on feminist supernatural fiction, Edgar Allan Poe, and M. Night Shyamalan.

Index